DAVE PELZ'S DAMAGE CONTROL

DAVE PELZ'S DAMAGE CONTROL

How to Save up to Five Shots Per Round Using All-New, Scientifically Proven Techniques for Playing Out of Trouble Lies

DAVE PELZ

WITH EDDIE PELZ
AND JOEL MENDELMAN

GOTHAM
BOOKS

GOTHAM BOOKS
Published by Penguin Group (USA) Inc.
375 Hudson Street, New York, New York 10014, U.S.A.
Penguin Group (Canada), 90 Eglinton Avenue East, Suite 700, Toronto, Ontario M4P 2Y3, Canada
(a division of Pearson Penguin Canada Inc.); Penguin Books Ltd, 80 Strand, London WC2R 0RL, England;
Penguin Ireland, 25 St Stephen's Green, Dublin 2, Ireland (a division of Penguin Books Ltd);
Penguin Group (Australia), 250 Camberwell Road, Camberwell, Victoria 3124,
Australia (a division of Pearson Australia Group Pty Ltd); Penguin Books India Pvt Ltd,
11 Community Centre, Panchsheel Park, New Delhi—110 017, India;
Penguin Group (NZ), 67 Apollo Drive, Rosedale, North Shore 0632,
New Zealand (a division of Pearson New Zealand Ltd); Penguin Books
(South Africa) (Pty) Ltd, 24 Sturdee Avenue, Rosebank,
Johannesburg 2196, South Africa

Penguin Books Ltd, Registered Offices: 80 Strand,
London WC2R 0RL, England

Published by Gotham Books, a member of Penguin Group (USA) Inc.

First printing, November 2009

10 9 8 7 6 5 4 3 2 1

Photo credits appear on page 329 and constitute an extension of the copyright page.

Gotham Books and the skyscraper logo are trademarks of
Penguin Group (USA) Inc.

LIBRARY OF CONGRESS CATALOGING-IN-PUBLICATION DATA
Pelz, Dave.
Dave Pelz's damage control : how to save up to five shots per round
using all-new, scientifically proven techniques for playing out of
trouble lies / by Dave Pelz, with Eddie Pelz and Joel Mendelman.
p. cm.
ISBN 978-1-592-40510-7 (hardcover)
1. Swing (Golf) I. Pelz, Eddie. II. Mendelman, Joel. III. Title.
GV979.S9P45 2009
796.352'3—dc22
2009026390

Printed in the United States of America
Set in Sabon and Meta, with display in Foundry Gridnik
Designed by BTDNYC

For our future golfers.
May their games be free from disaster scores.

Contents

Introduction

GOLF IS IMPORTANT TO ME. I've played it for more than fifty years, studied it for forty, conducted research on it for thirty-five, and taught it professionally for thirty-three. Just recently, however, I've learned something new—and very important—about the game. In a research project (code named "Disaster") at the Pelz Golf Institute that involved thousands of players, we uncovered several interesting facts about how golfers score:

- Golfers play two to five strokes below their handicap for most of each round.
- They play badly (above their handicap) on a few "disaster" holes, bringing their scores back up to handicap level.
- There is an easy way to avoid these disaster scores, and thus lower a golfer's handicap.

Working with the staff at the Institute, we've discovered a new and important way to eliminate disaster scores from your game. We call it **Damage Control.**

By way of an introduction to **Damage Control,** please consider the following six questions and answers:

Question 1: What's the problem?

Answer 1: Golfers play well for most of the round, but then ruin their score with a few bad holes.

Think about your game. You play well most of the time, but consistently seem to mess up a few holes that ruin your score. This doesn't happen once or twice a year. You do it often, almost like it's an unwritten law: "You can't put together a complete 18-hole round without a disaster hole." It's just the way you play the game!

See if you recognize these circumstances. You:

- Play well (below your handicap) for most of each round (fourteen to seventeen holes)
- Have a few "disaster" holes, with seriously high scores
- Are disappointed with your score and know you're capable of playing better
- Blame your disaster holes on errant shots that got into trouble
- Believe you must practice more, improve your swing, and learn to avoid trouble if you want to improve your game

Research into disaster scoring has shown us the following:

- All amateurs hit multiple errant shots every round, but they manage to get away with most of them.
- Errant shots usually don't cause disaster scores—they present opportunities for them.
- Disaster scores occur after a failed recovery attempt (the shot played after an errant shot) flies out of trouble into even worse trouble. Golfers often play out of the frying pan and into the fire.

Question 2: What's the answer?

Answer 2: Damage Control is the answer.

Recovery shots from trouble often fail because golfers don't know how to swing from weird stances on uneven terrain, with a bush behind the ball, or with a tree limb in the way. They try to escape from trouble situations using normal swings. But normal swings don't work from trouble.

Golfers also aim at inappropriate targets without realizing it. These problems can be eliminated by **Damage Control,** which enables golfers to escape trouble without ruining their score.

Some facts about **trouble:**

- Golfers will never completely avoid errant shots (we're all human).
- Courses are designed to get you into trouble. You *will* get into it. You'd better learn to deal with it.
- Even if you don't hit bad shots, bad luck and bad bounces will get you into trouble.
- The world's best players consistently hit errant shots into trouble.
- Trouble is part of the game; always has been, always will be.
- **Damage Control** will get you out of trouble without ruining your score.
- **Damage Control** requires skills that are different from those used from good lies.

Question 3: What's the effect of Damage Control?

Answer 3: It limits scoring damage to less than one stroke each time you get into trouble.

Damage Control enables you to escape from trouble into a better position than you would have been in had your previous shot not gotten into trouble. It allows you to escape on the first try, and then recover with less than one stroke (on average) added to your score.

Question 4: What is Damage Control?

Answer 4: Damage Control is a set of five skills that eliminates disaster scores from your game.

The physical skills of Damage Control are different from normal golf skills such as long-driving and lag-putting. The Damage Control skills involve swings you have never practiced before, from lies you have never practiced on. The mental skills of Damage Control require a different mode of thinking based on a different set of metrics.

The **five skills of Damage Control** are:

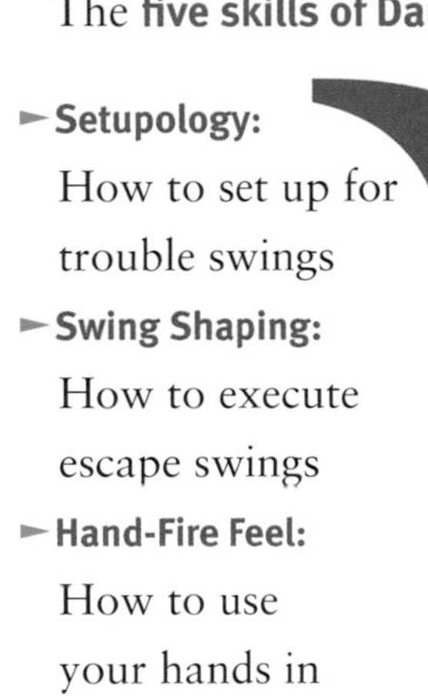

- **Setupology:** How to set up for trouble swings
- **Swing Shaping:** How to execute escape swings
- **Hand-Fire Feel:** How to use your hands in escape shots
- **Red-Flag Touch:** How to plan for the launch behavior of trouble shots
- **Damage Control Mentality:** How to think and plan when you are in trouble

Question 5: Who needs Damage Control?

Answer 5: All golfers need Damage Control, because "golf, as life, is full of unforced errors."

Golf deals us bad breaks and bad bounces all the time, sometimes even after we've performed well. The higher your handicap, the more trouble you get into—and the more strokes Damage Control can save you. The skills of Damage Control are unrecognized, unpracticed, and completely missing from most golfers' games. Damage Control cannot be learned in normal practice on normal ranges with flat practice tees.

Question 6: Why haven't you heard about Damage Control before now?

Answer 6: Because it's new. We just discovered and named it!

I played my entire career trying to get good enough to stay out of trouble, while never practicing getting out of trouble—which is what I actually needed. Simultaneously I've been coaching two of the world's best players, Phil Mickelson and Vijay Singh, and I've seen firsthand how they save their scores after their errant shots find trouble. Putting together the data from our research on amateurs with what I've seen from these pros, we've discovered why amateurs score disastrously from trouble while pros don't. We've identified five skills the pros have that are missing in amateurs' games: These are the five skills of Damage Control.

Damage Control will work for you, if you:

- **Step 1:** Read this book.
- **Step 2:** Practice Damage Control swings in your own backyard.
- **Step 3:** Play a few Damage Control practice rounds at your local course.
- **Step 4:** Make the emotional commitment to play with Damage Control.

I promise that learning to play with Damage Control will be worth your effort. **Damage Control will lower your scores by two to five shots per round!**

DAVE PELZ'S DAMAGE CONTROL

CHAPTER 1 The Concept of Damage Control

AVOIDING DISASTER SCORES IS what Damage Control is all about.

Six years ago, as a result of a pattern I observed in tournament scores at the Myrtle Beach World Amateur Championship, "Project Disaster" was started at the Pelz Golf Institute. After noticing the occasional but consistent appearance of double- and triple-bogey disasters on low-handicap amateur scorecards, we decided to determine how often and why they occurred. The initial results astounded us, and this prompted us to expand our study to include amateurs and professionals at all handicap levels. Naturally, we also began to study how such disasters could be avoided.

The data from this study show that virtually all amateurs get into some kind of trouble in almost every round—and they're not all that good at getting out of it. A few times each round they play shots from trouble into worse trouble, and this leads to disaster scores. The pros, however, are different. They also get into trouble consistently, but they're great at getting out of it.

Damage Control is the technique that can help you play more like the pros by teaching you how to avoid disaster scores. **Damage Control** is not about making perfect golf swings, improving the swing you have, or learning to stay out of trouble. **Damage Control** is about getting out of trouble after you're in it, without ruining your score.

1.1 The Big Picture

Golf is the greatest game. It's the game of a lifetime, a game of honor, a game for all ages. It can't be bought; it plays no favorites and offers a simple truth: The better you play, the lower you score, and the more fun you have.

The goal of my working life is to understand golf well enough to teach it simply enough, to help golfers shoot lower scores and have more fun. In pursuit of this goal, research first led me to putting, then to the short game, and now to Damage Control.

To fully understand and appreciate Damage Control, you must see the big picture of golf and the problems we all face in playing it. These problems include the statistics of shot patterns, trouble lies, and the snowballing effects that combine to keep you scoring two to five shots above your real ability, almost every time you play. If you'll take a few moments to examine these aspects of the game, it will help you to learn how Damage Control can help you score better.

THE CYCLE OF GOLF

Golf is played one shot at a time; the fewer, the better. We start at the first hole hitting and chasing the ball repeatedly, until we hole-out on the last hole. Then we add up our score and smile, frown, or feel something in between. Scorecards covering a wide range of skill levels show that golfers play reasonably well on most holes, but then waste shots on a few holes somewhere during each round. To understand this, let's look into the very core of the game: golf's fundamental cycle.

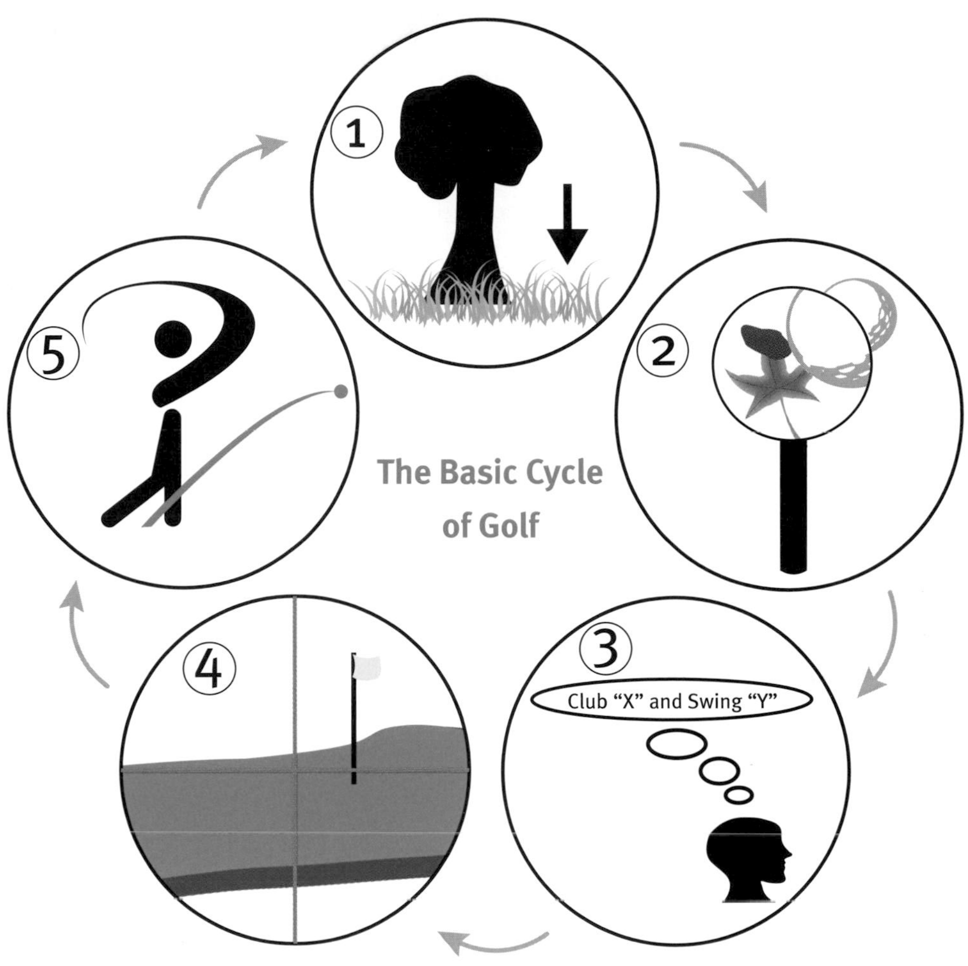

1.1

The essence of the entire game can be characterized in one cycle (Figure 1.1). In each cycle, the golfer must first find the ball (1), whether it's in his bag before the round starts, in his pocket between holes, or somewhere on the course in play. After finding the ball (2), its lie or condition of play is evaluated (including materials around the ball, stance requirements, and any obstacles to the upcoming swing that may be involved). Then the golfer selects the club and swing (shot) he or she intends to play (3), chooses a target (4), aims and swings (5). The ball flies off and the cycle is complete. To start the next cycle, the golfer moves out to find the ball again.

This sounds simple, and fundamentally, it is. We add up the number of cycles it takes to get our ball into the cup on each hole, record this number on a scorecard, and move on to the next hole. One shot at a time, one hole at a time. At the end of the day, the total of our hole scores is our score for the round. This is golf.

STATISTICS ENTER THE FRAY

The game would be incredibly simple (and boring) if every golfer hit every shot perfectly. We all know, however, that shots don't always fly the desired direction or distance. Instead, we scatter shots around our intended targets, and sometimes, all over the golf course.

Your shots usually land, bounce, roll, and stop some distance away from your intended target; the lower your handicap, the smaller your misses in general. Now imagine instead of playing one shot from each position on a hole, you hit a hundred. It would be very tiring, but after each hundred shots you would see a pattern of balls surrounding each target you chose on the course. These would be your shot patterns; they establish a generic picture of where you've hit shots in the past, and a statistical picture of where you are likely to hit shots with those same clubs in the future.

Before we proceed, let me assure you of something:

1. Shot patterns are real. They exist for all golfers. Your future shots will fly somewhere (statistically) into your shot patterns from every club in your bag. Which shot will come next? Only statistical probability knows. Your shot patterns can be improved and changed over time, but for now they are what they are.
2. From measuring the on-course play of amateurs and pros over the years, I've found shot patterns to be a good measure of their skill levels (on the practice range, too, if measured properly) in each area of their games. The tighter your shot pattern, the more skilled you are in any given area.

3. Every shot goes somewhere. Imagine plotting dots on a piece of paper that represent where every one of your last hundred fairway shots with a 7-iron ended up relative to their target. I know you can't really remember them, but imagine you could. You would see something like Figure 1.2 (golfer = start point for each shot, flagstick = target). Of course every golfer has their own unique skill levels (some slice, some hook, some hit lots of fat shots, etc.) and shot patterns for each club.

1.2

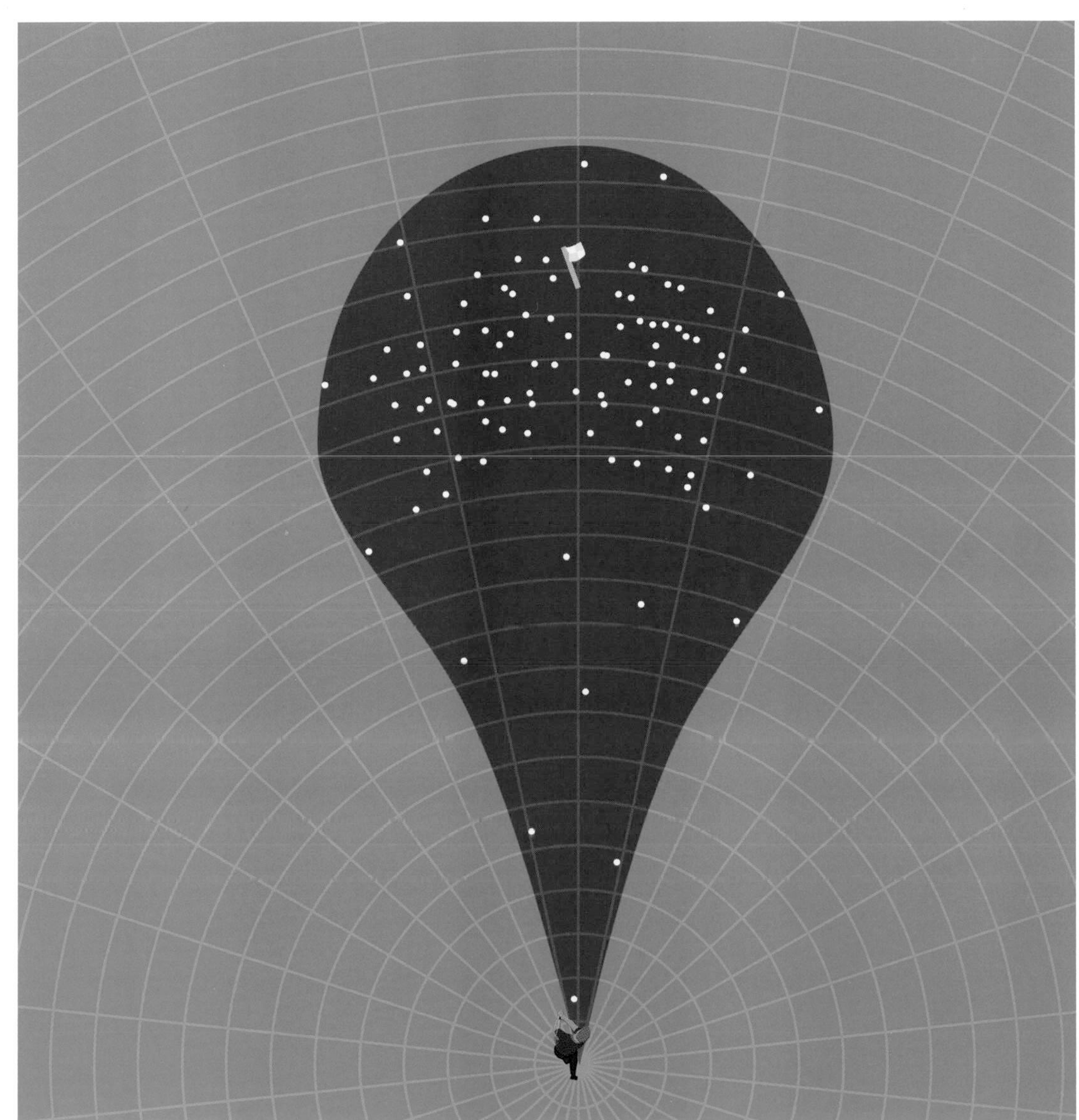

YOUR SHOT-PATTERN SIGNATURE

Shot patterns are golf's equivalent of your handwritten signature. Every shot pattern is different for every player (and for each of their clubs and types of shots). In general, individual golfers don't scatter their shots symmetrically around targets. Golfers will tend to miss left, short, or right, depending upon whether their swings tend to make their pull/hook shots left, hit them fat and short, or slice them to the right.

For those interested, the details of what shot patterns actually look like can be found in one of my earlier books, *Dave Pelz's Short Game Bible*. For the purposes of Damage Control, however, we use generic shot pattern shapes in our illustrations (as shown in Figures 1.2 and 1.3), which assume a generic golfer who scatters shots somewhat symmetrically. (In later illustrations, we will show only the outlines of shot patterns, eliminating the individual balls for clarity.)

All golfers make good, mediocre, bad, or awful swings on occasion, hitting shots in all kinds of directions and trajectories from all kinds of lies. To gain knowledge of your own shot patterns, how they're shaped and which way they're biased, you'll have to perform the tests suggested in Chapter 7 and observe your own results. Few golfers are aware of the size of their shot patterns from normal fairway lies. More importantly, most golfers have no idea of how fast and how badly their shot patterns degrade (and enlarge) when they hit from increasingly troubled lies.

The size of your shot pattern measures your skill with each club, much the way your scores measure your overall skill for the game. Of course, you need many shots to establish shot patterns, and remembering them is complicated, so don't try. Just remember: Where your next shot goes will be determined not only by your skill, but also by the statistics of your shot pattern from that lie.

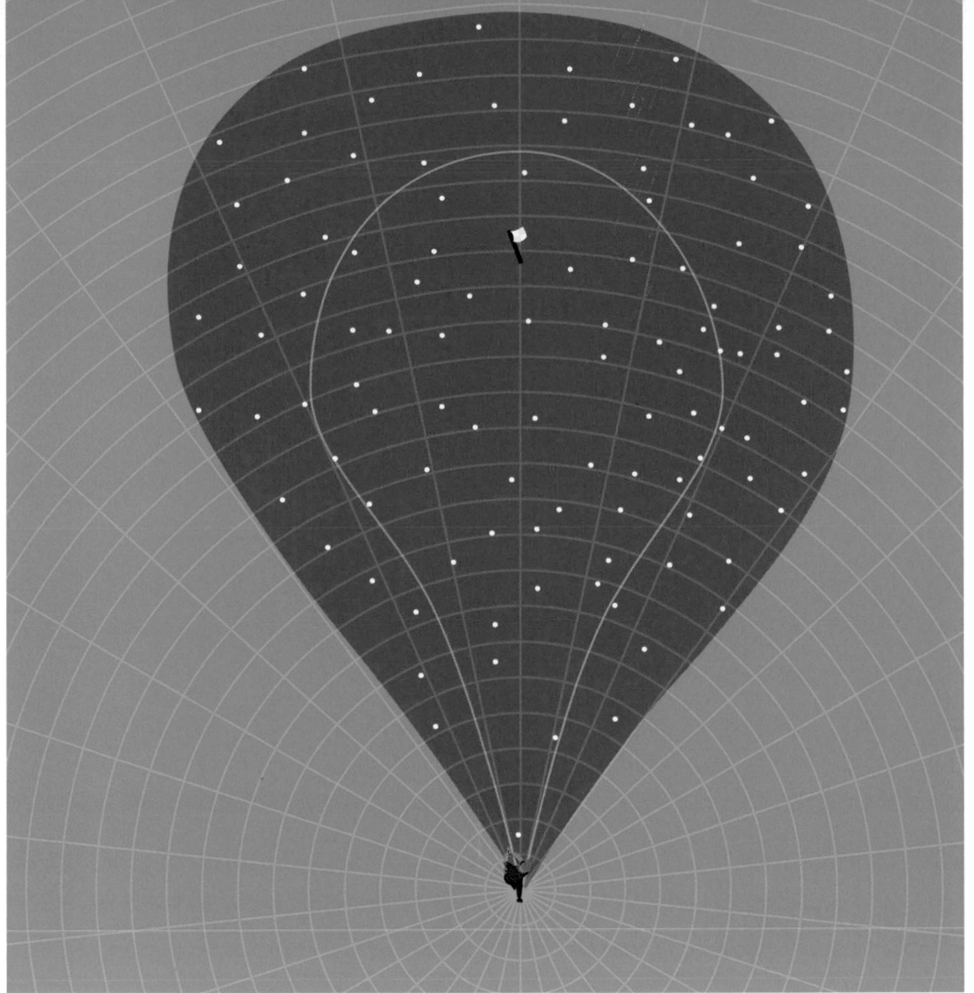

1.3 Your 7-iron shot pattern from trouble (4" tall grass on side-hill lie)

SEEING TROUBLE IS IMPORTANT

Golf courses are designed with trouble in mind. There are good reasons why shots end up in trouble, there's a lot of it out there. Golf course architects entice us into trying risky shots. They design holes to challenge both the physical and mental abilities of golfers who play their masterpieces. They offer a generally safe and beautiful pathway to play along—provided we hit nearly perfect shots. But since we often hit shots that are less precise and more scattered, these architects present us with lies and conditions that graduate from marginal to serious to extremely difficult. Please be aware, I'm not trying to make you worry about trouble: I want you to *not get upset* when you get into it, and to *get out of it quickly* after you find yourself in it.

Golf courses penalize errant shots with lies in long grass, slopes, water, trees, rocks, bushes, sand, and innumerable other trouble situations. In the Damage Control system, we consider the lie of a ball to include *all* the conditions of play that surround it. Therefore, when we consider the lie of a shot, we include the tree limb that might be in the way of a backswing, the lip of the bunker in front of the ball, or the side-slope on which a golfer has to stand. To categorize lie trouble in a simple way, we've broken it into four degrees of difficulty by color (Figure 1.4: green = safe, yellow = marginal, orange = frying-pan, and red = fire) and number (1–10). The designation of trouble areas as colors may be unfamiliar to you, but I'll explain its significance as we move through this chapter.

1.4

Lie

Degree of Difficulty	Color	Characteristics	Description
Safe (1, 2)		—on the tee —on the fairway —on the green —on the green fringe	**Safe Lies** are from which the normal, no-trouble game is played; as good as it gets.
Marginal (3–5)		—sitting up in light rough —good lie in green-side sand —on slight 2% slope —good lie in 4" rough	**Marginal lies** include some degree of difficulty over normal safe lies, but should not cause significant problems in scoring.
Frying-Pan Trouble (6–8)		—nesty lie in grass —down lie in 4" rough —sloping terrain 4% up, down, or side —6" rough	**Frying-Pan** trouble lies involve at least one degree of serious trouble, sometimes several, which leave the next shot possible but difficult to pull off without losing one or more strokes on your score, while being easy to hit badly into even worse trouble.
Fire Trouble (9, 10)		—tree limbs and tall grass —sloping terrain 5% up, down, or side —buried lie in sand with high lip —knee-high weeds; strong grass —creek banks, deep woods, shallow water at edge of ponds	**Fire Trouble** Lies are really bad problems all the way around; it may be difficult to get the ball back into play, in the extreme. Taking an unplayable lie penalty may be better than trying to hit it out.

Start by looking at an aerial view of a typical golf hole (Figure 1.5) in normal color, which should look familiar. Now look at the same hole through my eyes (Figure 1.6). This is how I see where the safe and the trouble areas are, with each area identified by its appropriate color. Again, I'm not trying to scare you with this view, but I like it because it allows me to see in a glance the situation a hole actually presents. This helps me and the players I coach to plan for the best way to play the hole.

Safe (green) refers to the relatively safe lies you get on tees, fairways, fringes, and greens. As you stray from safe areas into marginal areas such as green-side and fairway sand bunkers, light

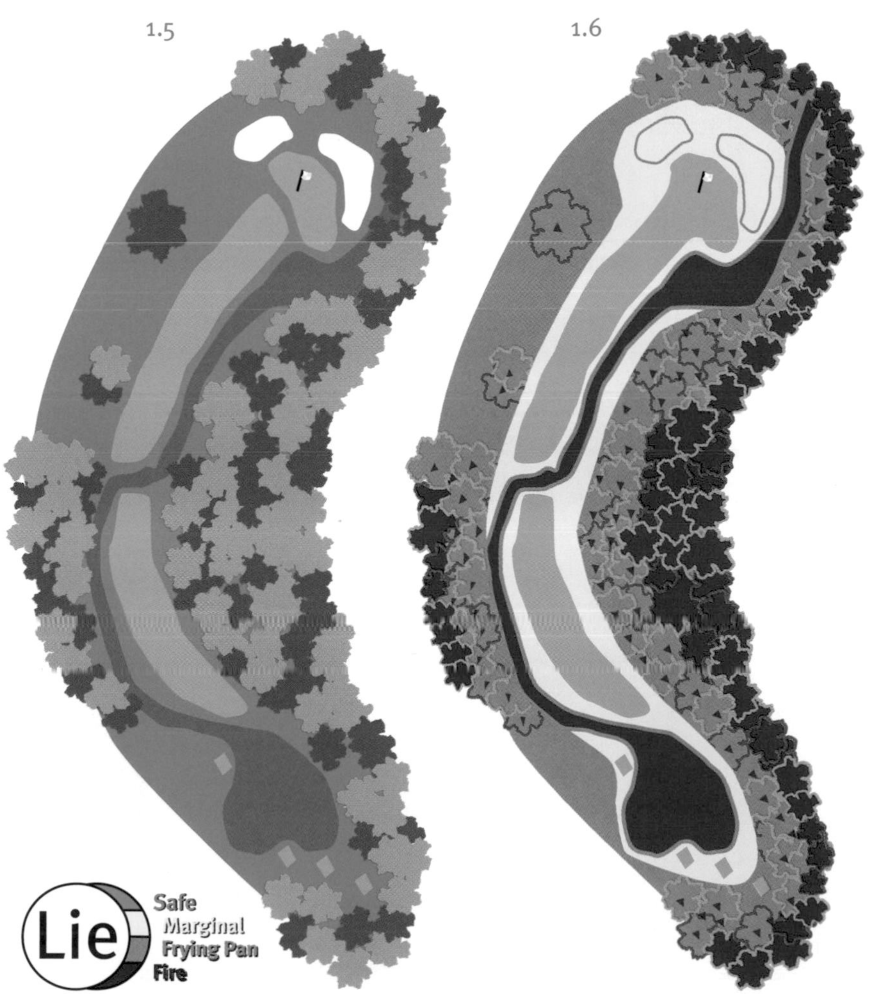

rough, and low-level slopes, the color changes to yellow. These locations present golfers with marginally more difficult lies to play from than those in safe areas. More serious rough, trees, deep and/or sloping sand traps, valleys with up/down slopes, and combinations of these conditions qualify as "frying-pan" (orange) areas. These are significantly more difficult lies, stances, and swing conditions from which it is easier to hit a bad shot out of the frying pan into the fire (that is, from a bad lie into an even worse lie). "Fire" (red) lies are defined as the really bad conditions on a golf course: severely sloped gullies, tall weeds, deep grass, creek banks, ditches, ponds, mud, lakes, fences, and any other extremely difficult lie.

Are you surprised that most of golf is not green and safe? Don't be; this arrangement—more trouble than safety—is generally true for most courses (the exact trouble/safe ratio is unique to every hole, and to every course).

Imagine how much yellow, orange, and red you would see in a lie-difficulty color view if you looked down the super-narrow fairways of a U.S. Open Championship course, to greens surrounded by 8- to 10-inch rough. A truly difficult course presents far more trouble to the golfer than the local municipal course, which specializes in providing safe (and fast) playing conditions. My purpose in showing you this view is to make you aware of how much trouble exists. Your association of color with trouble in your mind's eye will be useful later in using your Damage Controller.

TROUBLE AFFECTS SHOT PATTERNS

1.7. The world's best 4-wood player

You've seen where trouble is, and you understand how shots fly into shot patterns. Now let's examine how trouble affects results. Look at a typical amateur 4-wood shot pattern (imagine it might be yours) alongside a pattern of one of the best 4-wood players I've ever seen, Phil Mickelson (Figures 1.7, 1.8). Notice I left out all the shots

Your 4-wood shot pattern

Phil's 4-wood shot pattern

1.8

themselves and showed just the shapes of these two shot patterns. Phil's good 4-woods are longer and straighter than yours, and he hits a higher percentage of good ones than you. You, on the other hand, hit more shots into marginal, frying-pan, and fire lies than he does. He must be the better 4-wood player.

See what happens when we move both of you from safe lies into frying-pan trouble with your same 4-woods (Figure 1.9)? As you would expect, performance degrades from trouble. Uneven ground, grass between the clubface and the ball, or tree-limb interference changes the way swings must be made. From frying-pan lies it's natural to expect fewer good swings—and more bad swings—from anybody.

1.9 Your 4-wood shot pattern (frying-pan lie)

Phil's 4-wood shot pattern (frying-pan lie)

Why do trouble lies cause such troubled swings and degraded results? Because most of your practice time has been spent hitting shots from perfect lies on level ground. It's no surprise that this doesn't help at all when you're in trouble and must make "different" swings. Just look at some ways trouble can affect shots:

- Tall grass, clumps, and weeds limit your ability to get the clubface cleanly on the ball at impact.
- Surrounding bushes, trees, banks, and fences affect your ability to swing normally.
- Sloping and undulating terrain upsets your stance and balance.
- Your swing rhythm and timing are degraded by any (or any combination) of the above factors.
- Aiming (target orientation) is difficult when you can't see the target as you address your shot.
- Choosing a target is difficult when you can't predict how far or in what direction your shot is going to fly.

Every golfer is human, and no human is perfect. We all make good swings and bad ones, even from perfect lies. However, pros handle trouble lies way better than amateurs (Figure 1.10). Notice how much smaller Mickelson's change in shot pattern is (green vs. red) than yours.

1.10

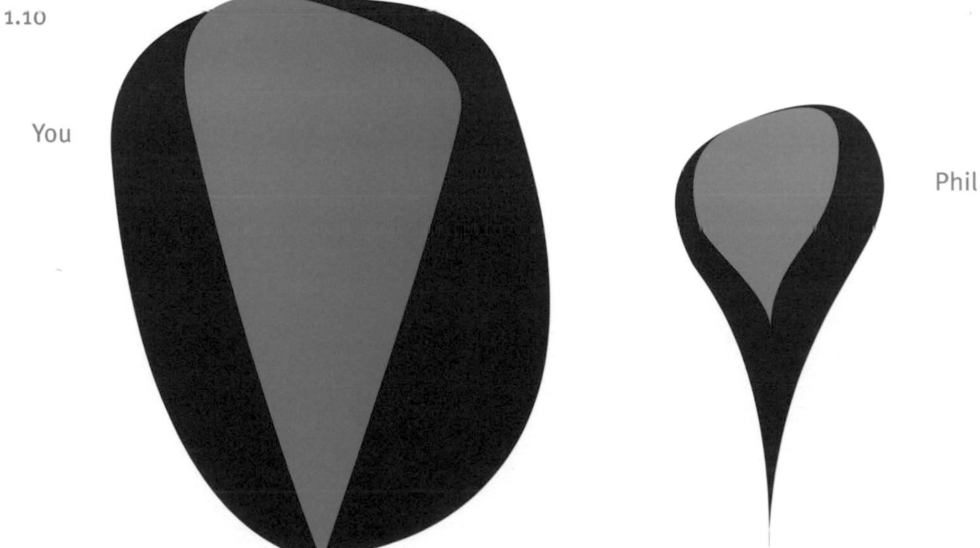

Recognition of this phenomenon, that trouble affects amateurs disproportionately more than pros, is important for you to understand. Pros get out of trouble on their first try; amateurs don't. It's no coincidence that amateurs record disaster scores frequently, while pros record them rarely.

TARGET SELECTION

Where you aim your shots is as important as how well you hit them. You should aim at a target that takes into account the size and shape of your expected shot pattern. Only after you've located your ball, evaluated its lie, selected your club, and established what kind of swing you can make (i.e., created an awareness of what your ensuing shot pattern might be) are you ready to think about how aggressively you want to choose your target. From perfect lies in the fairway, this choice is important. For shots from trouble, your target choice is way more than important. It's critical. It affects, even determines, your chance of successful escape . . . or disaster.

You may be a golfer who normally plays conservatively from good lies and already chooses safe targets when playing from trouble. Or you may be a riverboat gambler who can't resist trying almost impossible shots. In either case, your target selections will fall into one of four categories: Conservative, Aggressive, Risky, or Dangerous (Figure 1.11).

In the Target Selection Chart the colors green, yellow, orange, and red again represent shots that end up in safe, marginal, frying-pan, or fire conditions of play, respectively. The relative density of colors in each spectral band represents the probability that your shot will end up in those conditions.

Conservative target choices are those that receive and retain shots in safe lies at or above 80 percent of the time. Of course, the higher your skill level, the higher your percentage of shots that end

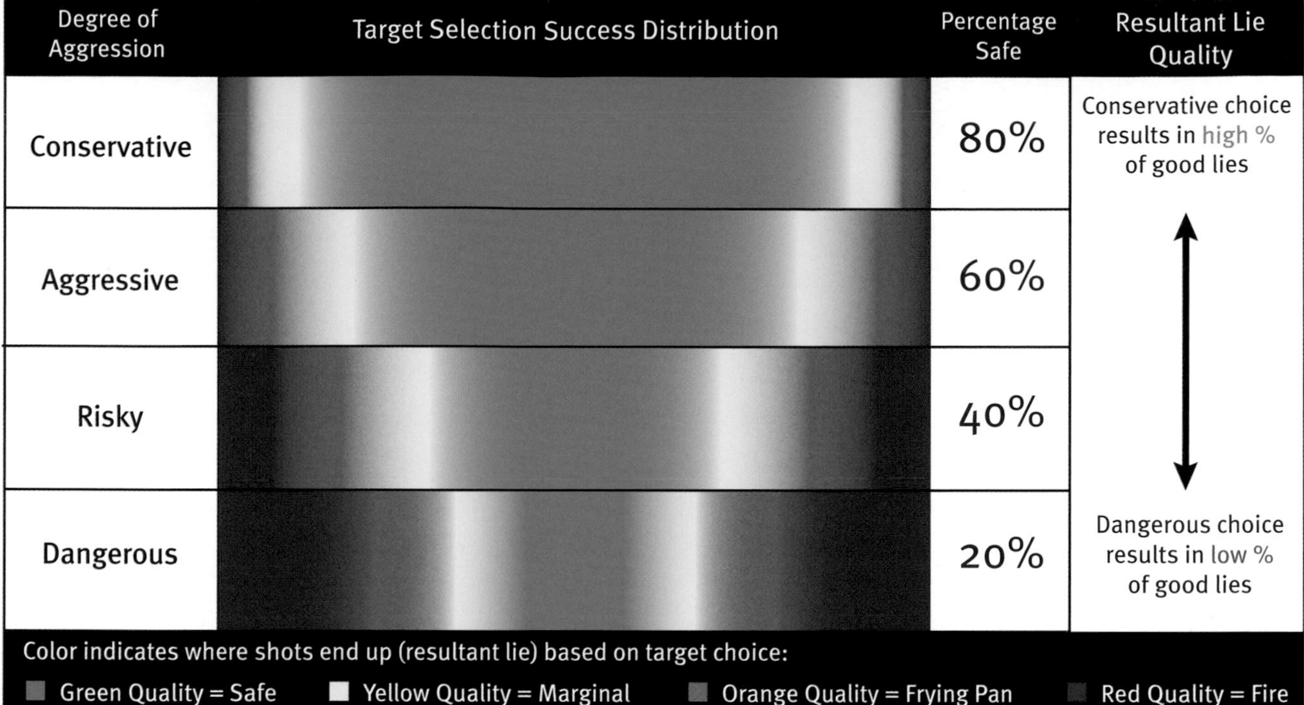

1.11 up safe when hit to any given target. So an aggressive target for you may be a conservative choice for Phil Mickelson.

If the chance that your escape shot will end up in a safe lie is only 60 percent, you are choosing an aggressive target. When you choose a 40-percent chance-of-safe shot, you are making a risky choice. And when you try a shot you believe will turn out safe only 20 percent of the time, your target selection is classified as dangerous. (If you choose a less-than-10-percent probability of a safe target, your strategy is reckless and silly; we don't even have a color for that.)

On a well-designed course, it is frequently the case that the closer you aim to the flagstick, the more dangerous the shot becomes. This is especially true for shots from trouble (which usually don't have much backspin) that fly into larger shot patterns. If you understand what the target-selection colors are telling you—"the more green a target choice has, the greater the chances are that you'll hit the ball there safely"—you understand their meaning!

THE OVERVIEW CONNECTION

What is the relevance of statistics, shot patterns, trouble, and target selection to your game? It's important to be familiar with these concepts because together they determine how you perform from trouble on the golf course. They all play a part, when combined with your skill, in determining how well or poorly you hit shots. When strung together shot after shot, these factors combine to determine how you score. I point this out because most golfers don't think this way—they think the skills they practice on the practice tee and putting green completely determine their scoring. My point is, when you find trouble (as all golfers do) the factors of statistics, shot patterns, and target selection (factors most golfers don't consider) not only degrade, but degrade dramatically enough to ruin your score and round.

A GOLF BALL IN TROUBLE IS LIKE A SNOWBALL

A golf ball in trouble can be like a snowball rolling downhill—it presages an "avalanche" effect:

- Trouble lies on uneven terrain affect a golfer's setup and posture.
- Troubled setups and postures (i.e., those that have never before been practiced) degrade a golfer's swing.
- As swings degrade, shot patterns expand.
- As shot patterns expand, target selection becomes more critical (when you don't know how large your shot pattern will be, you can't knowledgably choose the best place to aim, to statistically minimize your score).

Most golfers think their normal swing skills from normal lies determine their scores and handicaps. They believe if they groove their swing on the practice tee, they can avoid trouble on the course, and avoid disaster scores. They are wrong. They're not aware of how much trouble exists on a golf course, how often they are in trouble (during every round), how poorly they perform from trouble, or how consistently and significantly their bad shots from trouble effect (and ruin) their scores.

Pelz Golf Institute Research Results

Based on tournament scorecards from the DuPont and PGA TOUR Superstore World Amateur Handicap Championships, Myrtle Beach, South Carolina

Golfers:

- Play most of each round (14–17 holes) well below their handicap. On a few holes disaster strikes and ruins their score for the day.
- Blame a few errant shots, bad bounces, and/or bad breaks for getting into trouble
- Say they played well, but scored badly
- Blame "getting into trouble" for causing their disaster scores
- Vow to practice more, so they can learn to stay out of trouble
- Don't recognize disaster holes as a recurring part of their normal game

Golfers don't "get" what this disaster-score problem is, or that they have the problem. They don't understand that disaster holes are a normal part of their game, and so they can't very well look for an answer to a problem they don't know they have. They don't know that the setup postures and swings required from trouble lies are different from their normally practiced swings, and they have no idea where their shots are going when they execute really bad swings from trouble lies.

The result is that a few times each round, golfers hit into trouble and unwittingly use the exact recipe for disaster scoring. They stand in an unusual posture on difficult terrain, attempt a swing they've never practiced before, aim at a target they have almost no chance of reaching, and hit shots out of the frying pan into the fire. Disaster!

1.2 Why Disasters Happen

We've now established a few concepts to help you understand how the game of golf is actually played. I hope these concepts enable you to see how the lie of the ball interplays with a golfer's skill, shot patterns, and target selections (conservative, aggressive, risky, dangerous) to determine his scores. And you should be aware of how much more drastically trouble affects the performance of amateurs than it does pros.

It's time to look at what can be done about this. The truth is that PGA TOUR professionals don't have much of a problem with trouble lies, and you shouldn't either. I say this because I already know about Damage Control and what it can do for you. You don't understand this yet, but you will!

TROUBLE IS GOOD

Yes, you read it here: Trouble is good. The game wouldn't be as much fun or exciting without it. Courses are designed to get you into trouble, and to test how you escape from it. It's part of the challenge. Good course design graduates from providing safe, to marginal, to frying-pan, to fire lies, as your swings and shots go from good to bad to awful. Architects also design holes to mix in both good and bad luck. This makes for the wonderful and sometimes euphoric (when good luck comes) game we all play and love.

All golfers make bad swings from time to time. Even from perfect lies it's easy to hit shots into serious trouble (Figures 1.12, 1.13, 1.14). You must assume that you, too, will hit shots into trouble. Your mediocre, bad, and awful swings are as much a part of your game as are your good swings (just not as frequent, thankfully). And they will get you into trouble on occasion. This means trouble is waiting for you in your next round, and for the rest of your golf career. Embrace it—trouble is part of the game, and it's good.

How should you deal with trouble? The best way is to not spend all your time trying to avoid it, because that can't be done. The better way is to learn to get out of it (learn Damage Control) without letting it ruin your day.

1.12 TOP
If you're looking for trouble, you can find it from the sixth tee at Porcupine Creek.

1.13 TOP RIGHT
David Duval facing a trouble shot from pinestraw at East Lake Golf Club.

1.14 RIGHT
The hole is 22 feet above the sand at PGA West Stadium #16.

FROM BAD TO WORSE

What happens when your ball lands in trouble? Assume you drive your ball into an area of medium-high rough. If your next swing is well executed to a safe target, it should propel your ball out of the trouble and back into the fairway, to a better position than where a good drive would have ended up in the first place. You'll probably post an acceptable score on the hole, and no real harm will come to your round. This is what happens to most golfers after most errant shots in a normal round of golf.

However, if your shot from the rough doesn't escape and instead flies into even worse trouble, you've now jumped out of the frying pan and into the fire. It's easy to make a bad swing from a trouble lie. Once you play from a bad lie to a worse one, it's even easier to play a worse shot into an impossible situation. This sequence progresses from bad to worse, spiraling down into a true disaster hole. It sometimes even leads to a "ball in pocket" situation, the ultimate disaster.

1.15

Every trouble lie presents a potential for disaster. The scenario described above defines the pathway to a disaster score. Unfortunately, this sometimes happens several times in the same round. Trouble lies are part of the game by design—they have to be. But bungled escape attempts, fire lies, and disaster scores don't have to be!

A different pathway to disaster is brought into play when golfers try to hit "hero" recovery shots from trouble. They've seen Tiger and Phil hit these shots, so they try them too. Unfortunately, they've usually never practiced them before. The hero shot requires a trajectory so precise that even a relatively good swing can seldom carry it off (Figure 1.15). Hero shots rarely turn out well, and more frequently initiate the spiral to disaster.

HAVE YOU SEEN YOUR SHOT PATTERNS FROM TROUBLE?

Remember, we all have shot patterns with bad shots in them, even from perfect lies in the fairway (even from a tee). It's also true that none of us are immune to bad bounces, which can get us into trouble even after we've executed a good swing and launched a good shot.

There is even worse news, however. Everyone's shot patterns, regardless of skill level or handicap, get significantly worse when a golfer is playing from difficult conditions. If you think about it, this makes sense. Obviously the scatter of our shot patterns will be worse for shots hit from difficult stances and bad lies. We've never practiced them.

Look at the positions players get themselves into when trying to extricate balls from trouble (Figures 1.16, 1.17a–c). Can you imagine where some of these shots go? (Believe me; they don't all turn out perfectly!)

Have you ever practiced from these kinds of conditions, and do you know how to change your swing to produce good shots from

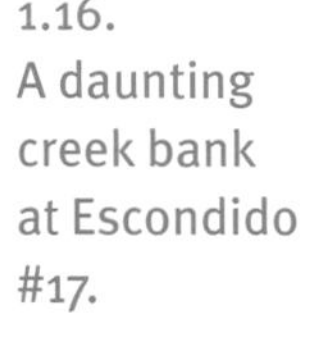

1.16. A daunting creek bank at Escondido #17.

1.17a TOP LEFT
From above my knees at the fourth hole, Pinehurst #2.

1.17b TOP RIGHT
Sometimes the best way out of jail is not a conventional swing.

1.17c LEFT
6' 4" tall PGA TOUR pro Tom Sieckmann faces a "low-ball" shot.

them? Your honest answers are probably "never" and "I have no idea." This proves my point: Given these two answers, you can't possibly know what your shot patterns from such circumstances will look like!

Imagine if you were asked about your shot pattern from a slight downhill lie just off the right side of the 18th green at Pinehurst No. 2 (Figure 1.18). Imagine that a hundred balls were dropped down around you on this tight (and, remember, slightly downhill) lie, and you're looking up at a super-fast green above you that's running (sloped) away from you. How large would your shot pattern around the flagstick be? Think especially where your marginal and bad shots would end up when the green is like a firm and fast upside-down saucer and balls run off the green as they near its edges. Have you ever run a test like this, hitting practice shots, just to see where they go?

Most golfers haven't and have no clue where their shots will end up, especially when they hit them from trouble lies with swings they've never tried before, from stances they've never swung from before, in normal rounds. How can anyone possibly plan and play reasonable escape shots from trouble when they have no idea where the ball is going after they hit it?

1.18

NORMAL SWINGS DON'T WORK FROM TROUBLE

This is why you shouldn't try a normal swing from trouble:

- Your posture on uneven terrain affects your normal swing mechanics.
- Normal swing mechanics can't be used when obstructions interfere.
- Shots behave strangely when poor clubface-to-ball contact is encountered.

1.19

Look at three examples:

1. When a high-lofted, open-faced cut-wedge shot is needed to pitch a shot over sand from a severe downhill lie (Figure 1.19), a normal swing with a wedge will not do the job. From a normal posture with your spine vertical, a normal swing will hit the ground behind the ball (Figure 1.20).

1.20

2. When you need a flat swing to hit from under a tree, standing up normally and taking a normal backswing that tips the tree and deflects the club off-line is no good (Figure 1.21a–b).

1.21a

1.21b

1.22 3. When backspin is impossible to impart to a ball from tall grass, golfers should not try stopping shots on a fast green with the flagstick on a downslope (Figure 1.22). Instead they should play away from the pin in a different (and safer) direction.

Whenever golfers get into trouble, it seems to be unique and different—because it usually is! They've never received instruction on setting up or making swings from trouble, never practiced from these conditions, and never noticed how shots react from such lies. Most golfers simply don't know how to make the swings and shots that will allow them to effectively escape from trouble. These are the facts. When playing the wrong swing or the wrong shot, the odds of escaping safely from trouble are not in your favor! But golfers routinely use normal swings from trouble and expect normal shot behavior in terms of backspin and stopping ability. This often results in badly hit shots getting into even worse trouble, and disaster scores follow.

ESCAPE SKILLS EXIST

The knowledge and skills needed to execute successful escape swings exist—the pros use them all the time. At the Pelz Golf Institute we have measured, tested, and proven this fact: Faced with a ball 12 inches above or below their stance, most golfers cannot hit a shot anywhere near where they are aiming. The same is true for uphill and downhill lies, tall grass lies, balls embedded in sand, under tree limbs, next to bushes, on hardpan dirt, and a wide variety of other troubled conditions we all (sooner or later) get ourselves into. Pros, on the other hand, don't perform too badly (worse than normal, but not really badly) from these same situations.

The truth of the matter is:

- Most golfers don't realize that normal swings don't work from trouble.
- Even if they are aware of needing a changed swing, they don't know how to make one.
- Special swings (those used to escape from trouble) are not taught by most golf professionals.
- Golfers don't realize that trouble shots don't usually spin or stop like normal shots.

Even after you understand all of this, you still may say to yourself, "I can't hit the ball well enough from good lies to stay out of trouble. Why not practice my normal swing and make it better, rather than work on learning something new like Damage Control?" But you are wrong to think this. No golfer has ever, in the entire history of golf, learned to avoid trouble on the golf course, and you are not likely to be the first! Even if you devote the rest of your life to improving your normal game, you'll still find trouble, and Damage Control can help you get out of it without ruining your score.

Normal practice will never prepare you for this. No matter how much you practice on the range from level terrain and perfect lies (Figure 1.23), it won't help you when you get into trouble (Figure 1.24). It's also of no help that most practice facilities do not offer the chance to practice from trouble-lie conditions. The result is that most golfers have never practiced the setups, swings, or shots needed to escape from trouble.

1.23

1.24

THE DEVELOPMENT OF DAMAGE CONTROL

Damage Control is a new and different set of golf skills. It is a real, meaningful, and important skill set. In the past, golfers only thought about trouble in terms of working on their normal game to better stay out of it. Staying out of trouble is impossible, however, and no one will ever do it! The game's ruling body, the United States Golf Association (USGA) keeps setting up courses to play longer, tighter, harder, and faster, all in an effort to make sure that everyone, even the pros, gets into trouble. This is as it should be, no matter how much better golfers learn to hit shots; trouble will always and forever be part of the game!

By studying how golfers perform from trouble, and then interviewing them afterward, we've learned why disasters happen and what must be done to avoid them. We've measured why amateurs are so bad at hitting trouble shots, and why they don't understand where their shots are going before they hit them. In this research we discovered that Damage Control requires five skills amateurs don't have (Figure 1.25). We have also developed drills to instill and develop these skills (Chapter 7), and formulated a fundamental philosophy: By escaping from trouble on your first try, and to a place better than your previous shot would have finished had it been well hit, you should lose less than one stroke—and almost never encounter disasters.

The Five Skills of Damage Control

- **Setupology** (Chapter 2: How to set up for trouble shots)
- **Swing Shaping** (Chapter 3: How to shape your swings for shots from trouble)
- **Hand-Fire Feel** (Chapter 4: Using your hands in escape shots)
- **Red-Flag Touch** (Chapter 5: Learning how escape shots behave once they land)
- **Damage Control Mentality** (Chapter 6: Using your Damage Controller)

1.25

CLOSE COUNTS

In Damage Control, like in horseshoes, close counts. One of the nice things about Damage Control is that your swings don't have to be perfect. They just have to be good enough to get the ball out of trouble and safely back into the game. If you can get back to a safe lie, in a position (blue area) that's better than what the previous errant shot (red X) would have been in had it been perfect (black X), you've done it (Figure 1.26). And Damage Control will lower your scores without requiring you to change your normal skills, swings, practice techniques, or habits.

1.26

1.3 Separate Thinking . . . and Almost Avoiding Disasters

"Almost" is a big word. No one can avoid disasters completely, always, and forever. Luck plays too big of a role in golf, and we're all human. We all make bad swings. All golfers, sometime, somewhere, will make a disaster score on a disaster hole in the future. If you don't want that to happen, then you'd better stop playing the game.

THE DAMAGE CONTROLLER AND TROUBLE GOLF

Through our study of amateur golfers and disaster scoring over the years at the Pelz Golf Institute, we have begun to understand not only how pros swing differently when they're in trouble situations, but that they also think differently than amateurs do. This realization led us to discover that the approach to thinking through or analyzing a trouble situation is different from the way most golfers think during a normal golf situation.

Forget for a moment the physical part of standing, balancing, and swinging to hit trouble shots; there is another aspect of playing from trouble that involves thinking, calculating, planning, and judgment. This mental aspect of playing from trouble takes place in a part of your brain that we'd like you to imagine is compartmentalized in a small package (something like Figure 1.27). We want you to imagine that it works like a small computer that has optics, intelligence, and memory so we can talk about it, describe its functions, and develop and train it to perform for you as if you were a pro. We refer to this part of your brain as your Damage Controller.

Your Damage Controller is where you actively (albeit subconsciously) process information and control your body and

1.27

swing for trouble shots. Imagine that it's separate from your normal golf brain. The Damage Controller is where you store the memories of all of your past trouble shots, including the lies, stances, obstructions, swings, and shot patterns, as well as your results from those particular circumstances. It also houses the judgment skills you use to imagine your results from such trouble situations in the future.

THINKING DIFFERENTLY?

Why is seeing and thinking differently when you encounter trouble conditions (that is, keeping your Damage Controller separate from the rest of your brain) so important? For normal play from the fairway or rough, the lie of the ball is usually reasonably good and often does not effect the selection of your target. Because lies are so often similar, your distance and club selection (with the hole as target) are usually your primary mental focus points. Bad decisions or poor thinking under normal conditions are usually penalized (on average) by less than one stroke.

When trouble shots are encountered, however, the conditions of lie difficulty and swing unfamiliarity become overwhelmingly important and frequently dictate not only different target selections, but also result possibilities. Strategic thinking and innovation become critical to fully evaluating situations relative to the conditions, your physical skills, and successful options. At these times, the consequences of making bad decisions or choices can suddenly become catastrophic.

It is the severity of these consequences that requires your play from trouble to be so different from your normal golf strategy, and requires thinking when in trouble to be so different from normal thinking. It is the dire consequence of disaster scoring that dictates how amateurs must change the way they see and analyze their play when confronted with trouble. To facilitate this change, we use the metaphor of the Damage Controller to compartmentalize what and how your mind's eye should perceive and process information for the unique situation of escaping from trouble. Our concept of training this part of your mind to compute in a logical and linear progression will also help to reduce your emotional responses in trouble situations.

HOW THE DAMAGE CONTROLLER WORKS

Look carefully at the photos on the next few pages to understand the three steps of how your Damage Controller should work (assuming you're thinking like a PGA TOUR pro):

Step 1: Imagine looking through your Damage Controller (Figure 1.28) and seeing a close-up view (Figure 1.29) of the lie and any swing limitations involved around the ball. You then scan back and see an overview (Figure 1.30) of the trouble you're

1.28

1.29

1.30

in. Almost immediately the Damage Controller in your mind determines which club and swing (Figure 1.31) to play in this situation, and how difficult (on a scale of 1–10) the shot will be.

1.31

Step 2: After "seeing" your situation, your Damage Controller enables you to visualize the escape shot-pattern (see white outline, Figure 1.32) you might expect from these conditions.

1.32

Step 3: As you survey the landing area you're considering for the shot, your Damage Controller sees your shot pattern with a color-scale overlay (Figure 1.33), which indicates how safe your target is to hit to (only 20 percent safe in this case)!

1.33

You might think I'm exaggerating how precisely pros think when they're in trouble, but I'm not. The examples shown here are no stronger or clearer than the imaginary pictures pros see when they evaluate the trouble they find themselves in during tournament play.

It is this process and this level of clarity we hope to instill into your Damage Controller, to help you learn to play with Damage Control. No matter how difficult a situation you may play into in the future, we can help you learn to play out of it like a pro.

IT IS NICE TO KNOW

You may not have thought of these kinds of things before, but they are the considerations you should weigh when you're playing from troubled conditions. You should be aware of not just how to hit trouble shots, but where they are likely to go after you hit them. And you should be able to estimate the probability of success in hitting safely to any target you look at.

Of course, no one is perfect. You can never be 100-percent sure you will escape to your target spot in the fairway, just short of the green. You can only determine the odds of getting there. And you must also realize that to take full advantage of your Damage Controller decisions, you need the skills to make good Damage Control setups and swings.

PLAY WITH PROBABLE, NOT POSSIBLE

For years I've been trying to convince TOUR professionals to only attempt shots they believe they can pull off successfully 90 percent of the time. Why 90 percent? Because I've seen too many golfers try risky shots, with disastrous results. Remember, the best players in the world occasionally make bad swings, and even they aren't immune to the wrath of the "Golf Gods" when they combine trouble lies with poor swings and high-risk targets.

At this point let me introduce another piece of information we've garnered from our research. After studying the play of both amateurs and professionals (almost without regard to skill level or handicap) we've found that if golfers think they can hit a shot, they will try it. And when I say *can*, I mean if they think they *possibly* can, or are *physically capable* of hitting the shot.

Too many golfers attempt shots they *possibly can* hit, rather than those they *probably will* hit. Golfers play the game expecting to hit the most perfect shot they are physically capable of hitting, rather than one of the shots from their normal shot pattern. They expect to hit their best shot when they need it, even when a penalty awaits them if they don't.

What are they thinking? Do they think bad shots only come when they aren't trying to hit good shots? How many golfers try to hit bad shots? Nobody is perfect, and you must recognize the probability is high that you will hit shots commensurate with your current shot pattern. Your pattern can be improved over time, but it is what it is for now. In any situation, trouble or otherwise, you should play the game expecting and allowing for shots from your current shot patterns.

LESS AGGRESSIVE IS SOMETIMES MORE AGGRESSIVE

An example you may identify with is a 23-handicap alumnus of my Scoring Game School (who shall remain anonymous). I had measured his driver shot pattern and was then playing a round of golf with him. He swings hard, hits lots of long hooks and slices, and about twice in ten drives unleashes a really nice, long, straight one. We were on the toughest hole on the course, a very difficult 430-yard par-4. This hole would take a perfect drive and a perfect 5-iron for him to reach in two. It has out of bounds down the left and a lake along the right in the driving area (Figure 1.34).

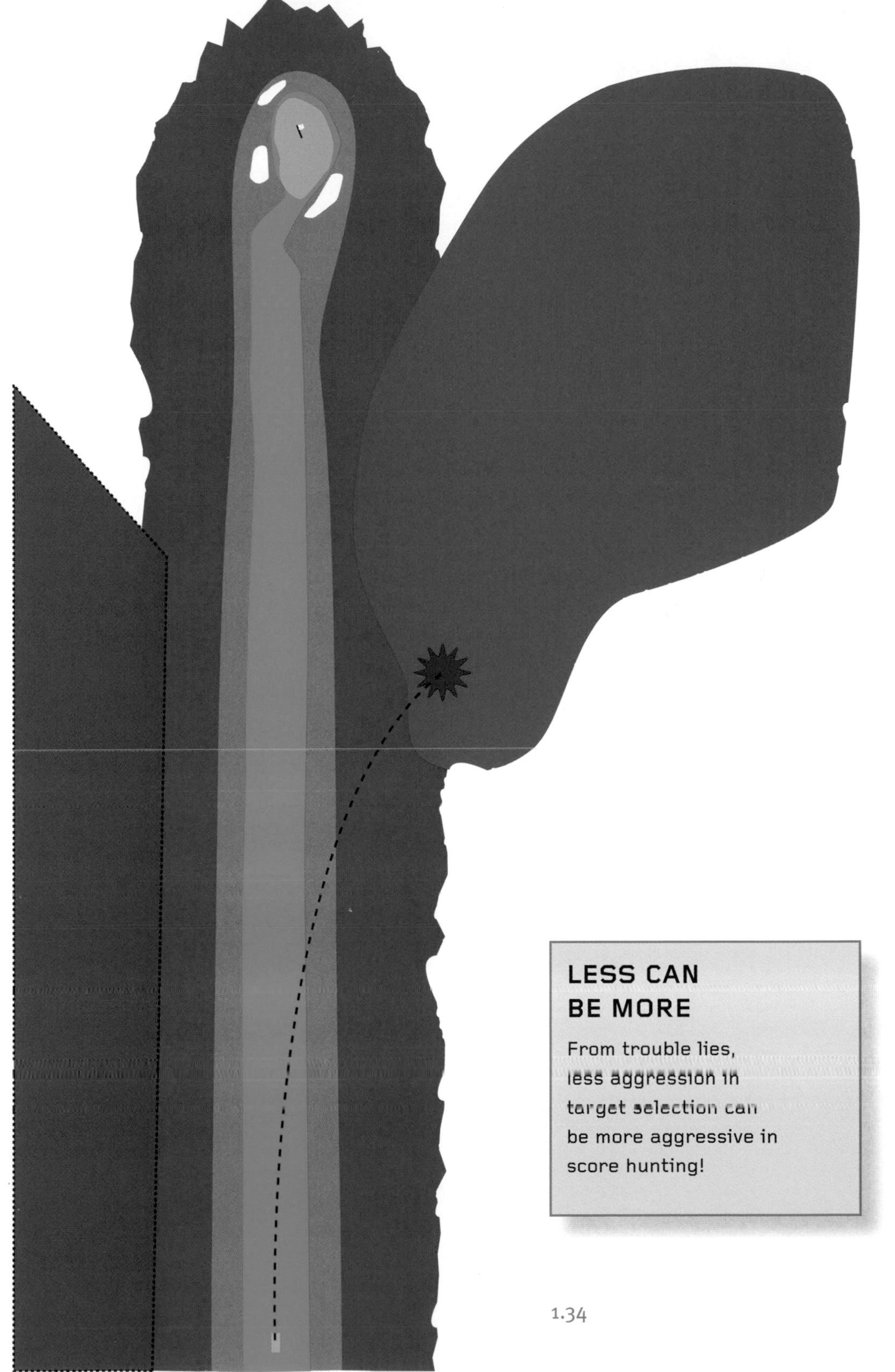

LESS CAN BE MORE

From trouble lies, less aggression in target selection can be more aggressive in score hunting!

1.34

He hit a reasonably good, solid, 250-yard drive, which landed at least 20 yards in the water on the right.

To my amazement, he exclaimed "Damn it, I can't believe I hit that shot. I just can't get water out of my mind; it must be a mental thing. Water is like a magnet to me." As I looked at him and smiled, I visualized his driver shot pattern on the practice range (with no water in sight). He had absolutely no recognition that *at least 50 percent* of the best drives from his drive-pattern would land in that water. To my way of thinking, he had just saved one stroke by at least not hitting it out of bounds to the left!

His expectation (hope) was to hit one of the few good straight drives he knows he *possibly can* hit, at just the right time. Would he ever consider hitting a 5-wood off the tee safely short of the water, then another 5-wood to the green on this hole? Not a chance! When he stands on any tee it is bombs away, no matter what lies ahead.

To see this, look at the trouble situation in the next series of photos. Too many golfers would try a miraculous recovery shot here (Figure 1.35), aim at the flagstick, hit the ball short or into the water, and score at *least* 6 (Figure 1.36). Instead, wouldn't it be smarter to acknowledge the trouble you're in, escape from it, then try to minimize the damage by getting up and down from the fairway short of the green to score a 4, or at worst a 5 (Figure 1.37)?

1.35

Too many golfers would try a miraculous recovery shot here (Figure 1.35, previous page), aim at the flagstick, hit the ball short or into the water, and score at *least* 6 (Figure 1.36, below).

1.36

Instead, wouldn't it be smarter to acknowledge the trouble you're in, escape from it, then try to minimize the damage by getting up and down from the fairway short of the green to score a 4, or at *worst* a 5 (Figure 1.37, below)?

1.37

LESS THAN ONE STROKE IS KEY

Most golfers aren't aware of their shot patterns from good lies on level ground, except in a very general way. Even fewer realize how bad (large) their shot patterns become from trouble lies, so they are not aware of how easily they may move from the frying pan into the fire.

To control damage you must accept this fact: Every time you get into trouble, you will add a fraction of a shot to your score, on average. The lower you make that fraction, the better player you will become. In this regard, the farther forward you can advance your safe escape toward the green, the lower that fraction of a stroke lost should be (on occasion it can be zero, when you save the stroke with a one-putt).

There is seldom a reason you should lose more than one stroke because you hit a shot into trouble. Just by escaping back into the fairway ahead of where you should have been in the first place, you should be able to average losing *less* than one shot. The process of playing with Damage Control is not much different from the process you normally use on most shots (the fundamental cycle of golf). To see this, imagine you just hit an errant tee shot onto a sidehill lie under a tree:

1. Look at your lie and evaluate the trouble; determine your best shot (club and swing).
2. Now visualize the shot pattern of your escape shot.
3. Select the target for escape that gives you the combination of:
    - A 90-percent certainty of successful escape to a safe lie
    - A position closer to the green than your previous shot *should* have been in the first place.
4. Take a Damage Control setup and stance, appropriate for your sidehill lie.
5. Make a Damage Control (flat or upright) swing that misses the tree limb.

6. After your ball lands back in the fairway (out of trouble), focus on recovering to save the stroke you might lose due to the trouble you were in.

> **LESS THAN ONE STROKE**
>
> When you escape from trouble on the first try, and get back into the game in a better position than you would have been in from a good shot in the first place, you are free to recover and save the stroke you are in danger of losing.

1.4 Subtleties of Damage Control

Great players play with Damage Control. When you see them face difficult, challenging shots on television, they usually do quite well getting themselves free without losing strokes to par. They succeed because they've learned the skills of Damage Control through their own on-course experiences.

They've practiced the shots that cost them strokes, to be ready to better execute them in future tournaments. Based on vast experience (they all hit lots of bad shots into lots of trouble), TOUR professionals have learned the setup and posture, swing shape, hand action, touch, and target selection required to extricate balls from trouble on their first try on a regular basis. They usually only hit into worse trouble when they get greedy and try the hero-shot approach. It is critical to their success to have Damage Control skills and to know what shot patterns to expect from trouble lies.

WHO NEEDS DAMAGE CONTROL

Sam said it best: There is a famous story about a discussion between the great Sam Snead (Figure 1.38) and baseball's best-ever hitter Ted Williams. Each was making a case for the difficulty of his sport when Snead said, "But Ted, in golf we have to play our foul balls." Sam got it right. In golf you have to play your foul balls—and it helps when you do it with Damage Control!

1.38

Damage Control is so important because we will all need to deal with trouble for as long as we play the game. Because you'll periodically make bad swings, and occasionally get bad bounces, you never know when Damage Control will be needed to minimize the damage to your score.

Disaster holes are not fun for anybody. The best players in the world practice Damage Control. Vijay Singh, who may practice his normal swings more than anyone else, also works on his Damage Control skills: Figure 1.39 shows him practicing at East Lake Golf Club before the TOUR Championship; he's got a tough greenside lie with water behind the flagstick.

Vijay is a good example of how PGA TOUR players use Damage Control. He is an aggressive player and hits driver off most tees. Although he is very straight considering his distance, he drives his ball into trouble in almost every round he plays (I've walked many rounds with him, and believe me, this is true). Once in trouble, however, he has incredible escape skills, and seldom hits shots from the frying pan into the fire. His escape shots usually get him into a position from which his wonderful short-game skills can eliminate the potential lost stroke. This is in contrast to average golfers who don't practice as much on the practice tee, don't play nearly as much on the course, and *never* practice trouble shots. This is a gigantic

1.39

difference between the games of professional golfers and weekend players. This book offers you the chance to learn these skills (they are relatively easy to learn) and begin to bridge this gap.

DAMAGE CONTROL MAKES THE GAME EASIER

Scoring seems difficult to golfers (and maybe to you) because most golfers try to play the game without having the proper tools. Trying to get out of trouble with a normal swing is like trying to do home repairs without the right tools. Can you imagine trying to unscrew a screw without a screwdriver? Or pound a nail without a hammer? Learning the skills of Damage Control, however, changes all this, because now you have the tools necessary to successfully play shots from trouble. And all Damage Control requires is swinging "good enough" to escape on your first try. You don't have to hole your shots from trouble or even hit them close to perfectly. You simply must get them back into play in one try.

Once you've mastered the skills of Damage Control, there's no reason why you won't be able to:

- Play from uphill plugged bunker lies
- Splash the ball out of water hazards
- Hit from under tree limbs, off hardpan, pine needles, or cart paths
- Blast shots from U.S. Open–style rough

GO FOR IT

There are thrills in golf you shouldn't miss. I realize it's fun to try, and occasionally pull off, a miracle shot. When your score is not important and you have plenty of time and golf balls, you should "go for it." Why not try a miraculous recovery for fun? It can truly be a thrill and worth the expense of time and a few balls. I warn you, however, against trying these shots when your score really counts. It's easy to get addicted to the thrill of the "almost impossible," so be careful. It can work itself insidiously into your attitude, and if it ever gets in there, it will cost you dearly, both in your scoring and handicap.

> **SAVING STROKES**
>
> You'll probably save more strokes in three weeks from learning Damage Control than you would from practicing your long iron swing for three years.

I often hear the following question from students: "Why should I practice Damage Control when my normal game is so bad? Wouldn't I be better off learning how to hit the ball better, so I can avoid trouble in the first place?"

The answer is NO! The inadequacies in your normal game are the reason you need Damage Control. The worse your normal game is, the more you need and will benefit from Damage Control. Damage Control will always stay with you and always be needed. Your normal game is never going to be good enough to avoid trouble completely. Trouble is designed into the game, and you need to learn to make the best of it. Damage Control will improve your scores, no matter how good the rest of your game gets.

WHEN IS DAMAGE CONTROL NEEDED?

Whenever your ball finds trouble, you need Damage Control. You need it to bring your good scores all the way to the house, lower your handicap, score the best you can on any given day, and smile as you walk off the 18th green.

If you are a struggling professional, Damage Control can help you win more tournaments, miss fewer cuts, lower your scoring average, and win major championships. If scoring is important to you, you need Damage Control, but don't try to extend it over the entire golf course. Level lies in light rough are in-the-game. Damage Control is necessary only when you worry about hitting the next shot into worse trouble than you're already in.

But forget about Damage Control on the practice range. Normal practice time on the normal flat range is for your normal

swings, and you will always need some of this. Damage Control development is not to be substituted for normal practice. You can't practice the swings of Damage Control when you're on the perfectly level practice range anyway. When you practice normal swing techniques, don't even think about Damage Control.

If you want to score better the next round you play, work on your Damage Control skills immediately. I know you're going to get into trouble in your upcoming round and I want you to get out of it without ruining your score. Don't cancel any lessons you have scheduled with your pro; just do your Damage Control work first. Then you'll have the best of both worlds, playing better for most of your round, plus getting out of trouble when you stumble into it.

CHAPTER 2

Setupology

SETUPOLOGY IS THE SKILL of setting up properly for trouble shots. It's the first skill of Damage Control because setup comes before the backswing, downswing, or follow-through of any trouble shot, and a bad setup affects everything that follows. Whether they're caused by an unusual stance on difficult terrain, tree limbs that inhibit the golfer's stance or swing, or "stuff" around the ball, trouble lies require different setups than normal shots do. And setting up poorly is often the first mistake golfers make when they're in trouble.

Research shows that awkward stances and improper setups dramatically increase the odds of creating bad swings and errant shots. But data also indicate that when golfers understand and internalize good Setupology, they significantly improve their ability to escape from trouble.

Setting up in bad posture for a trouble shot is like tying one hand behind your back before trying to swing. Even from perfect lies on level tees, bad setups make swinging properly difficult. But from a trouble lie on difficult terrain with a bush limiting your backswing, setting up in the wrong posture is the golfer's equivalent of shooting oneself in the foot.

2.1 The Fundamentals of Your "Normal" Swing

Before getting into Damage Control Setupology, I want to make sure you appreciate the concept of your "normal" swing. It's what you think of as your golf swing, the swing you normally use on the golf course. Whether you're trying to hit the ball long distances with a power swing, short and accurate distances around the green with finesse swings, or into the hole with putting strokes, these are the swings from normal lies you usually think of as your normal golf swing.

WE NORMALLY PRACTICE OUR NORMAL SWINGS

Every golfer tries to make perfect swings and hit perfect shots all around the golf course. When those swings and shots turn out to be not so perfect, we take lessons and practice to improve them. These lessons often deal with our posture, ball position, grip, or wrist hinge; the shape of our swing; or where we take divots. This is good and as it should be. Most of our practice shots are hit from near perfect lies on the flat and level practice ground of a practice range. This practice helps to refine and groove our normal swing for the normal shots we encounter most often on the course. Again: This is good.

But please beware: None of the above does anything to improve your Damage Control skills, which are the skills you need to extricate your ball from trouble.

IT'S DIFFICULT TO MAKE A GOOD SWING FROM A BAD SETUP

To make a good swing, one must be physically able to make good shoulder and hip rotations, arm swings, and wrist hinges, without being restricted by some internal (arthritic) or external (trees, bushes) interference. For example, your body can't make a good swing while you're lying on your back, because the ground won't allow you to turn your shoulders or hips enough to create good motion, and there's no room to swing your arms or club behind you (as I demonstrate by lying on the ground on my back for the "hands and wrists only" swing, Figure 2.1). These restrictions provided by

2.1

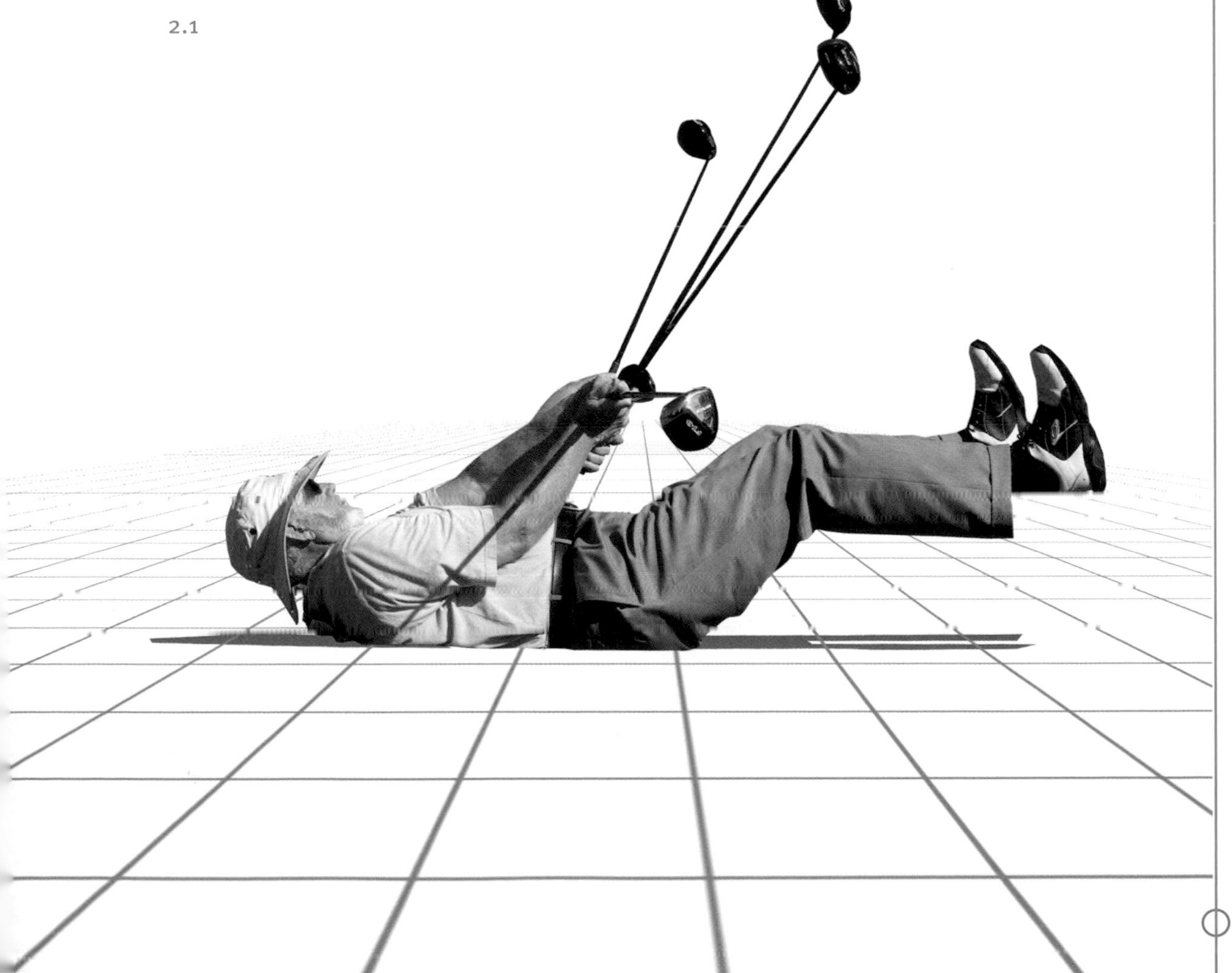

the ground are even more obvious when you see them rotated into an upright position (Figure 2.2), a situation that a tree behind you might create. On the normal practice tee, however, there are no trees, and you can turn freely and make your normal driver swing (Figure 2.3). Good body rotation is crucial to a good golf swing.

2.2

2.3

It's also difficult to make effective swings without good balance, because losing balance means moving your body in strange ways and getting into restrictive positions. Obviously, bad balance can destroy any golf shot (as Eddie learned trying to hit a shot from off a balance board, Figure 2.4).

2.4

THE SWING IS NOT A CIRCLE

When viewed face-on, the cocking of your wrists relative to your forearms increases gradually as you swing back away from the ball. The wrists don't become fully cocked until you're near the top of your backswing, but they should stay fully cocked in the downswing until shortly before impact. This difference in wrist-cock timing produces a larger radius for the arc of the clubhead in a normal backswing, as compared to the downswing (demonstrated by one of the best wedge players of all time, Tom Kite, Figure 2.5). It's important to be aware of this difference in your normal swing radius, because it can be important when some kind of obstacle is crowding in behind your golf ball.

2.5

EVERY SWING HAS A "BOTTOM"

Every golfer's swing has a low point, or "bottom," relative to the ground, and this is where a normal divot is taken. Different players with different swing-timing and weight-transfer actions will have slightly different bottom positions on shots from level ground.

From a lie on level ground, the divot taken by most golfers starts near the middle of their stance, which means the center of their swing-arc bottoms out about two to four inches forward of their stance center (Figure 2.6). The precise location of where a player's club first strikes the ground can be dramatically affected by the terrain of the lie, the stance, and the setup of the player. This can have a significant effect on where the ball should be positioned (forward or back) in the stance for a shot from trouble.

To ensure clean contact with the little ball (the golf ball) before contact with the big ball (the Earth), the little ball should always be positioned either exactly on or slightly behind where the golfer's divot will commence (and this sometimes means the ball should not be in the middle of the stance).

2.6

YOUR SWING PLANE

When you track a golfer's clubhead (not the shaft or hands) and it travels in a single plane throughout the entire swing, the player is said to be swinging "in plane." The angle measured between the plane and the ground is the player's swing-plane angle. If you put a camera lens (or your eyes) at the right place behind a golfer's in-plane swing, you'll see something like Tom Kite's swing (Figure 2.7).

2.7

Although most golfers try to swing their clubheads in the same plane on both their back- and through-swings, not too many actually do it. It is also true that most golfers address shots with their hands somewhat below this plane, and then the faster they swing and the more clubhead speed they generate through impact, the closer their hands come to moving up into their swing plane at impact.

Most golfers swing in two planes: one for their backswing, and then a different plane for their down-/through-swing. Some golfers have no distinct planes in their swings at all—they swing in a constantly changing loop of di-

SWING PLANE

You can't see if golfers are swinging "in plane" when you're standing behind them, unless your eyes are in the swing plane (which they will not be, if you are standing on an extension of the ball-to-target line). This means you can't tell if a golfer is swinging in plane from a photograph, unless you know the camera lens was precisely positioned in plane when the photo was taken.

rections. Generally (although not always), the less complex and more in plane a golfer's clubhead motion is, the more consistently solid and repeatable swings, and the higher the percentage of solidly hit golf shots will be.

As club length changes, it forces the golfer's swing-plane angle to change, as seen for my driver and wedge swings in Figure 2.8. Longer clubs require flatter (lower-angle) swing planes, while shorter clubs require more upright (larger-angle) swing-plane angles for any given golfer.

2.8

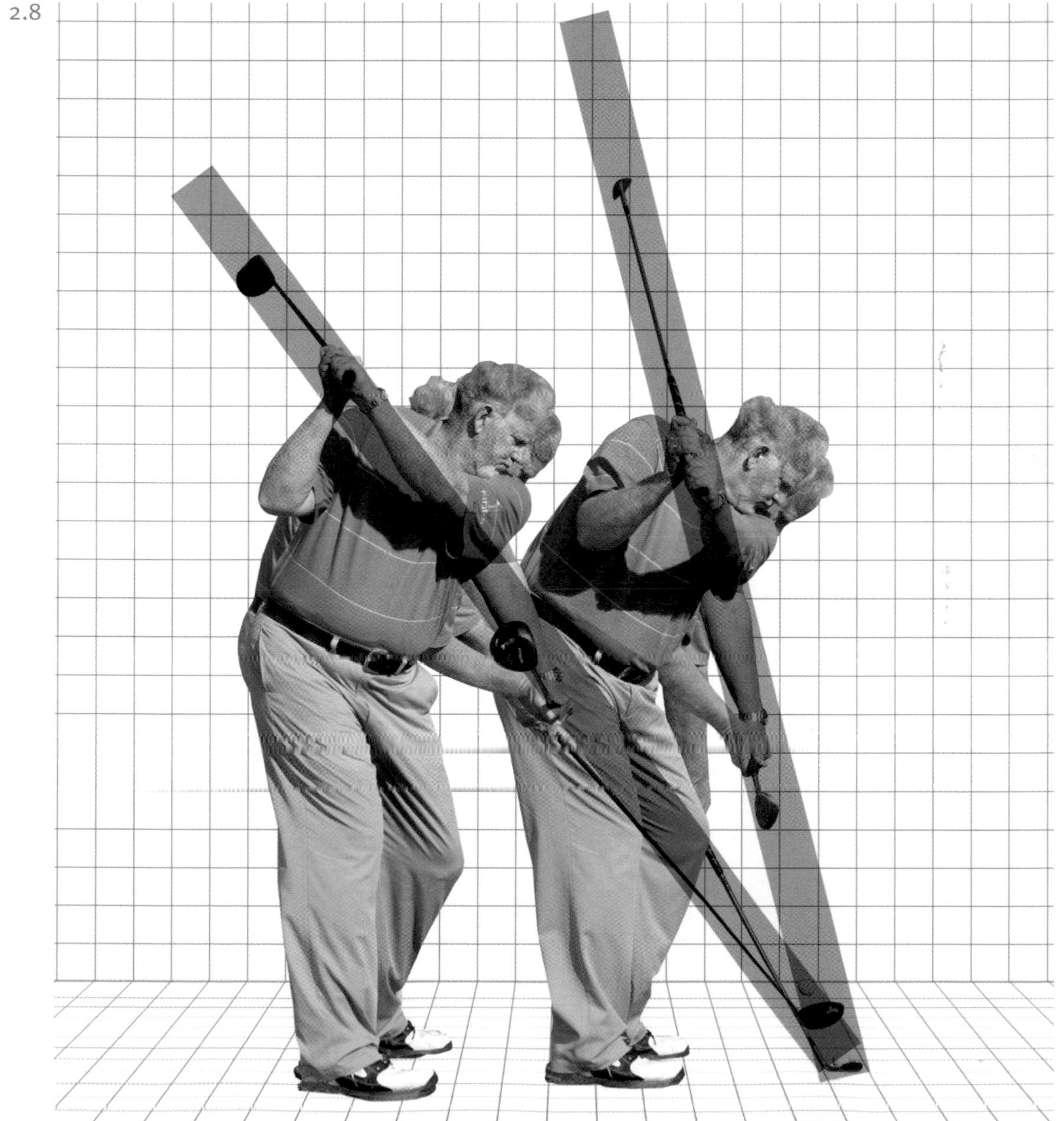

YOUR SWING IS UNIQUE

Your normal power swing is what it is, and it's yours. Whatever swing characteristics you have, they are probably uniquely yours, and they're almost certainly not perfect. But that's not a problem—it's just golf. You can improve your swing if you work on it, especially if you work on it consistently with an experienced golf professional.

While your normal setup and swing may not be perfect, you groove it on the practice range and in everyday play. You develop subconscious compensations to adjust for its deficiencies, and then incorporate them into your normal play. Your normal swing, including compensations, is the "heart" of your normal game.

2.9

An example of how a setup deficiency can be compensated for is when a golfer normally positions his ball too far forward in his stance. From good lies in the fairway he can learn to "chase after" the ball through impact and hit reasonable shots (Figure 2.9). Notice the dip of Eddie's head (some golfers also employ a late-release wrist cock) through impact, as he demonstrates the "chase" move. Depending on how often you practice it, you can get reasonably proficient at hitting shots from level lies with a chase swing.

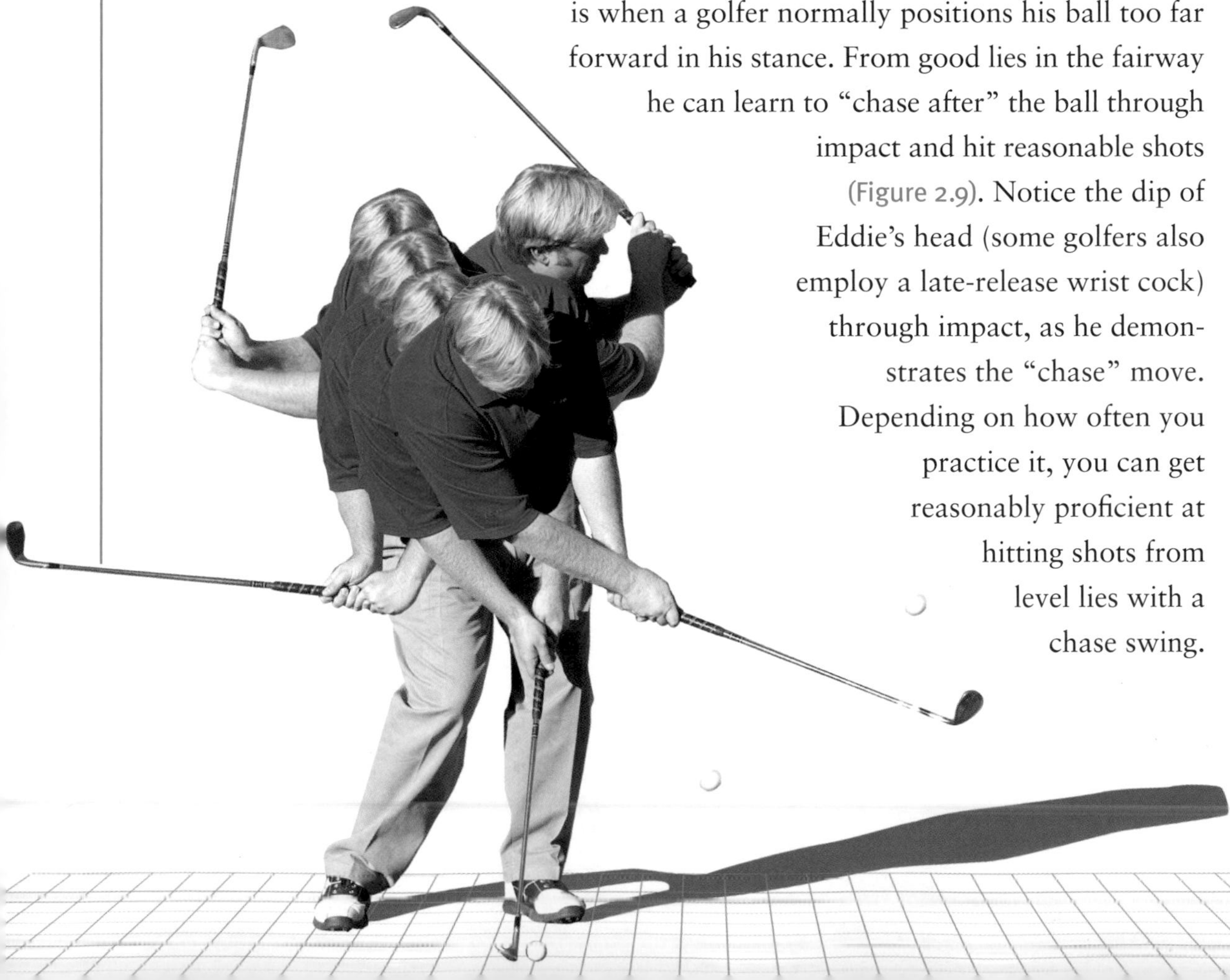

DIFFICULT LIES UP THE ANTE

A chase swing ultimately limits a player's game, however, because it becomes difficult to execute from sloping terrain lies (and even from level lies under pressure, when the hand and wrist muscles get tense and swing timing gets fast). Watch Eddie's chase swing try to hit a ball from a severe downhill lie. With that same setup error (ball too far forward), the chase swing can produce a "flub" (Figure 2.10) of epic proportions. Who knows where this ball will go? For sure, it won't fly dead to the target with good trajectory and backspin, as originally intended.

2.10

Different courses also present difficult setup challenges. Every time a golfer changes his normal setup posture—thereby putting his muscles, bones, and joints into different relative positions—his swing undergoes significant changes. Look at the obviously different setup positions that Ken Venturi gets into for shots from greenside moguls in Figures 2.11, 2.12, 2.13 (moguls by architect Pete Dye, TPC Sawgrass, Ponte Vedra, Florida). Just imagine the different swings and swing feels he has to make to successfully execute from these different setups.

2.11

2.12

TROUBLE LIES REQUIRE SPECIAL SWINGS

Golfers produce their normal shot patterns from perfect lies on level terrain. Add to this a non-level stance on uneven ground, and the quality of both their normal setups and swings degrades, causing the spread of their shot patterns to grow significantly. When you then add additional trouble around the ball (grass clumps, weeds, roots, or tree limbs) that gets in the way of their normal backswings or downswings where their shots will go becomes anybody's guess.

This is exactly why normal swings—even the best normal swings—won't work from trouble. Trouble-lie interference can cause bad swing planes, shot contact away from the sweet spot, and even the introduction of foreign substances between the clubface and ball at impact. Attempts to compensate for unique lies, stances, and setup positions, with never-before-practiced in-swing adjustments, lead to shot patterns that expand exponentially—often to disastrous proportions.

2.13

NORMAL SWINGS DON'T WORK FROM TROUBLE

I hope this picture of your "normal" swing, and what happens to it when your ball is in trouble, is clear to you. Your normal swing from your normal setup:

- Is not a circle
- Has a wider backswing than downswing arc when the clubhead is behind you
- Has an arc bottom that occurs just forward (toward the target) of the middle of the stance
- Moves the clubhead in your unique swing plane
- Has deficiencies and compensations that are grooved for good lies on level terrain

THE PROS MAKE IT LOOK EASY

A number of trouble shots probably look easy when you see them played on TV from the proper Damage Control setup by the world's best players. The swings look simple, the players escape with no penalty and save par, and you're convinced to try the same shot the next time you find yourself in similar trouble.

The problem is:

1. You didn't notice the setup change the pro made or the ball position he used before executing his escape swing; and
2. You don't have a feel for how to make the swing, turn through the shot, or keep your balance. There is a chance you've never made such a swing before, never even once in your life. If you try this shot with no change in your normal setup or swing, you could very possibly unleash a badly off-line ball . . . and be looking at a chance for the disaster hole that ruins your round.

Understand that you set up and play with your normal swing from good lies on level terrain most of the time. No matter how good your normal swing is, however, it won't help you get out of trouble when you can't use it because of difficult stances, different postures, and obstructions around the ball.

Also, your normal swing thoughts, keys, feel, or balance don't produce their normal results from trouble lies, because you can't make normal swings from abnormal body positions. To see why all of this is true, it's time to look at how changing your setup in terms of spine position, stance width, and ball position affects your swing and shot results. In other words, let's look at Damage Control Setupology.

2.2 Spine Angles Influence Swing Mechanics

Your spine is the heart of your golf swing. It is the axis around which your golf swing turns.

While your posture may have been of little interest to you in the past, to play with Damage Control you need to understand how your spine angle affects your ability to swing. Having the proper spine angle is fundamental to Damage Control and critical to your swing performance from trouble.

YOUR SPINE-TO-SWING-PLANE ANGLE AFFECTS THE NATURAL EFFICIENCY OF YOUR SWING

The power of a golf swing is similar—yet different—from a baseball swing. The swings are similar in one sense: In both movements, power is more natural and easier to generate when the clubhead (or bat) swings perpendicular to the spine (Figure 2.14). There is maximum and fairly consistent power around the perpendicular (90-degree) angle, but power decreases dramatically as the swing plane moves far away from perpendicular. The swings differ in that baseball swings are usually closer to perpendicular to the spine than golf swings (except when baseball players go after bad pitches). This is because golfers play with the ball on the ground, while a pitched baseball approaches a batter somewhere between the shoulders and knees.

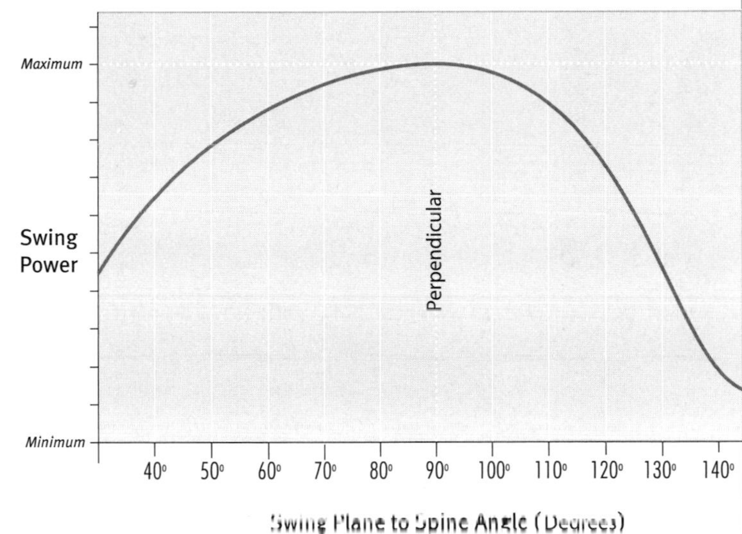

2.14

If you don't understand this, grab a golf club or a bat and make some swings as shown in Figure 2.15. In either game, as the clubhead (or bat) swings far above or below the perpendicular to the spine—the swing gets more difficult to make, and less powerful.

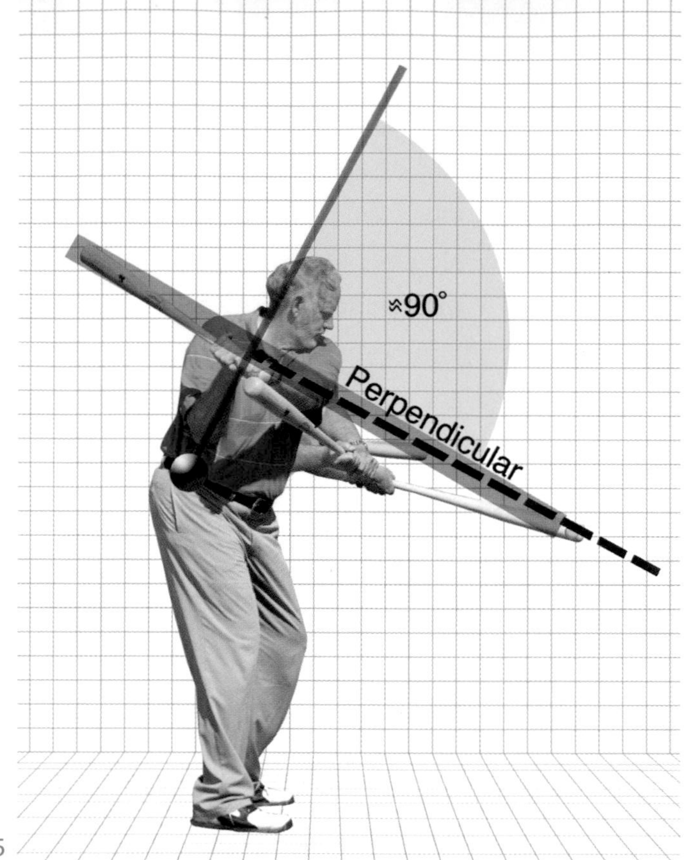

2.15

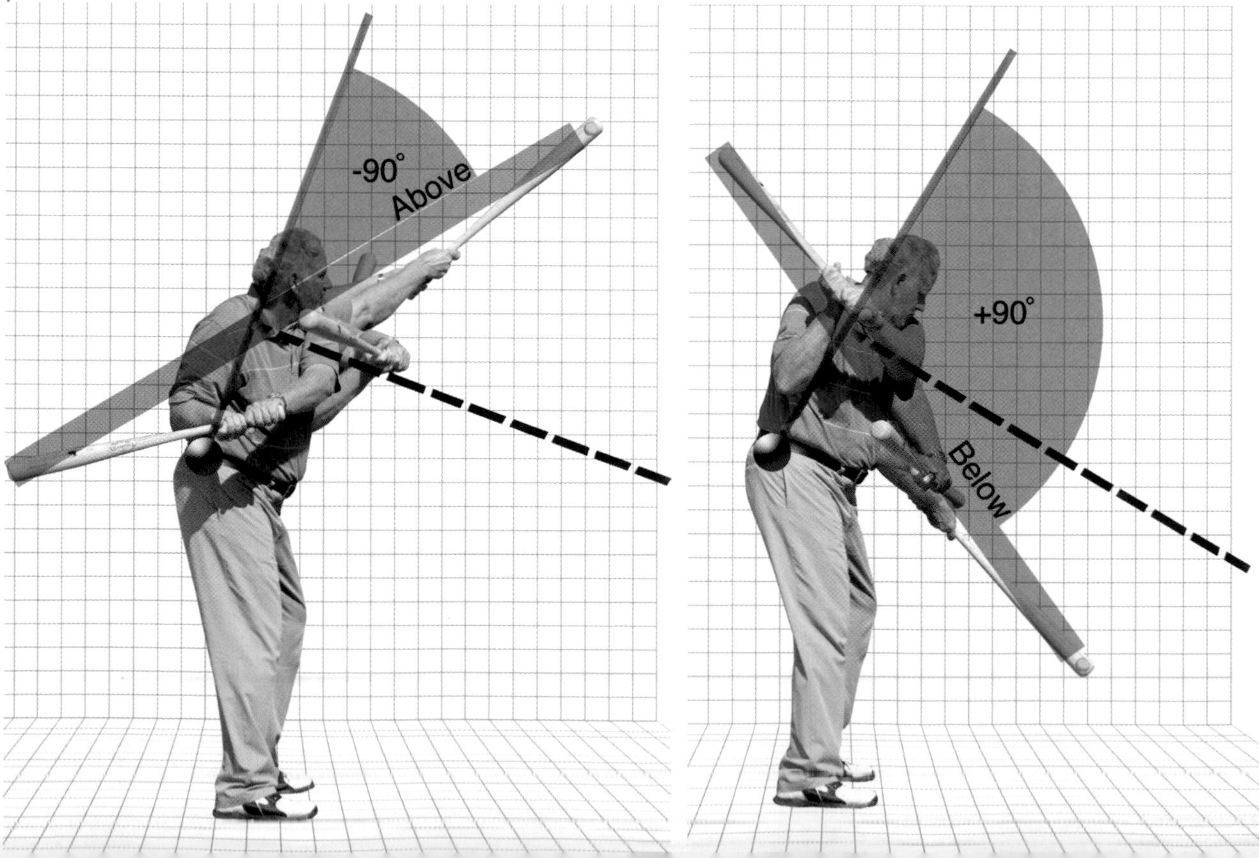

BENDING OVER OR STANDING UP AFFECTS THE SPINE-TO-GROUND ANGLE

Your spine-to-ground angle is measured (looking down-line from behind) as the angle between your spine and the ground. It can be made smaller by bending over closer to the ball, or increased by standing up straighter and moving your spine into a more vertical position (Figure 2.16).

2.16

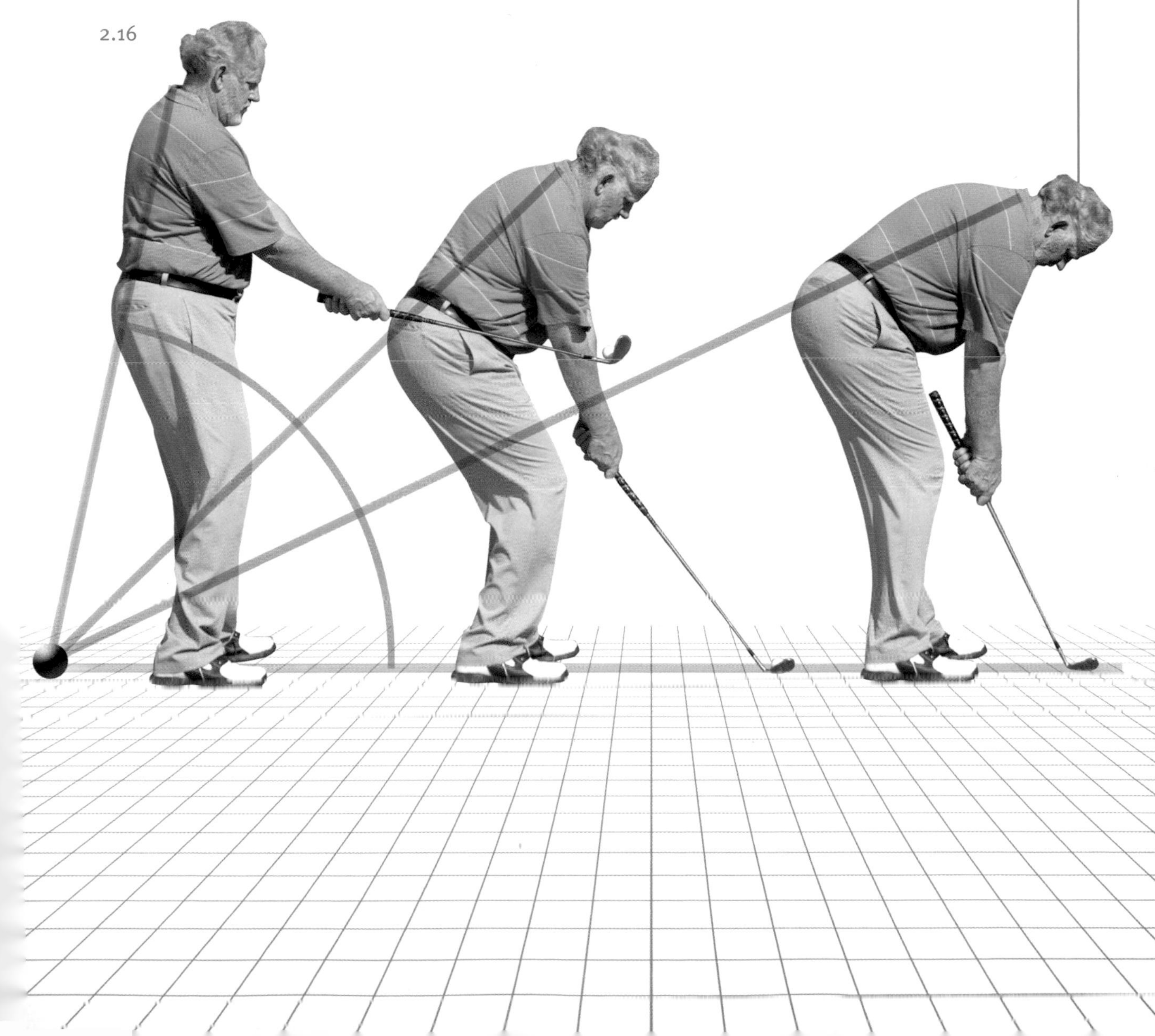

On level ground, the more vertical the spine is, the easier it is to make flat swings, all other things being equal. As you can see, when a golfer stands upright with his spine nearly vertical, it's easy to swing in a more horizontal (flatter) swing plane (Figure 2.17). When he bends over, putting his spine in a more horizontal position, the opposite is true. In this case a vertical swing becomes the more natural and easier swing to make (Figure 2.18).

2.17

2.18

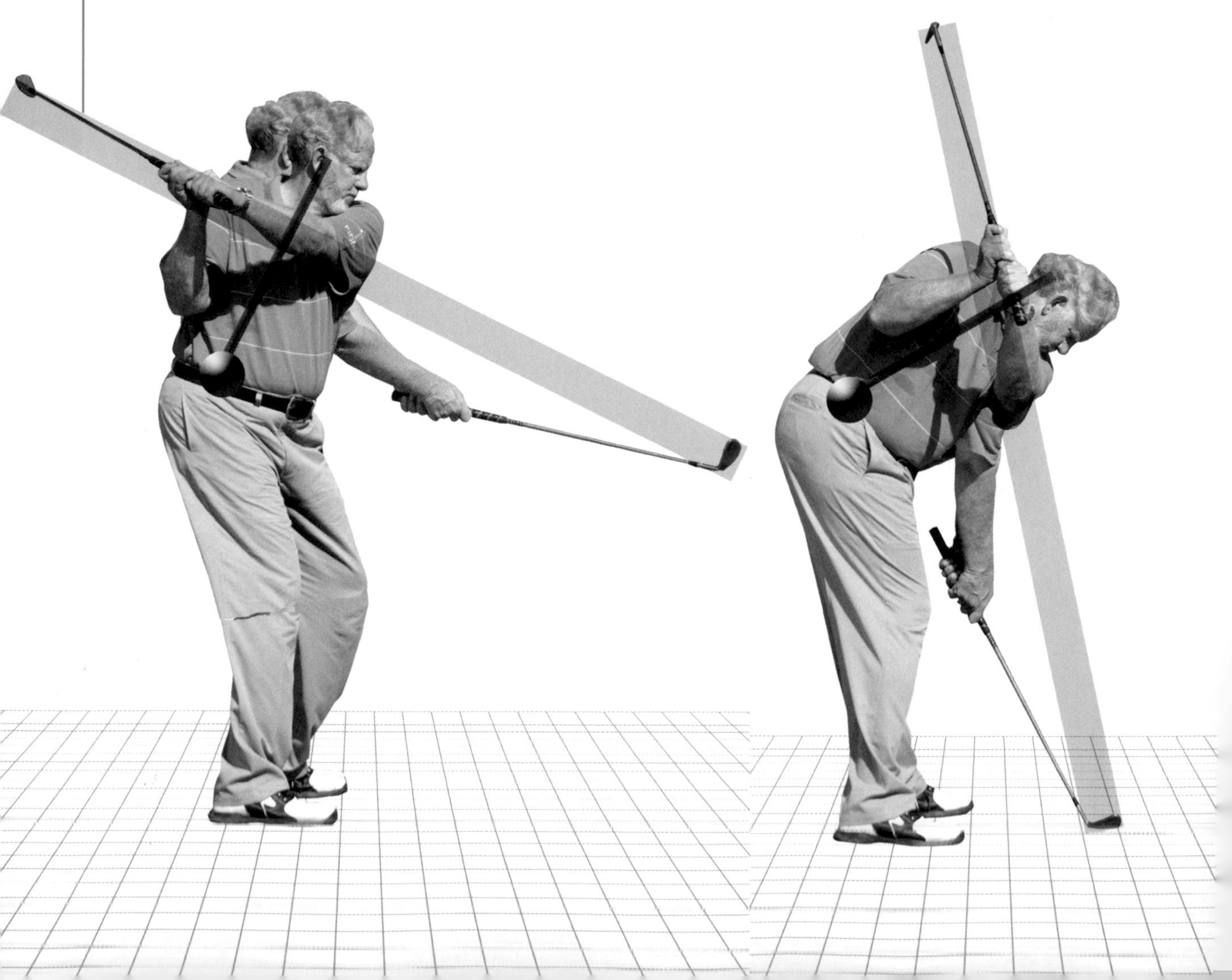

Applying this principle to a shot under tree limbs, it's better to make a flat swing from "on your knees" (Figure 2.19, spine more vertical), than from a standing-but-bent-over position (Figure 2.20).

2.19

2.20

Your spine-to-ground angle, height, arm, and club length all influence your swing plane. The shorter you are, and the longer your arms and clubs are, the more upright you will stand and the flatter you will swing (Figure 2.21).

2.21

Upright swings require the opposite spine-to-ground-angle relationship that flat swings do. Bending over encourages a more horizontal spine and makes swinging a club vertically much easier. It also helps to use the shortest workable club (Figure 2.22) when making an upright swing.

2.22

THE SPINE-TO-TRUNK ANGLE AFFECTS HIP ROTATION

The spine-to-trunk angle is the angle between the spine and the lower body (hips and thighs), as seen looking down-line from behind a golfer. The closer to 180 degrees, or a straight line, this angle becomes, the more easily and powerfully the lower body can be rotated. Conversely, the more bent-over a golfer stands, the smaller this angle becomes, and the more difficult it is to rotate the hips and lower body.

Even when the spine is upright, the hips are difficult to rotate if the spine-to-trunk angle is small. Such a position is required if you must squat to hit a shot from under a tree limb (Figure 2.23). If you don't believe this, try rotating your hips while swinging from a deep-squat position, sitting in a chair, or sitting on the ground.

2.23

TAKE YOUR SPINE ANGLES TO THE MIRROR

Now lay this book down, stand in front of a mirror, and internalize these three fundamentals of Setupology:

1. **Standing up = vertical spine = flat swing.** All other things being equal, the more vertically you position your spine, the flatter (more horizontal) your swing plane will become. Set up as you would for a "normal" swing with any club and watch yourself swing in a mirror. Notice the angle of your swing plane relative to the floor. Then stand up a little more vertically, imagine a ball on the side of a hill about a foot above your feet, and swing again. Notice that your swing plane gets flatter. Finally, stand perfectly straight up, imagine your ball in a bush at shoulder height, and see how easily and powerfully you can swing at it in a flat, almost horizontal swing plane (Figure 2.24a–c).

2.24a

2.24b

2.24c

2. Bending over = horizontal spine = upright swing. The more you bend over, the more horizontal your spine is, and the more naturally upright (vertical) your swing plane becomes. Start again from your "normal" address position and watch yourself in the mirror. As you bend over more, getting your spine closer to horizontal, your swing plane motion becomes more upright (Figure 2.25a–b).

2.25a

2.25b

3. Squat = locked hips = minimum power. The smaller the angle between your spine and trunk, the more difficult it will be to rotate your lower body during the swing, and the more upper-body power you must rely on in these conditions. To feel this, start from your normal address posture and swing in a flat swing plane with your eyes closed, concentrating on how easy and natural the swing feels. Then, keeping your spine-to-ground angle constant, squat lower to decrease your spine-to-trunk angle and swing again. Notice how the swing gets more difficult. Squat down even lower (making your spine-to-trunk angle even smaller) and repeat the same swing. Feel how much more restricted your hips feel, and how much less powerful your swing feels. Notice how it takes more effort to rotate your lower body and make a full swing back and through (Figure 2.26a–c). Now take the final step and sit on the ground. This will be your smallest spine-to-trunk angle, and it will surely create your most difficult lower-body rotation position, and least powerful swing.

2.26a

2.26b

2.26c

2.3 Spine Tilt vs. Lean

Spine tilt and lean angles refer to the angle of your spine forward or back (toward or away from your target) in a 90-degree different direction from your spine angle. Spine tilt is the side-to-side tilting of your spine toward or away from the target relative to your lower body, as seen from a face-on view (Figure 2.27). Spine lean occurs when a golfer leans his entire body forward or back along the target line, while maintaining zero spine tilt (Figure 2.28).

2.27

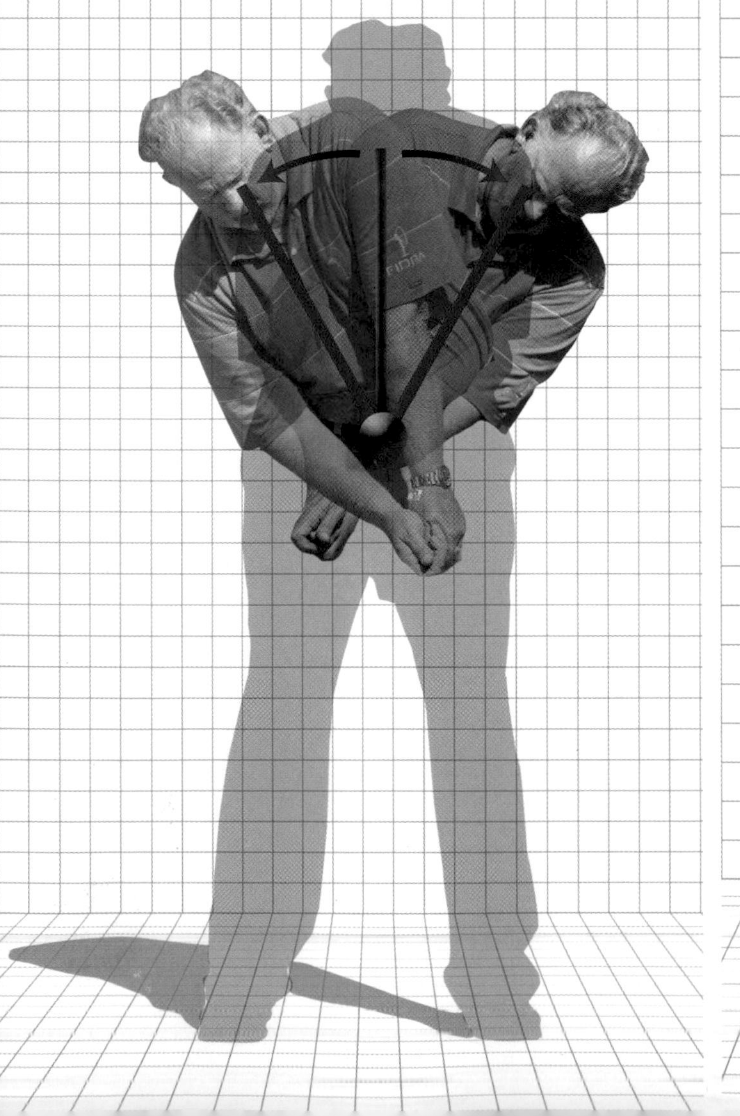

2.28

SPINE TILT IS NO GOOD

Spine tilt on level ground affects how the swing arc encounters whatever the ball is sitting on (Figures 2.29, 2.30), and is generally not recommended. There should be little or no spine tilt in your normal setup for shots with good lies on level terrain. Spine tilt also creates a second problem: The farther your spine tilts away from your lower body centerline, the more difficulty you will have rotating your lower body and producing power in your swing (Figure 2.31).

2.29

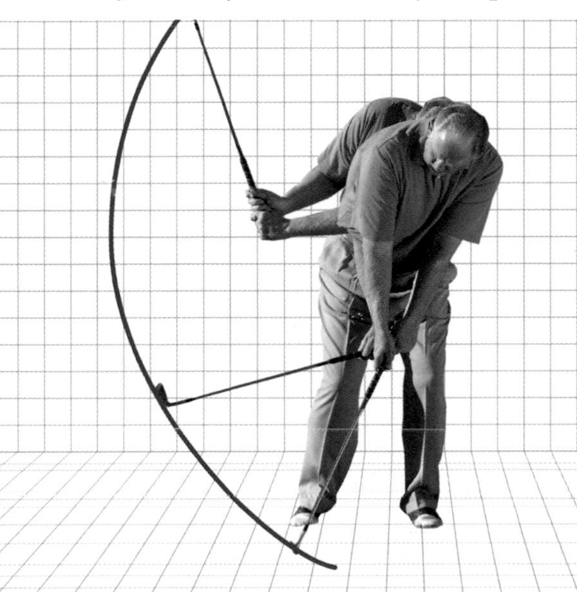

2.30

So for two reasons, spine tilt is not good when setting up your posture for a golf swing—in fact, it's something to be avoided. Many golfers do it all the time, however, because for some it's a natural and instinctive thing to do.

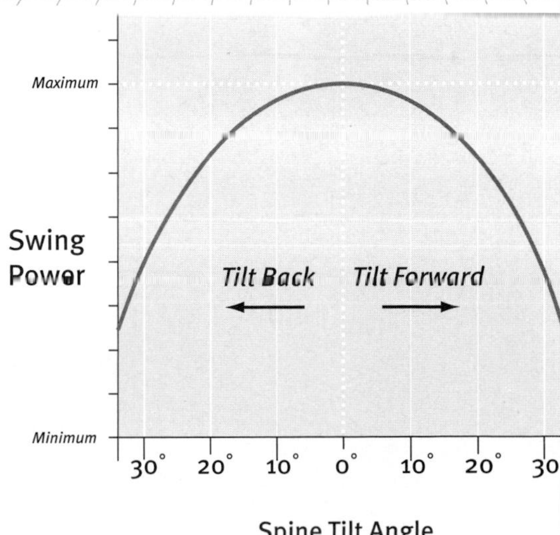

2.31

LEAN SPINE FORWARD ON DOWNHILL SLOPES

Golfers tend to lean back on downhill lies. Your head is heavy and your instinct for balance always influences you to keep your spine vertically under your head and balanced above your feet. Sometimes, however, you can't hit good golf shots from the most balanced position. For example when your ball lies on a downhill slope, to keep your head in good balance you instinctively stand more vertically (Figure 2.32). This leans your spine away from being perpendicular to the ground, making it more likely you'll hit the ground behind the ball.

2.32

The proper setup for downhill slopes is to spread your stance (feet) more than normal to provide a wider base, then lean forward to get your spine (and lower body) closer to perpendicular to the ground (Figure 2.33). This will also place a disproportionate and unusual loading on your forward leg, knee, and ankle, which makes keeping your balance as you swing a real challenge.

2.33

But just because this forward weight distribution is unusual doesn't mean it's wrong. In fact, for downhill trouble lies, it's exactly what you need to maintain through impact to execute a successful shot (Figure 2.34). Of course, after impact you need to walk forward to catch your weight and balance.

2.34

There are exceptions to this setup, however. Setting your spine perpendicular to the ground is not always necessary. For some small hand- and arm-controlled wedge swings used for short pitch or chip shots, it may be more comfortable to use a normal (vertical spine) stance. A perfect setup illustrating this normal, vertically balanced posture for a short pitch is shown by short-game great Seve Ballesteros in Figure 2.35.

2.35

LEAN BACK ON UPHILL TERRAIN

On uphill shots your instinct for good balance again wants your spine to be vertical (Figure 2.36). This is exactly the same as your instinct on downhill lies (except in the opposite direction), but if accommodated during setup, makes your swing arc dig straight into the ground at impact. Such impact can be very hard on the hands and wrists and is not conducive to good shotmaking.

2.36

If, however, you take an extra-wide stance and lean back so your spine is perpendicular to the ground (maintain your spine-tilt = zero) as shown in Figure 2.37 below, you can make a good escape swing. That is, you can make a good swing if you can keep from falling backward as you swing the club forward through impact. This is quite difficult to execute, because most of your weight is on your back foot in this setup, and a less-than-normal amount of weight will transfer forward onto your lead foot through impact (because of gravity), unless you force it to do so.

2.37

CHECK YOUR BALANCE IN THE MIRROR

Okay, now lay this book down again, stand up, grab a club (any club), and stand in front of a mirror. You need to make some swings so you can see, feel, and internalize the effects that spine lean and tilt can have on your swing mechanics. Consider it just another quick drill in your study of Setupology.

Spine tilt inhibits lower-body rotation. First, make a few of your normal swings from a level lie. Close your eyes and swing, focusing on the feel of your swings. Now tilt your spine forward (hold your lower body still) and swing. Then tilt it back from normal (again keeping your lower body still) and swing again. Can you feel the decrease in swing power produced as your spine tilt angle increases in either direction from zero?

2.38

Now find an object that's about 6 inches high, and imagine that you're going to hit a shot from a downhill lie. Place your back foot up on the 6-inch object, keep your spine vertical for good balance, imagine a ball in the middle of your stance on the severe downhill slope, and swing. Are you aware you would have hit 6 inches to a foot behind the ball with that swing (Figure 2.38)?

Next widen your stance and lean toward the target, to remove any spine tilt angle (Figure 2.39). This gets your spine perpendicular to the ground you're standing on (and hitting from). Now swing again. Notice how bad this balance

2.39

feels, but also notice how you would have hit the downhill shot solidly, without hitting the ground behind the ball. The key to remember here is to get your spine as nearly perpendicular to the ground (your shoulders parallel to the ground) as possible, so that your spine-tilt angle is close to zero.

Experience the uphill lie in the same way. This time put your forward foot on the 6-inch object—from an extra-wide stance you'll have to lean away from the target instead of toward it, to avoid creating a bad spine angle with the ground (Figure 2.40). Again, feel how difficult it is to keep your balance in this posture, but how much better the swing feels (relative to hitting a good shot) if you force a good body turn through impact.

With these swings you should be getting the feel of putting your body into position (wide stance with minimum spine tilt) to make good solid swings from sloping lies. If so, you've become aware of an important fundamental of Setupology.

2.40

2.4 Stance Width

There is no perfect stance for all golfers for all golf shots, but there is a perfect stance for every golfer for every individual shot. This is especially true for shots from trouble. The perfect stance in each case is the one that balances your stability, power, and balance, while also making the swing easy enough for you to create the solid contact required to escape from the circumstances involved.

There are as many stances as there are lies, shots, and players in the game. Therefore, it would be essentially impossible to remember the exact perfect stance for every lie and shot, even if we could give them to you in this book. Instead, for good Damage Control, you need to learn the "principles of stance," which will then serve you for the rest of your golf career (and all your escapes from trouble).

NARROW STANCES VS. WIDE STANCES

Turning or rotating your body around your spine is easy when your feet are close together. You can put your feet as close together as you want and feel almost no resistance to rotating your body. A very narrow stance may not be too stable, however, and won't provide a good base to push against to produce maximum power.

2.41

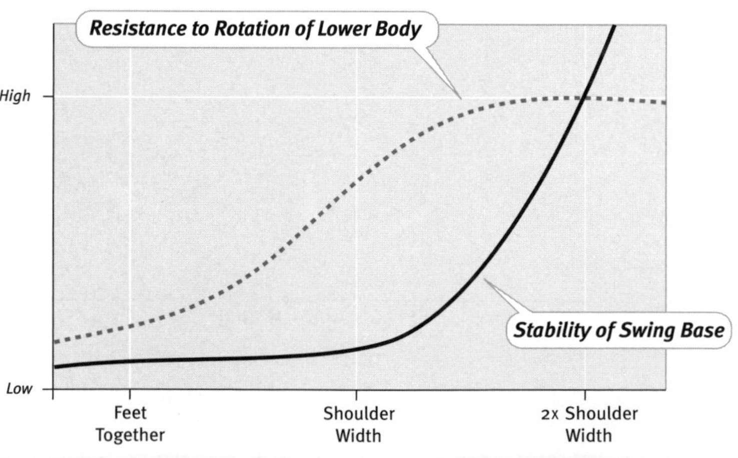

As your feet get farther apart your stance becomes more stable and creates greater resistance to your lower-body rotation, until you get them too far apart (Figure 2.41). A stance that's too wide limits your ability to turn your lower body, decreases your ability to generate power, and degrades your balance by restricting knee flexibility and your ability to maintain an athletic position. Also, the position of your toes and feet—either turned inward toward each other (pigeon-toed) or outward (duck-toed)—can have an effect on your ability to rotate your body around your spine.

The general rule is, the wider the stance, the more stable the swing base and the more power you can generate, up to a certain width (see Greg Norman in Figure 2.42a–b: very wide, stable, and powerful). Most golfers prefer a stance somewhere close to—but wider than—shoulder width for power shots. A less-than-shoulder-width stance usually feels better for short-game finesse shots. But because golfers differ so much in stature and every trouble lie is different, there is no specific rule for stance width in all situations.

2.42a

2.42b

INTERNALIZATION TIME AGAIN

Internalizing the effects your stance can have on your swing is easier to accomplish by feel than by reading about it in a book. For this reason I ask you to get up again, grab a club, and try the swing sequences described below in front of a mirror.

You need to feel the difference your stance width makes in a swing. There is no right or wrong here; no one stance is perfect or another bad. They're just different—sometimes quite different from your normal stance on level lies. The important point is that one particular stance width will be best for every different trouble shot you encounter. What you want to do is internalize your stance fundamentals well enough so you'll know when you've found the best stance once you're in, and trying to escape from, trouble.

Stand with your feet together and a club across your shoulders as Eddie is doing in Figure 2.43. Swing (rotate) your body around your spine. Close your eyes so your attention is tuned completely to the feel of your rotation motion. Now feel how almost your entire lower body is swinging in rhythm with your upper body, back and through, back and through, as shown. There's not much resistance to turning, but also not much of a base to generate power from.

Widen your stance in steps, and feel your lower body begin to provide resistance to your swing rotation as your stance gets wider. Imagine and feel the base that provides good lower-body resistance to coil against, and more power.

Then keep on widening your stance and swinging. When you get your feet far enough apart, you can hardly turn your hips at all. Your swing will then be essentially all upper body: not too bad, but not your most powerful. This feel of stance width versus power will now stay with you forever. It's like riding a bicycle—once you feel it, you'll never forget it. When you next get into trouble, move your feet between practice swings until you've found the width that gives you the best combination of balance and power.

2.43

This fundamental aspect of Setupology is to get your stance into the best "compromise" position to allow you to 1) make enough of a free swing to create solid contact with the ball; 2) keep your balance and stability through impact; and 3) generate enough clubhead speed to escape safely from the trouble you're in.

2.5 Solid Contact, Ball Position, and Face Angle

One of the most important parts of a shot from trouble is the contact your club makes with the ball. Without clean clubface/ball contact, proper ball position relative to your swing arc bottom, and the proper clubface angle through impact, your shot is not likely to escape on the trajectory or with the velocity you desire. That is, if it escapes at all. While this may seem obvious, clean and solid contact is accomplished in surprisingly few trouble shots. It is often of no great concern to golfers—if it even enters their mind—before they swing at trouble shots.

IMPACT CONDITIONS ARE CRITICAL

When something behind your ball prevents your normal swing from contacting the ball cleanly, you have a problem. This something could be a clump of grass, a bulging tree root, a ridge of sand, a bush, or any number of obstacles on the course (Figure 2.44a–e).

2.44a–e OPPOSITE: Golf balls and clubs

Your problem could even be the "big ball": the Earth. On a downslope, with your back foot above your front foot (Figure 2.44f), it is incredibly easy to hit the big green ball before you make contact with the little white one. Even if you heed the advice offered in Section 2.3 (lean to match your shoulders to the slope, eliminating spine tilt), I still recommend setting up with the white ball a little back in your stance on downhill lies, to give yourself a safety margin against hitting the ground first. You will also need to take several clubs' worth of extra loft to compensate for the slope and the fact that the ball is farther back in your stance.

2.44f OPPOSITE LOWER RIGHT: Downslope

More importantly, however, if you don't make solid contact with a trouble shot, you're not likely to enjoy the result. It doesn't matter what's preventing you from hitting the ball solidly. You must figure a way to get around, under, over, or through it if you want to pull off a good escape shot.

2.44a
2.44d
Callaway
GOLF
2.44b
2.44e
2.44c
2.44f

BALL POSITION

At the Pelz Golf Institute we define forward versus back ball position as the position of the ball along your swing line, relative to the center of your stance (Figure 2.45). Golfers often ask us where they should position their ball for this or that shot off level ground, and we can answer them precisely once we've seen them swing.

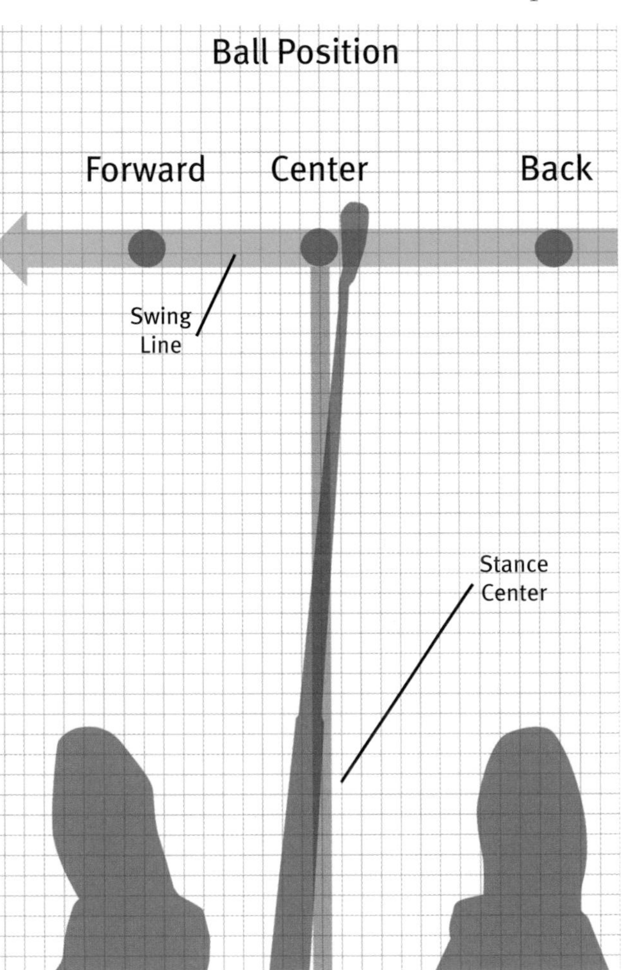

2.45

But we can't do this for Damage Control shots, which require you to play the ball far forward in some trouble lies and way back in others. The most important thing about ball position in any trouble shot (except sand) is that the ball should sit exactly where you can hit it (Figure 2.46) before you hit anything else or the ground. This means that no matter what stance you take, or the shape, plane, or path of your swing, your club will contact the golf ball before it hits the ground, and create the cleanest contact possible.

If your ball position is forward of where your club contacts turf, the fat shot that results will not be good (Figure 2.47). No matter where you think you have your ball positioned, if it is wrong for the trouble swing you are preparing to make, you're looking for disaster.

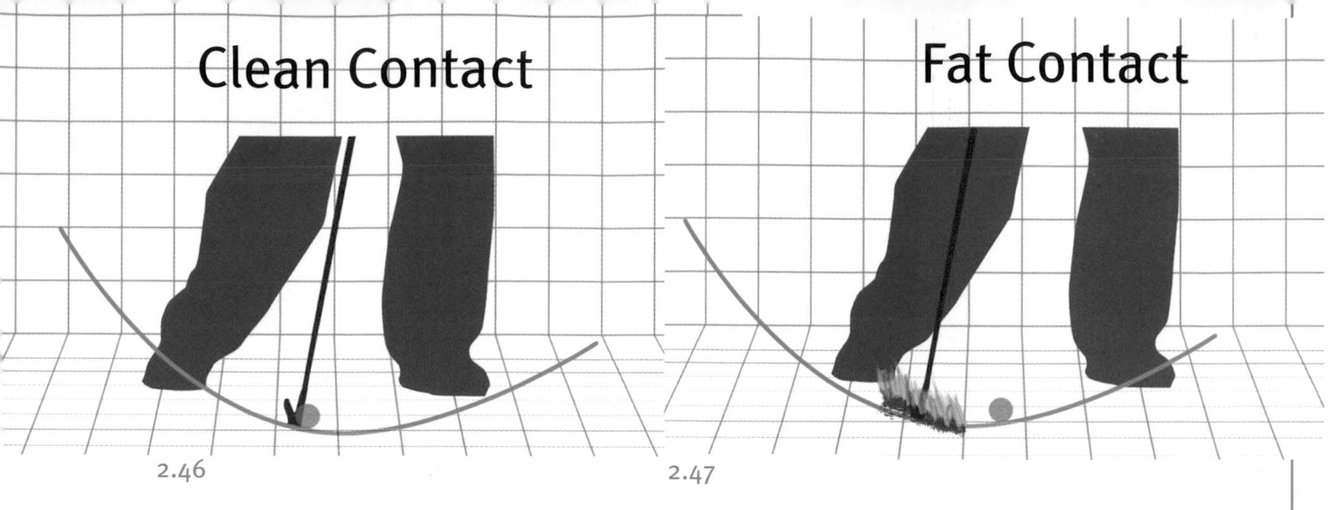

2.46 2.47

VERIFY YOUR DIVOT . . . BEFORE YOU POSITION THE BALL

2.48

Awkward stances on uneven terrain don't produce the same swing shapes as normal swings from level lies. Therefore, you can't know exactly where your ball should be positioned on trouble shots until you've taken your stance and know what the shape of your swing will be.

The Damage Control system to accomplish ball position is simple: Verify the spot at which your club will contact the turf by making a good, realistic practice swing from your same setup position. Duplicate the exact same stance and setup you're anticipating for the real shot in this practice swing. Then, look carefully and notice exactly where your divot starts (Figure 2.48).

Once you see the start of your practice-swing divot (that is, the back of the divot, not the center), move into position for the shot by moving your body position until your ball is exactly on or slightly behind that spot in your stance. This placement is important for solid contact, and will save you from many disaster holes in the future.

FACE ANGLE INFLUENCES BALL FLIGHT

Many golfers have been told that the golf ball starts on the swing-path line of the clubhead through impact, then spins and curves from that line based on the face angle of the clubhead at impact. As a result, these golfers spend their entire careers working on the path (and swing plane) of their club through the impact zone.

The truth is that the ball actually starts in the direction the face angle of your club is aimed at impact. You can demonstrate this to yourself on the practice tee by hitting a few shots in three different ways:

1. Down-the-line path, square face. First, set a two-by-four on edge and aim it at your target. This will allow you to make sure the clubhead is basically traveling along the two-by-four line through impact. Hit several 7-iron shots from your normal stance, with your normal grip and with the clubface aimed squarely at your target. This should be your normal down-the-line swing path that hits your normal shots toward your target. Hit enough of them to be assured that everything is behaving normally (Figure 2.49).

2. Down-the-line path, open face. Next take the same normal stance and grip position at address with the same club, but this time lay the clubface of your 7-iron open by 30 degrees to the right of the target (Figure 2.50) before you grip it. Double-check that the clubface is open when your grip is normal, then make the same normal swing along the two-by-four line as you did before (when your clubface was aimed at the target). Your shots will fly immediately to the right because the clubface was open at impact, not because your swing path went over there!

3. Down-the-line path, closed face. Now close the clubface at address (again using your same normal stance and grip) and make some more swings along the same two-by-four swing path. See how the shots fly to the left now because of the closed clubface, even though your swing path is still along the same two-by-four line direction (Figure 2.51)?

2.49

2.50

2.51

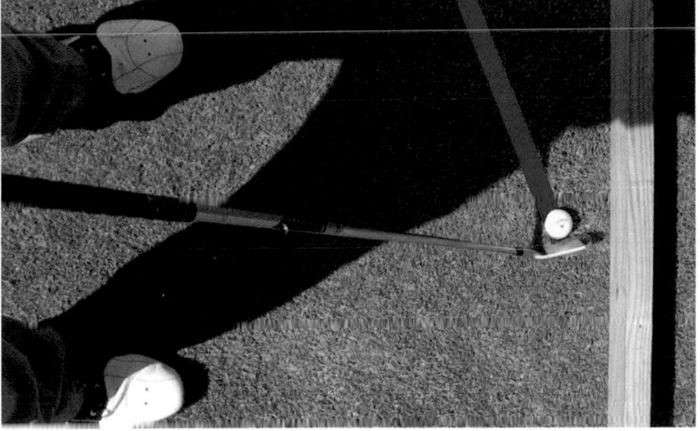

Understand this: Your clubface angle at impact controls your initial shot direction. This will be a tremendous asset when you're planning and aiming escape shots from trouble (as you read this today, golfers all over the globe are hitting trouble shots straight into the trees in front of them, because they expect their ball to start on their swing-path line instead of where their clubfaces are aimed).

FEEL IMPACT

We've just shown you how clean contact, ball position, and face angle are important for successful escape shots. But you need to feel and internalize this importance, so you won't forget it when you're in the heat of battle.

To do this, address a ball in your normal setup position and pick a target off in the distance, but don't swing. Imagine smacking the ball solidly and hitting a perfect shot at your target, with your normal square clubface position. Now loosen your grip and rotate the shaft with your right hand while not moving your left hand, so that the clubface is open by 30 degrees. Put your right hand back on the club and check to make sure your hands are in your normal grip position, but that the clubface is still 30 degrees open. Imagine how far right the shot would fly from a normal swing with this setup (Figure 2.52).

2.52

Imagining where your shot is going to fly off the clubface is something you should do before every trouble shot. Now try the opposite shot. Rotate the clubface closed, take your normal grip, and this time imagine how far left the shot would start from this impact position. This feeling of accurately knowing your shot starting line relative to your clubface position before every trouble shot is paramount to Damage Control.

While you have a club in your hand, I want you to learn to feel something else. Turn the clubface back to square (without moving your feet) and move the ball way back in your stance (away from the target) until it is opposite your back ankle. Now address an imaginary ball as if it were up in the middle of your stance. Imagine making a perfect swing at the imaginary ball, and imagine and feel the shot (Figure 2.53). You'll probably either whiff completely, swinging right over the top of the ball, or hit just the top part of the ball and dribble it a few yards out in front of you. Now try to feel the kind of swing you would have to make to hit the real ball—which is sitting so far back in your stance—solidly without moving your feet. This is the kind of feeling you never want to have before a trouble shot.

2.53

If you're ever standing over a trouble shot and feel you have to make a really weird swing like this to hit it—STOP! Step back and change your stance, ball position, spine angle—change *something*—to give yourself a good, solid swing feel. Then take another practice swing from your new position to ingrain this new feel before you swing at the shot.

The point is, before every trouble shot, you should feel as though you are set up to hit the shot with the easiest, most consistent, most powerful, swing you can muster under the lie conditions you are in.

2.6 Setupology Is Fundamental

Okay. By now I hope you understand how important your posture, spine angle, stance, ball position, and face angle are when you're setting up to hit a trouble shot. I also hope you're committed to getting all of these as good as you can before swinging at any future trouble shots. You need to understand that setting up for the best possible escape swing is two-thirds of the battle in escaping from trouble. You can't make a good escape swing from a bad body position, and that's a fact.

I also want to make sure you don't think I'm trying to get you to swing a golf club like a baseball bat, or to change your normal swing in any way. It's just that golf's trouble shots are often played from extremely uneven terrain—the ball often sits on strange levels relative to your feet, the angles of your body parts may be in weird positions, and normal swing thoughts and normal swings won't work in these conditions. We must contort our bodies, bend over, lean our spines, and position our joints into new and different positions during swings from trouble, in almost every round we play. And to play with Damage Control, you need to know how these changes will affect your ability to swing and hit shots.

None of the setups or postures in this chapter are impossible to swing from. They're just different from the normal setups you practice and use from level lies. Once you learn to put your body in the best position to deal with the trouble you encounter, and then practice making such swings (which we'll do later, in Chapter 7), you can execute them quite well.

So that's it for Setupology for now. It affects how your setup and posture can influence your ability to swing, and you've experienced the feel of some of these changes. You'll learn more and internalize more Setupology in Chapter 7 when you actually set up and hit shots from different lies and postures. And you'll also feel and see how changing your stance, ball position, and clubface angle affects your impact and shot direction from real trouble swings in your own backyard.

As you develop the physical skills to become a Damage Control player, you will stand, bend, lean, imagine, and feel impact before every escape-shot attempt. You'll always make a realistic practice swing to verify your ball position precisely at or behind the start of your divot, before every trouble shot. And you will always be aware of this fact: Your setup (Figure 2.54) will either *enable* . . . or *prohibit* . . . your escape-swing success.

2.54

CHAPTER 3

Swing Shaping

When Your Normal Swing Won't Get You Out of Trouble, Create One That Will!

NORMAL SWINGS DON'T ALWAYS WORK PERFECTLY, even from perfect lies. But put golfers in trouble, with difficult stances, tall grass around the ball, and obstacles interfering with their swings, and their shot patterns go to hell.

Hitting bad shots from trouble is understandable. The rocks, trees, creek banks, tall grass, mounds, waterfalls, and bushes that make golf courses some of the most beautiful places on earth also present severe swing difficulties to golfers who get too close to the beauty.

The second skill of Damage Control is Swing Shaping. This skill allows golfers to change the shape of their swing and hit screaming shots from trouble lies with Tour pro consistency. Whether it's changing the radius of your backswing, making your swing plane flatter, or terminating your follow-through early, shaping your swing to make solid contact with the ball is paramount to escaping from trouble. The guiding fundamental of Swing Shaping is: When your normal swing won't get you out of trouble . . . create one that will!

3.1 Changing the Shape of Your Swing

In the last chapter you saw how to setup and position your body to make swinging from trouble easier. Now it's time to learn how to create the swing shapes needed to extricate balls from trouble utilizing those setups.

The size, circularity, and symmetry of your swing can be changed in many ways. Changing the timing of your wrist cock changes the position of your clubhead along its swing path. Gripping down on the shaft changes the radius of your swing path, and you can also lengthen or shorten your backswing or follow-through.

While these swing changes sound easy, they're not necessarily easy or repeatable if you try to make them for the first time during actual play on the golf course. In fact, just the opposite is true. Most golfers have never thought about changing the shape of their swing in these ways, or how it feels to do so. And they've certainly never practiced doing it.

When in trouble, golfers understand that their clubshaft must miss the tree limb hanging over them, but they don't know the feel of the move that would make it happen. So they swing, trying to change the club path with only their hand and wrist muscles, just hoping to miss the tree. All too often this creates a bad swing, a tree collision, and a bad shot that flies out of the frying pan into the fire.

THE CONCEPT OF AVOIDANCE

It's better to avoid hitting things other than the ball—save all the swing energy you can for the ball. Whether the trouble is in front of, beside, or behind the ball, try not to hit it. That's the purpose of Swing Shaping: to hit the ball cleanly without hitting other things. If you absolutely can't avoid hitting them, then avoid it for as long as you can—hopefully until after you've made contact with the ball.

When hitting obstacles is unavoidable, it's better for your follow-through to swing into them than for your downswing to pass through them. Any time your club contacts trouble before it gets to the ball, your odds of getting a good face angle at impact, sweet-spot contact, and accelerating velocity through impact are degraded, while your chances of moving the ball into worse danger are greatly increased. Hitting a tree limb in your backswing is much worse than hitting it at the end of your follow-through, when it won't affect your shot (although it could bend your shaft).

Give yourself a margin for swing error. It's better to play shots intentionally off the toe of your club to avoid contacting a tree root than it is to try to execute a perfect swing and just barely miss the root with no margin for error. Understand that human instincts are strong and deeply ingrained. If your subconscious thinks you might hit a tree root or rock in your swing, it might flinch away at the last moment, resulting in a poor shot. It's better to choose more club and plan for toe impact than it is to expect a solid shot but instead get one unexpectedly off the toe with a flinch swing.

TIGHT QUARTERS BEHIND

When there's not enough room behind the ball to take a normal backswing, a good swing can often still be made. This kind of trouble comes in many forms, and in various levels of severity.

Bushes, trees, and fences are frequent culprits. Let's say that a bush is impeding your normal backswing by only a few inches (Figure 3.1a–d). You can still hit this shot using an "almost" normal swing by playing the ball farther back in your stance. You simply move your body forward to create extra space. You'll also have to close the clubface slightly to keep the ball from launching right of the target, and use more loft to compensate for this closed face.

3.1a The problem: bush behind the ball

3.1b Normal ball position

3.1c Ball back position

3.1d

Another way to combat trouble from behind is to grip down on the club. This decreases the radius of your swing and the amount of room you need behind the ball, by as many inches as you grip down (Figure 3.2a–b). Of course the shorter the radius, the less powerful the swing, so you may have to make a more powerful swing on a gripped-down shot so it'll fly the required distance.

3.2a

3.2b

As trouble closes in even tighter behind, more extreme changes can be made to create a swing that's sufficient to extricate the ball. Look at my situation in Figure 3.3, where my clubhead hits a tree shortly after takeaway (Figure 3.4). I don't have nearly enough room if I cock my wrists gradually, as I do in my normal backswing.

3.3

3.4

1. Pre-Cock (lift club vertically)

3.5

2. Take backswing

3.6

3. Normal downwing

3.7

By fully cocking my wrists before takeaway (called "pre-cock"—Figure 3.5) and then keeping them fully cocked up to the top of my backswing (Figure 3.6), a normal downswing will fit just inside the tree trunk (Figure 3.7). This shot is not as dangerous as it looks—the downswing is exactly the same as normal, but it takes some practice to get used to the feel of making your backswing with completely cocked wrists. It's a confidence thing: First cock your wrists, then make a good backswing, and finally swing down and follow through normally (Figure 3.8).

3.8

3.9

When trouble is even closer, a different change can allow you to still hit the shot. When a fence, for example, provides absolutely no room for a backswing, a shot can still be played forward to a green off to the left. Set up with both your body and swing-to-come aimed down the fence line (as in Figure 3.9), well right of the green. Then close the clubface to the left (Figure 3.10). Use lots of extra loft, and make a normal swing down the fence line (Figure 3.11). After trying a few of these shots with different clubs, you'll quickly see how low, left, and far the shots will fly. You'll also see how little backspin they have and how far they roll. With practice you'll learn when (and when not) to use this escape technique.

3.10

3.11

OBSTACLES AND TROUBLE AHEAD

3.12

When a normal setup causes your clubhead or shaft to hit trouble after impact, you've got a problem (Figure 3.12). If simply aiming left or right solves the problem, then it's easy. But when neither of these is an option, changing your swing shape is the only answer.

To stop your club after impact may sounds simple, but it's actually quite difficult. To hit a ball hard and then stop your hands, arms, clubhead, and follow-through almost always takes more time and room than you might expect. This scenario often ends up bending or breaking the shaft, or hurting the golfer's hands and/or wrists. It's especially difficult in the heat of the moment when you want to hit an important shot to save a stroke and win a hole.

The hit-and-stop technique will work only if you have enough room. The general guideline is that you should never hit a shot if you don't have enough room to follow through (Figure 3.13a–b) at least half as far as the length of your backswing. And even if you follow this guideline, stopping in time to avoid shaft damage takes practice and good hand-eye coordination.

3.13a

3.13b

3.14

If you're faced with a more serious follow-through problem—such as that posed by a solid rock in front of your ball—you need to stop your club quickly after impact (Figure 3.14). With proper Setupology you can use the ground to stop your club, as I demonstrate in Figure 3.15. But *do not* try this swing or shot without going through the proper instruction (sidebar below) *and* backyard practice first (this is detailed in Chapter 7).

3.15

WARNING: TRY THIS SHOT ONLY AT YOUR OWN RISK.

This shot can be dangerous. It can injure your hands and wrists, break your club, or cause the ball to ricochet back and hit you.

If you insist on learning this shot, sneak up on it in stages: first try stopping your club with nothing in front of your ball. After you learn how quickly you can stop your club and how high you can launch the ball, try the shot with a soft ball over a soft obstacle such as a sponge (see Chapter 7). Don't play with solid objects (real balls, real rocks) until after you're experienced and know you can hit the shot safely.

AGAIN, I WARN YOU: BE CAREFUL.

3.16

You must first practice in your backyard with a foam rock to develop the setup, knowledge, and swing skill necessary to pull this shot off, so you don't hurt yourself on the golf course!

Position the ball 8 inches farther back in your stance than normal (see normal footprints in grass, Figure 3.16) and lean sharply forward. Use a club with lots of extra loft to compensate for both setup changes. Then swing severely down into the ground and lighten your grip at impact (almost let go of the club, to protect your hands and wrists). Let the ground stop your club.

TROUBLE ON THE TOE OR HEEL SIDE OF YOUR BALL

When your ball decides to snuggle up alongside trouble, you must focus on making a swing that will a) maximize contact with the ball; b) minimize contact with the trouble; and c) optimize the tolerance for shot pattern scatter. In many cases perfect contact is not an option; you simply have to do the best you can and allow for the consequences in shot reaction. A number of different items can cause trouble: rough, bushes, rocks, tree roots, even the edge of a low-lipped sand bunker. Such problems can require different solutions, depending on which side of the ball they're on, where they align themselves relative to your target direction, and how solid they are (Figure 3.17a–f).

THE IMAGES ON THE NEXT SIX PAGES (Figure 3.18a–k) illustrate a number of trouble scenarios that occur first off the toe, and then off the heel of a club. Don't try to memorize how to play from any of these situations. Study each trouble circumstance until you understand how it should be handled, then move to the next example. You just want to pick up the principles of obstacle avoidance.

NOTE: ASSUME YOU ARE IN ADDRESS POSITION (see your toes, hands, club)

- The gray bar represents a trouble obstacle—it may be soft like grass (it's okay to hit through it) or hard like a rock (hitting it would cause injury).
- The green arrow represents the line-to-target direction.
- The blue arrow represents the clubhead swing line direction.

3.18a

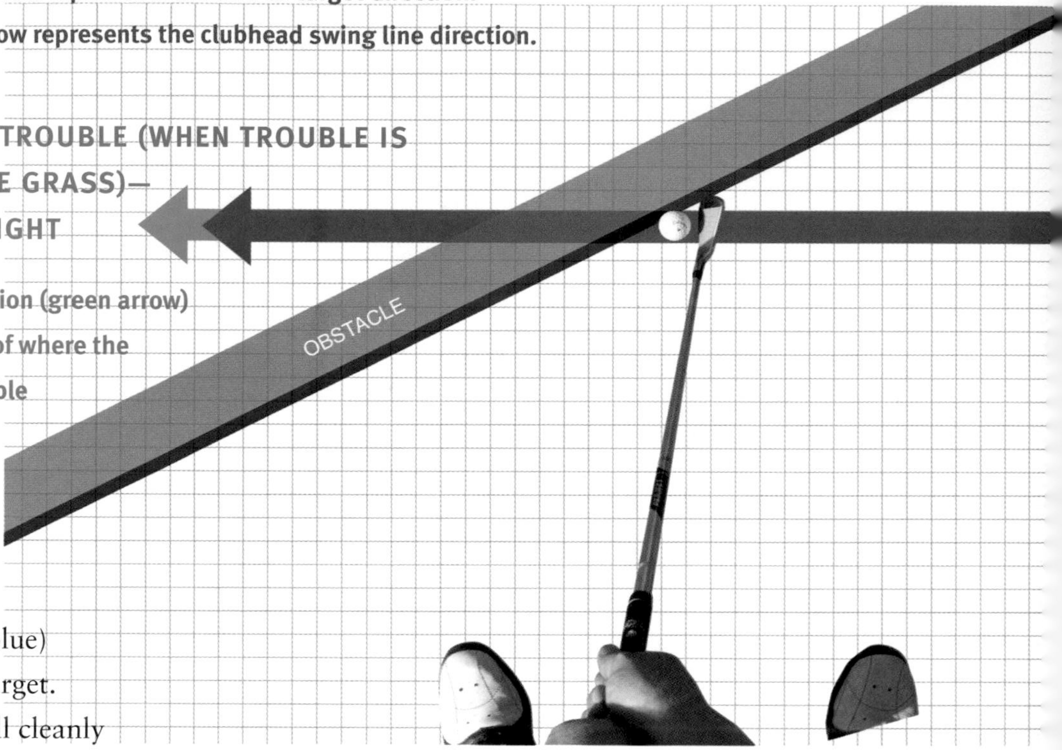

1A. TOE-SIDE TROUBLE (WHEN TROUBLE IS SOFT, LIKE GRASS)—TARGET RIGHT

Target direction (green arrow) to the right of where the edge of trouble points (gray bar)

OBSTACLE

- Set up and swing (swing line blue) straight at target.
- Club hits ball cleanly before contacting trouble.

3.18b

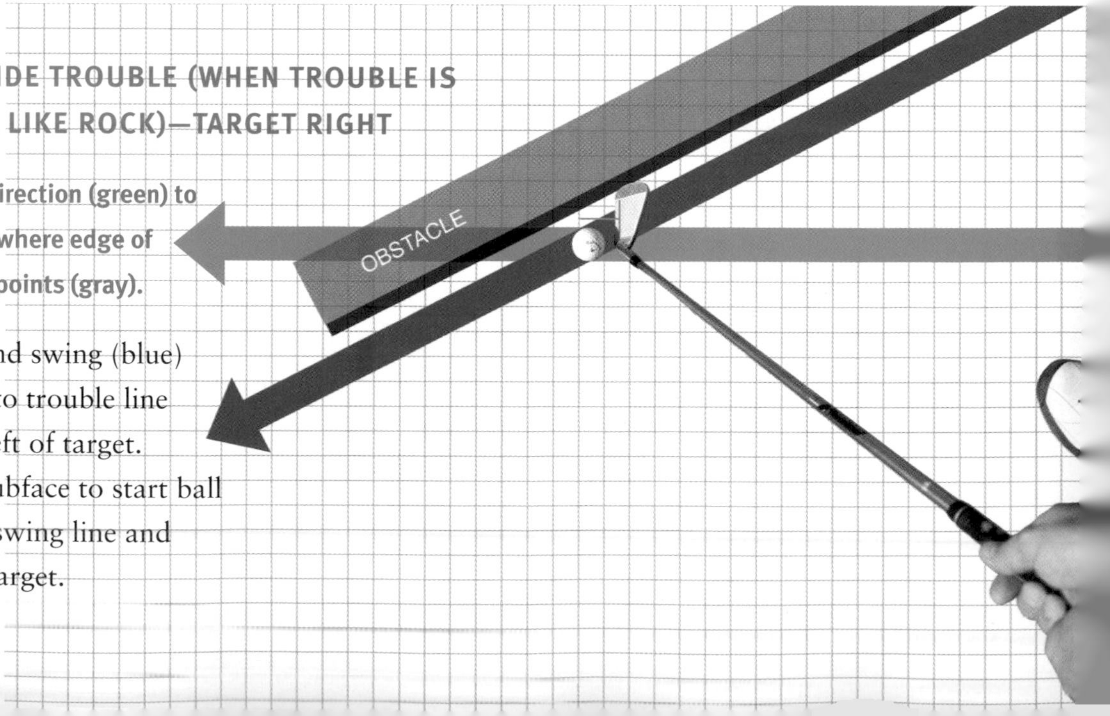

1B. TOE-SIDE TROUBLE (WHEN TROUBLE IS HARD, LIKE ROCK)—TARGET RIGHT

Target direction (green) to right of where edge of trouble points (gray).

OBSTACLE

- Set up and swing (blue) parallel to trouble line (gray), left of target.
- Open clubface to start ball right of swing line and fade to target.

2. TOE-SIDE TROUBLE (WHEN TROUBLE IS EITHER HARD OR SOFT)—TARGET STRAIGHT AHEAD

Target direction (green) same as trouble edge direction (gray)

- Set up and swing (blue) parallel to trouble edge (gray), straight at target (green).
- Use extra club and play shot off the toe of your clubhead; assume shot will travel 75 percent of normal distance and spin less than normal.

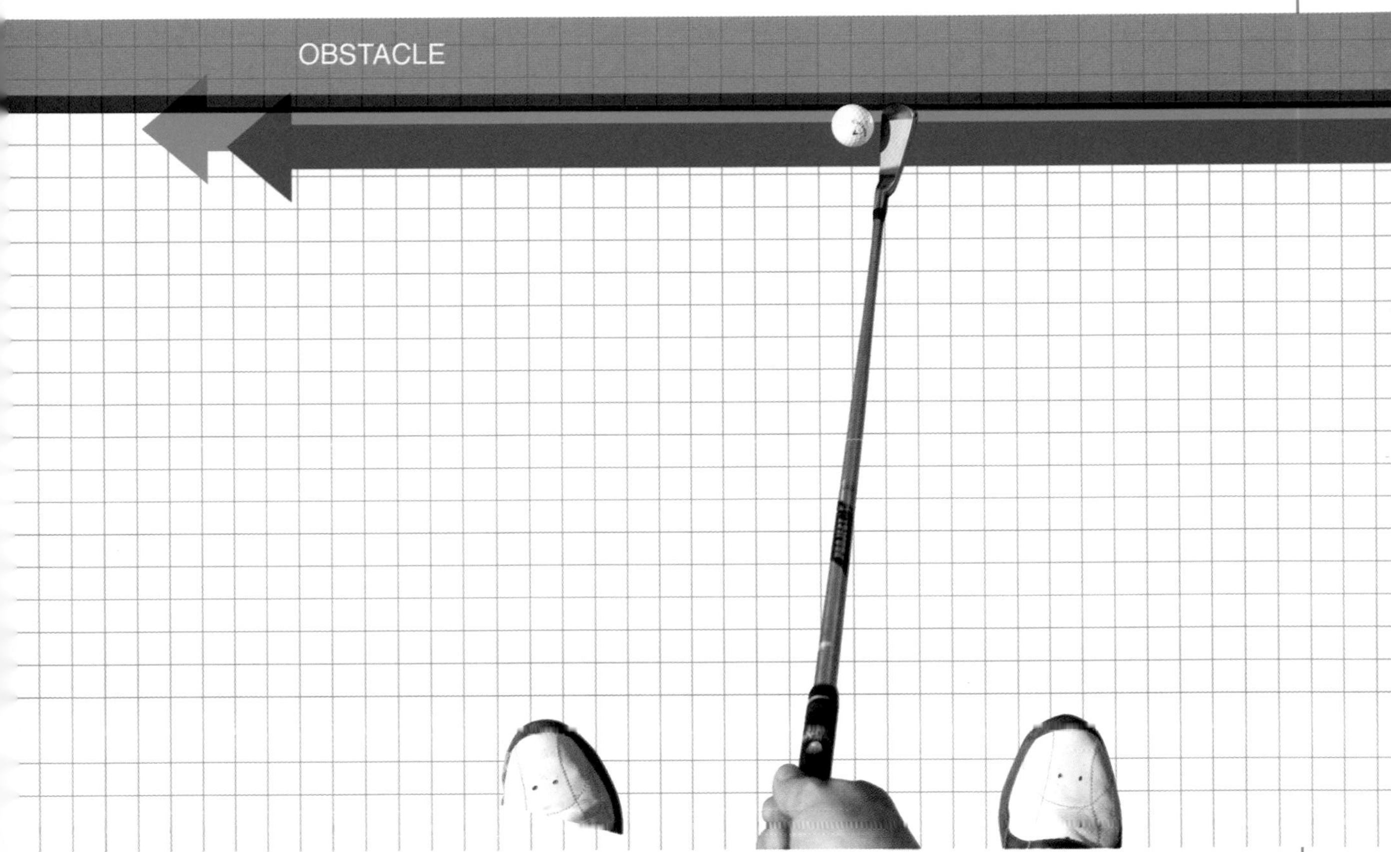

3.18c

REMEMBER: The blue arrow denotes swing path; the green arrow shows the path that the ball will follow; and the gray bar simulates the problem obstacle, which could be soft like grass, meaning you can hit into or through it without hurting yourself, or hard like a rock, which means that hitting it could cause injury.

3A. TOE-SIDE TROUBLE (SOFT OR HARD)—TARGET LEFT

Target direction (green) left of trouble edge direction (gray)

- Do NOT aim straight at the target and try to power through trouble before hitting the ball.
- Even when trouble is soft, this seldom produces good shots.

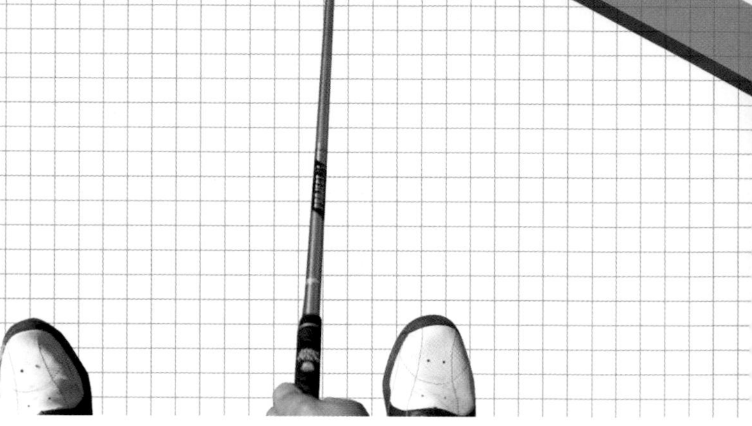

3.18d

3B. TOE-SIDE TROUBLE (SOFT OR HARD)—TARGET LEFT

This setup will allow you to hit a solid shot without ever touching the trouble. If you get the clubface angle correct, the ball will start to the left of your swing line with some hook spin, and draw to your target.

Target direction (green) left of trouble edge direction (gray)

- Set up and swing (blue) parallel to trouble edge (gray).
- Close clubface to start ball left of swing line and hook to target.
- Use extra loft to compensate for closed face.

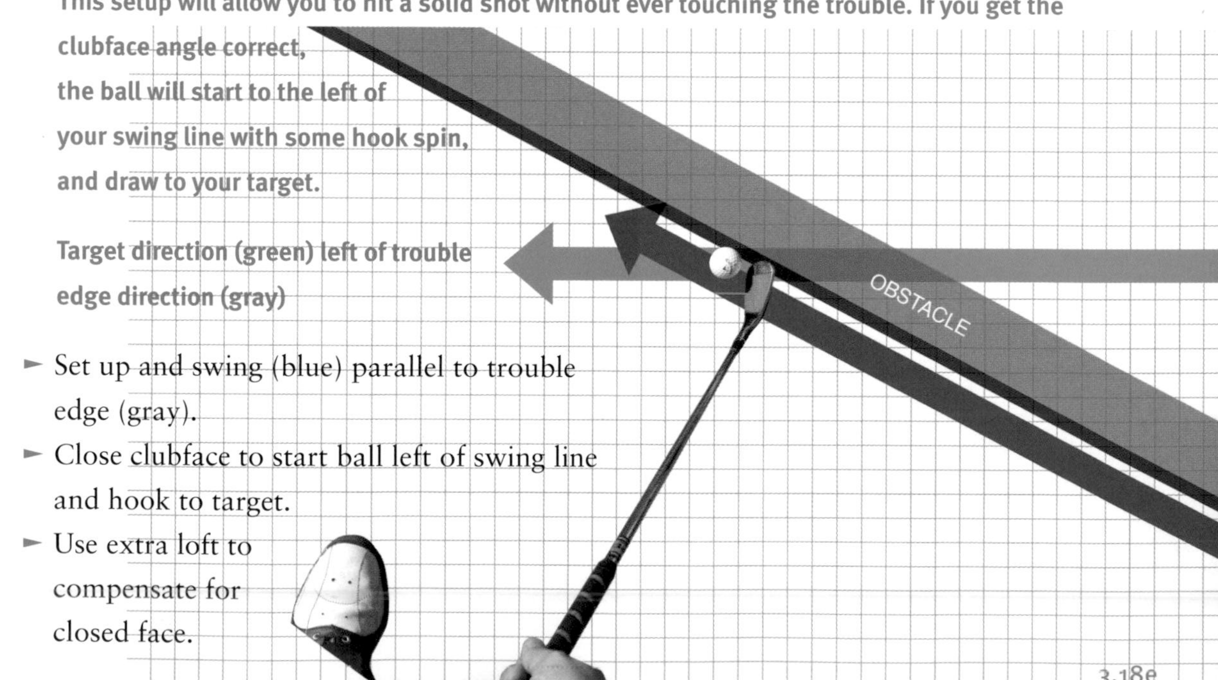

3.18e

4A. HEEL-SIDE TROUBLE (SOFT OR HARD)— TARGET RIGHT

Target direction (green) right of trouble edge direction (gray)

- Do NOT set up directly at the target and try to swing through the trouble.
- Even if trouble is only tall grass, it will affect your clubface and shot trajectory.
- This technique usually does not turn out well.

3.18f

4B. HEEL-SIDE TROUBLE (SOFT OR HARD)— TARGET RIGHT

If your ball is so close to a hard surface that you might shank the shot, either take an unplayable lie or try to hit the shot with a left-handed swing (see Chapter 7: opposite-way swings).

Target direction (green) right of trouble edge direction (gray)

- Set up parallel to trouble edge and swing (blue) parallel to trouble edge (gray).
- Open clubface to start ball right of swing line and slice to target.
- Use less loft to compensate for open face.

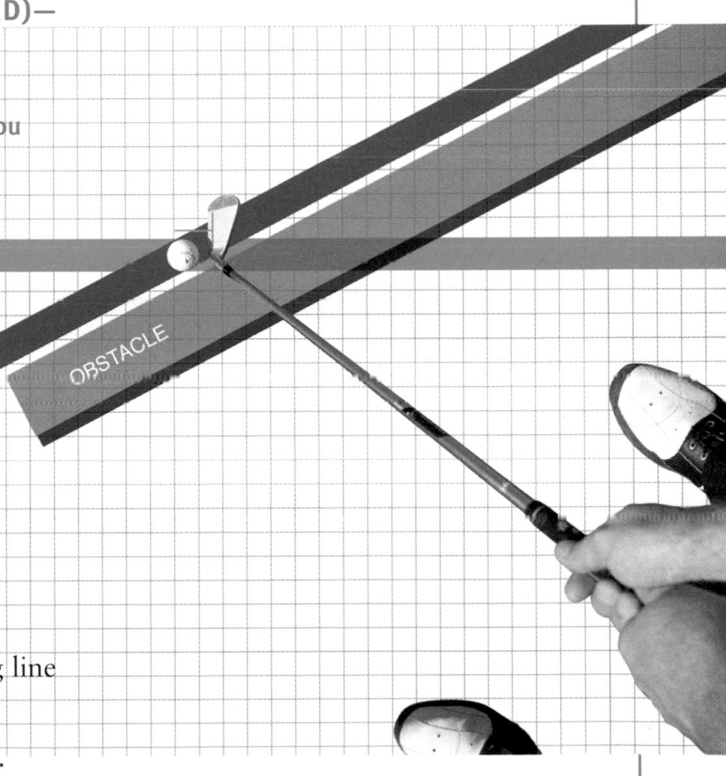

3.18g

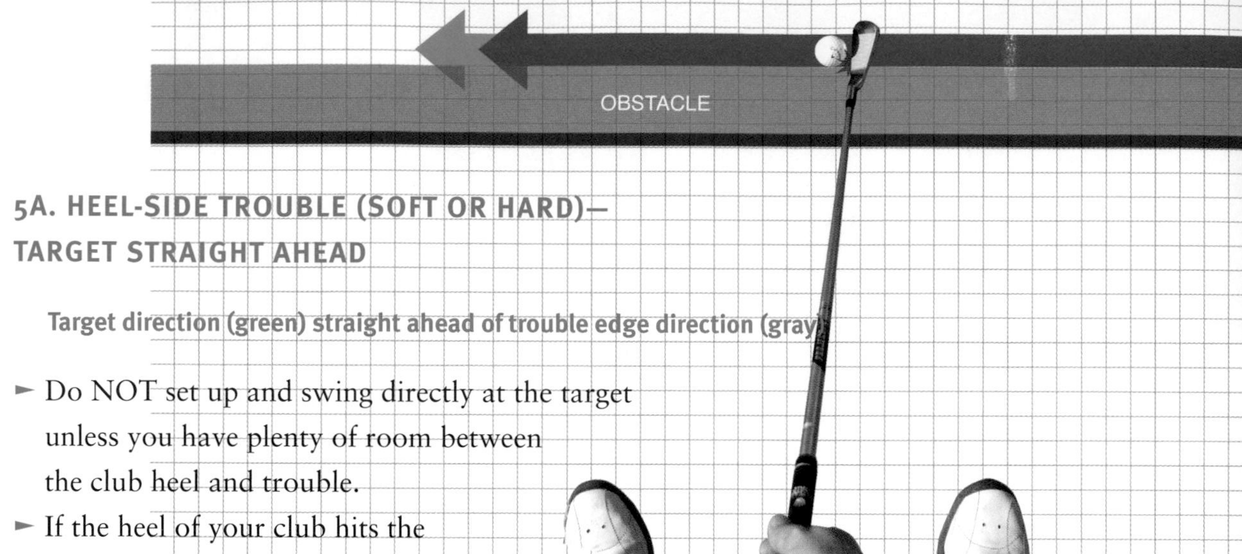

5A. HEEL-SIDE TROUBLE (SOFT OR HARD)—TARGET STRAIGHT AHEAD

Target direction (green) straight ahead of trouble edge direction (gray)

- Do NOT set up and swing directly at the target unless you have plenty of room between the club heel and trouble.
- If the heel of your club hits the hard trouble, you have a disaster.
- If the heel catches up in soft trouble and flips closed, you have another disaster.

3.18h

5B. HEEL-SIDE TROUBLE (SOFT)—TARGET STRAIGHT AHEAD

This technique gives you a margin of error so that you'll never hit the dreaded hosel shot from this lie. If the trouble is too hard to hit into, however, you might try a left-handed swing.

Target direction (green) straight ahead of trouble edge direction (gray)

3.18i

- Set up aimed slightly left of trouble edge and swing (blue) slightly into trouble (gray) after impact.

OBSTACLE

- Open the clubface slightly to start ball slightly right of swing line and fade to target.
- Use slightly less loft to compensate for the open face.

6A. HEEL-SIDE TROUBLE (SOFT)—TARGET LEFT

Target direction (green) left of trouble edge direction (gray)

- Set up and swing (blue) directly at target (green) with square clubface.
- Hit the ball first, then swing into and through trouble (gray), as long as it won't hurt your hands or wrists.

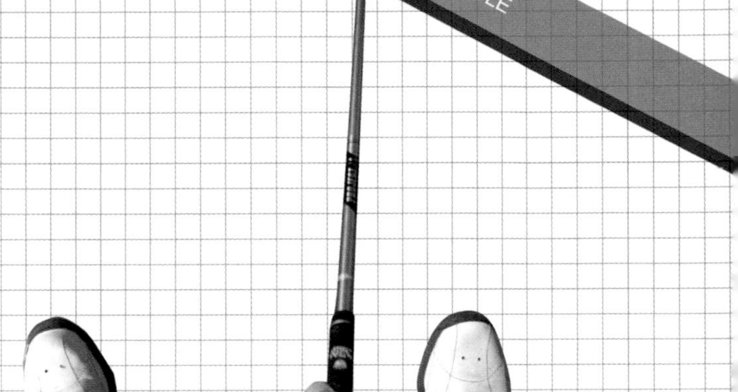

3.18j

6B. HEEL-SIDE TROUBLE (HARD)—TARGET LEFT

Target direction (green) left of trouble edge direction (gray)

3.18k

- Set up and swing (blue) along trouble edge, to right of target (green).
- Close clubface to start ball left of the swing line, and hook to target.
- Use extra loft on club to compensate for closed clubface at impact.

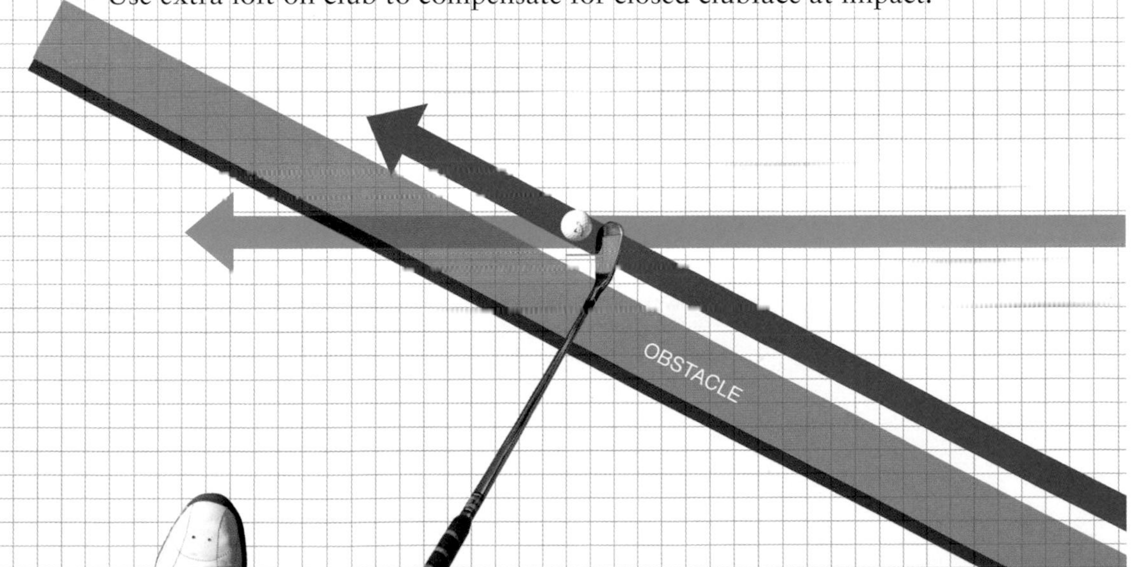

3.19

When grass is everywhere around the ball and there is no way to avoid it, you've got to get your club into and out of it as quickly as you can. From really tall grass, your goal should be to use a compact and powerful swing with the shortest club you can possibly use that will still provide enough power to get through the grass and muscle the ball out. The tighter the swing radius, the less grass you have to swing through.

As you can see in Figure 3.19, I'm gripping down about 3 inches on my wedge, and I have the face slightly open to help the club slide through the grass with less resistance. I'm also using a high-lofted wedge to get the ball up and out of the grass as quickly as possible. Remember, the lower this shot launches, the more grass the ball has to pass through, and that means the more power you must provide.

3.2 Changing the Swing Plane

There are right and wrong ways to change the plane of your swing. Unfortunately, the natural and intuitive way for most golfers is often the wrong way.

Left to their natural instincts, golfers in trouble situations usually set up normally, then use their hands and arms to swing weakly into a more upright or flat swing plane in an attempt to miss the trouble. Such swings are usually inconsistent, don't hit solid shots, and frequently produce awful results. A better way to make an "off-the-normal-plane" swing is to change your initial setup body positions, then emphasize good upper- or lower-body rotation to produce strong and solid swing power.

A FUNDAMENTAL SOME GOLFERS DON'T UNDERSTAND

Two principles of the golf swing escape the attention of many golfers. The faster and harder a golfer swings, the more strongly centripetal forces will pull their swing into a plane perpendicular to their spine and pull their hands into that swing plane through impact. In other words, the most powerful swings that most golfers make come close to a plane perpendicular to their spine. Examples of this can be seen in some of the powerful (only kidding in my case, but Charles Howell and Phil Mickelson hit it pretty well) driver swings in the game (Figure 3.20a–c). While this position is not always possible to achieve from trouble, the closer you can get to it, the more powerful and stable such a swing will be.

3.20a–c

3.20a

3.20b

3.20c

A natural consequence of this is the opposite effect—the farther your swing plane moves away from perpendicular to your spine, the less powerful or repeatable your swing will be. You can see this in the funky swing I'm making after my ball gets stuck up in a tree (Figure 3.21). My swing plane is nowhere near perpendicular to my spine, and is also at the bottom end of the power spectrum.

It is important for the sake of good Damage Control to position your body to swing in a plane that's as nearly perpendicular to your spine as possible. This may mean contorting your body at address into a strange position or getting down on your knees and emphasizing upper-body rotation to produce the highest percentage of normal power you can under the circumstances. But if this is what it takes to produce a consistent escape swing from a trouble situation, then you need to learn how to do it.

3.21

HOW TO CREATE FLAT VS. UPRIGHT SWINGS

In Chapter 2 you saw how setting up with your spine angle more vertical makes swinging in a flat plane easier, while a horizontal spine makes swinging in an upright plane easier. It was also discussed how the spine lean, spine-to-trunk angle, and stance width of your setup affect your ability to rotate your upper and lower body. Now I want to show you how these adjustments work when you're trying to shape your swing on the golf course.

Let's start by looking at what happened to Eddie when he hit his drive off to the right in the rough on a par-5 hole (Figure 3.22). All he needs to do is punch the ball a few yards forward and back into the fairway to make saving his par routine. From his normal posture, however, it's clear he can't hit his ball solidly. Several tree limbs will surely deflect the clubhead as he moves into impact and disrupt the shot badly.

3.22

3.23

If he instinctively bends over and lowers his hands to get the clubshaft low enough to miss the tree limbs (Figure 3.23), he puts himself into an even worse posture. Any shoulder rotation from this position would produce a very upright swing, so he must use his hands and wrists alone to keep the clubhead swinging below the branches. He cannot possibly generate significant power by swinging the club from this position.

The better solution, although not instinctive or natural, is to get down on his knees (Figure 3.24). From this position his swing plane can be almost perpendicular to his spine, and he can generate some real clubhead speed and power through impact. Notice that Eddie's spine angle becomes almost vertical, so he can make a more natural shoulder turn to generate the flat swing required to avoid the tree limbs.

You should also notice that Eddie changed clubs when he went to his knees. By using his utility club (which has a smaller heel and exposes no hosel to the ball), he eliminated the possibility of hitting the ball off the hosel of an iron club. Also, whenever you swing in a really flat swing plane close to the ground, it's easy to catch the clubhead heel on the ground, which will flip the clubface over and cause you to flub the shot. With a little practice in just brushing the ground rather than digging into it, however, the flip-over flub can be avoided.

3.24

3.25

3.26

Exactly the opposite solution works best when you need to make a truly upright swing (Figure 3.25). In this case you need to move closer to the ball, bend over more to position your spine more horizontally, and grip down on the club shaft. Then work hard to get your shoulders to rotate from that position (Figure 3.26). Although you'll never generate as much power from an upright swing as you would from a flat swing, it's invaluable when you're in a tight situation between trees.

As you can see in Figure 3.27, even when my hips and lower body can't turn optimally (I was too bent over to allow maximum hip rotation), decent upper-body rotation can be maintained. When a good upper-body swing of the shoulders can be achieved, you can still generate adequate power in the shot. 3.27

BACKHAND SWINGS CAN MAKE DIFFICULT SHOTS EASIER

When the ball is well above your feet (Figure 3.28), a normal swing is not easy to execute without hitting behind the ball or hitting it way left. In this case, you need the backhanded shot. It's not that difficult to execute, but it feels strange the first time you try it.

The backhand swing allows a good stance in this situation. Keep your shoulder anchored with your free hand to provide a stable anchor point for your swing. Play the ball out in front of your feet to contact it cleanly before scuffing the turf (Figure 3.29). You'll need to try a number of backhand shots before you can feel the direction the ball comes off your clubface and how much loft, carry, and roll you'll get from this swing.

3.28

3.29

3.30

Look how easy a shot from the water's edge becomes when you hit it backhanded. With a simple 7-iron swing (instead of risking a fall into the water and possibly an alligator encounter Figure 3.30), I can chip this shot close enough to have a good chance to save par (Figure 3.31a–b).

3.31a

3.31b

SWINGS FROM THE OPPOSITE SIDE CAN SAVE STROKES

When your ball comes to rest on the wrong side of an obstacle and leaves no place for you to stand, another stroke-saving option is to learn to swing from the opposite side of the ball (Figure 3.32). Anyone can learn to swing the opposite way, left-handed vs. right-handed, and it's actually easier than it was when you were learning to swing for the first time (your brain already knows most of the swing principles involved).

Don't, however, think you're going to hit good shots this way at first. A little practice will go a long way toward improving the feel of your opposite-side swing and making you capable of swinging like PGA TOUR pro Tom Sieckmann (Figure 3.33), who is also the Director of Instruction in our Scoring Game Schools. You have to find which clubhead works best for your swing when turned upside down. When I tried this for the first time, my instinct told me a low-lofted club would work best. The opposite was true, however, because higher-lofted clubs allowed me to hit better shots. Understand, however, that the first few times you try this technique (in Chapter 7), you'll probably get some pretty awful results.

But be patient. You'll be surprised how easily it will come to you. You'll never have to play many shots, or hit perfect shots with this technique. You just have to swing well enough to make solid contact and get your ball out of trouble and back into the game!

3.32

3.33

3.3 Swings for Sloping Terrain

Lies on sloping terrain are an important part of the game. I'm sure you've experienced many of them. The farther your shots stray from the center of the fairway, the greater the slopes and the more rugged the terrain they tend to come to rest on. Golf course architects design slopes and undulating terrain into their trouble areas because they know golfers have trouble handling them. They make the "garden spot" of each fairway level to reward the well-struck tee shot with a perfect approach to the green. There are good and valid reasons why golfers have problems from sloping lies, and overcoming them is part of the skill of Swing Shaping.

Swing alterations must be made to accommodate sloping terrain by changing your stance, adjusting your ball position, and leaning your body and spine. These alterations are fraught with balance difficulties, however, and they must be made with care and determination based on experience.

SIDEHILL LIE: BALL ABOVE FEET

When the ball is more than 3 inches above your feet at address, several things happen. Your spine-angle tends to become more vertical, you stand farther from the ball, the club feels heavier, and your swing plane becomes flatter than normal. The clubface (because of its loft) also aims to the left of your normal alignment (for right-handed players), as shown by the "floatie" plastic tube stuck on my wedge (pointing perpendicular to the clubface, Figure 3.34).

3.34

CLUBS HELD HORIZONTALLY FEEL HEAVIER

Hold a club with one hand by the end of its grip. First let it hang vertically straight down below your hand; it feels very light. Then balance it vertically above your hand; again it should feel very light. Now hold it out horizontally from your hand—you'll immediately notice it feels much heavier. In golf, the greater the lever arm of a clubhead is positioned out horizontally from your hands, the heavier the club will feel (and swing).

If your ball is above your feet and you swing using your normal feel, your clubhead will swing through impact lower than you want (sometimes missing under the ball). This happens because your clubhead feels and swings heavier than normal (see sidebar above). To compensate for this effect, simply imagine that the ball is slightly higher than it really is. Address the ball with your clubhead slightly above it (Figures 3.35, 3.36), and actually try to hit above the real ball. This technique allows you to use your normal swing feel and still achieve solid contact with the ball.

3.35

3.36

3.37

When you find your ball waist-high in a tree or bush (Figure 3. 37), this extra-heavy feel becomes a really serious issue. Many golfers swing and miss such balls completely, usually swinging under them by several inches. Again, I recommend using your normal swing feel, but imagine that the ball is several inches above where it really is (Figure 3.38). I know this may sound silly or bizarre to you, but don't discount it until you've tried it. I've seen it work for many golfers!

3.38

As with so many Damage Control skills, this shot is easy once you experience the heavy-club effect, understand it, and compensate for it (Figure 3.39).

3.39

SIDEHILL LIE: BALL BELOW FEET

When a ball is below your feet, stand closer and lower your body down to it (squat). If the ball isn't too far below your feet, you can keep your spine-angle normal while squatting and make a good escape swing by using only a little less lower-body rotation than normal (Seve, Figure 3.40).

A common misconception is that when the ball lies below your feet, you must aim left of your target because the slope will send the shot to the right. This sounds reasonable because the opposite condition is in fact true (when the ball is above your feet, you must aim right of the target to compensate for the clubface aiming left). The truth in this situation, however, is that your clubface aim should remain normal, because as you squat down with your knees to reach the ball, your shaft angle and clubface aim don't change (see floaties, Figure 3.41).

This shot does create problems, though. As the ball moves farther below your feet, care must be taken to avoid catching the heel of the club in the turf, which will cause the clubface to flip over closed and send the shot left. Another danger is losing your balance during the swing and hitting the shot off the hosel of the club.

As the ball continues to move farther and farther below your feet, this shot becomes more and more difficult. At some point you'll have to bend over more at the waist to reach down to the ball (because eventually, squatting no longer works—your knees stick out and get in the way of your swing). This means your swing will consist mostly of upper-body power, and staying in balance will become the key to hitting the shot well.

3.40 ABOVE
3.41 BELOW

DOWNHILL SLOPE: BACK FOOT ABOVE THE FRONT

From Chapter 2 you may remember that standing vertically using normal balance makes for a bad setup on a downhill slope. For downhill lies, you should widen your stance, lean forward to level your shoulders with the slope, use a more lofted club to compensate for the downslope, grip down on the shaft, and position the ball back in your stance.

With forward lean, more weight than normal is thrown onto your forward leg and foot, creating a difficult balance situation during the swing. To make good swings from a downhill slope, put more emphasis on your upper-body turn, because your lower body will be somewhat restricted by your wide stance. Focus on staying down and through the shot until you're past impact, then release from your stance and walk through to your finish (to keep from falling). From a downhill slope, make sure you can release your body after impact (especially when you're making a powerful swing) and walk down the hill without stepping into something harmful (Figure 3.42).

You will learn your "lean-limit" when you start doing downhill drills in Chapter 7. This is the maximum amount of forward lean you can tolerate to get your spine more perpendicular to the ground

3.42

(and shoulders parallel to the surface) while still producing good swing speed. There is always the danger of hitting behind the ball from a downhill lie, so make sure the ball is positioned a little back in your stance. Also be aware that these shots can carry a good distance when hit well, and that they fly lower and roll farther than similar shots from level lies.

UPHILL SLOPE: FRONT FOOT ABOVE THE BACK

When hitting a shot from an uphill slope, the golf swing gets much more difficult to finish. This is because gravity is pulling your weight back away from your target, down the hill during the swing. From a wider-than-normal stance you must lean back to set your shoulders parallel to the sloped terrain, so the bottom of your swing arc won't hit into the ground. On an uphill-lie shot, use a club with less than normal loft to compensate for the up slope, and grip down on the shaft (Figure 3.43).

The difficulty of this shot comes from having to force your body rotation (and resulting weight transfer) to move *up* the hill through impact. This action takes both understanding and practice, because it requires significant extra effort to transfer your weight uphill, and you must delay any thought about catching your balance until after the ball is gone (Figure 3.44).

3.43

Just as you do for downhill lies, you have to learn your "lean limit" for a good swing. Remember, exaggerating your body turn to produce clubhead acceleration past impact (which requires rotating your weight uphill through impact) is not an easy or natural thing to do. (But whatever you do, don't fall back until after impact.)

As your downswing starts and proceeds forward, gravity will pull your body backward. The weight on your back foot will be intense and your balance will really feel off. If you can learn to deal with all of this, you can hit excellent uphill shots. They will launch higher, carry shorter, and stop quicker, so remember to use more club (that is, a club with less loft). After the ball is gone it's okay to fall back, catch your balance, and watch the beautiful fruits of your labor.

3.44

3.4 Launch Direction and In-Flight Curvature

"I can't hit the ball straight . . . so why should I learn to hit it crooked?" I've heard this question many times, and I have two answers for it:

1. Learn to hit it crooked so you can get out of trouble.
2. Learning to hit it crooked will teach you something about *not* hitting it crooked (which helps you hit it straight).

You need to be able to curve shots to successfully play with Damage Control. No doubt, no question, no choice! You need to be able to curve shots to avoid disaster holes. The good news is, learning how to curve your shots means it will be a lot easier for you to learn how *not* to curve them!

Both the launch direction and sidespin (curvature) of your shots are controlled by the angle of your clubface through impact. Learning how to hit shots with your clubface reliably open or closed makes it easier to curve shots around obstacles and escape from trouble like the pros.

THE CLUBFACE CONTROLS LAUNCH DIRECTION AND SPIN

Three facts all golfers must deal with are:

1. The launch direction of a shot is controlled by the alignment of your clubface at impact.
2. Clubface alignment at impact can be controlled by changing either your clubface aim or your grip at address.
3. In-flight curvature is determined by clubface angle relative to swing-path direction through impact.

The simplest way to curve shots is to set the clubface at address in exactly the impact position desired for the shot, then grip it normally and swing away. The shot will launch in a direction determined primarily by the clubface angle at impact. The ball will then spin and curve away from that direction, based on the severity of the glancing blow caused by the clubface angle relative to the swing-path direction (Figure 3.45).

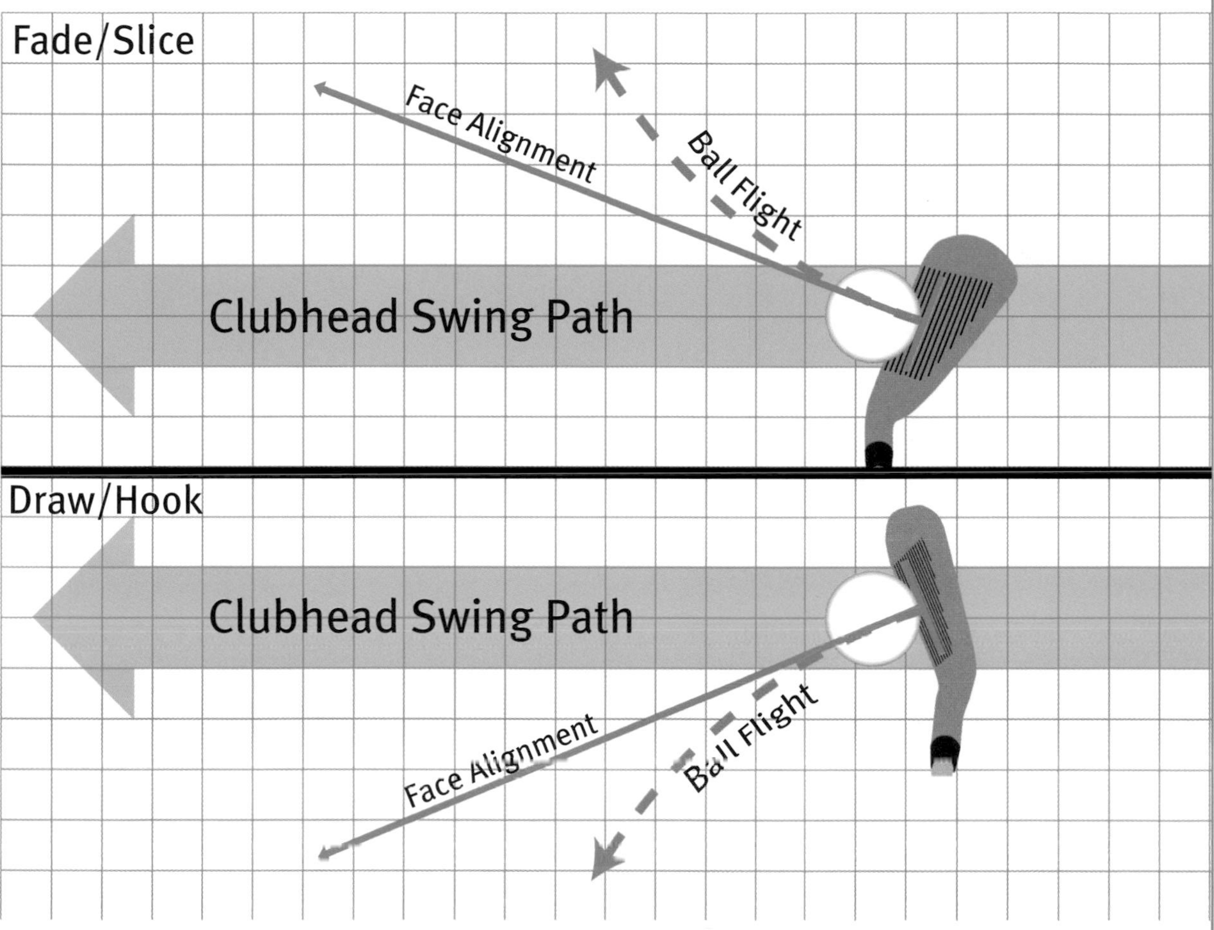

3.45

Many Tour professionals accomplish curving shots using a different technique. They leave their clubface square at address but preset their grip to different positions (Figure 3.46a–c), so that the clubface turns to the angle they want as their hands return to their normal impact position. They've practiced swinging with a square clubface alignment so often that their hand positions are grooved to return to square through impact, creating the cut or draw face angles they desire.

Normal

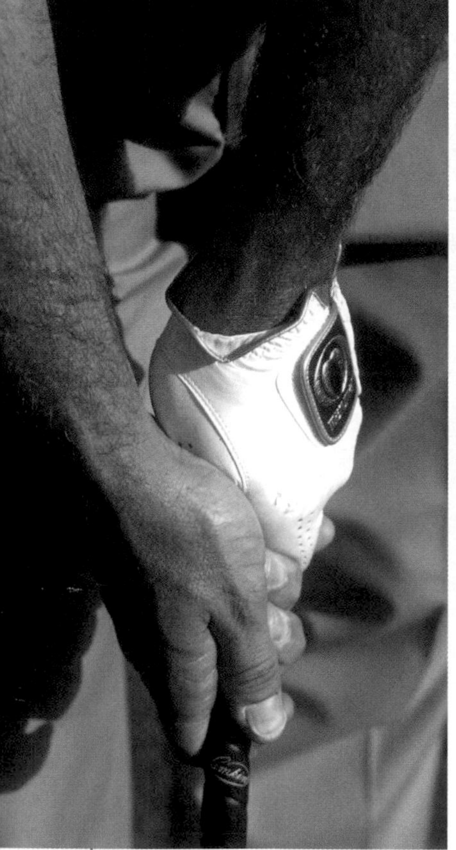

3.46a

Cut

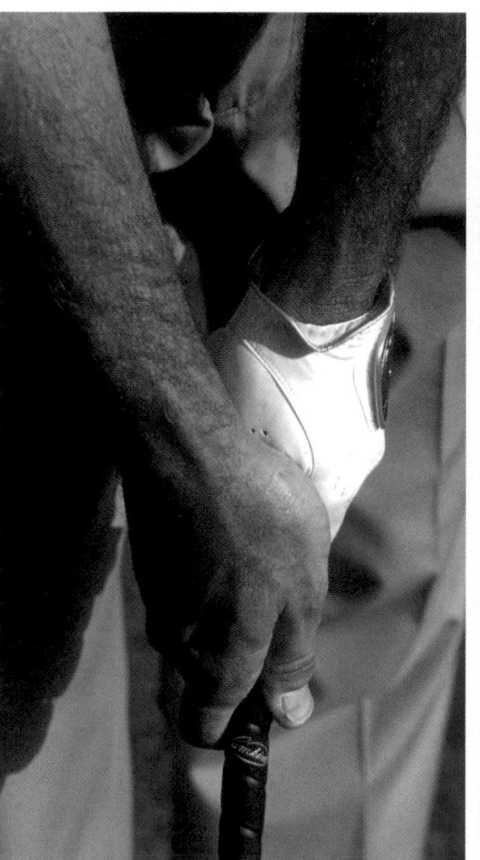

3.46b

Draw

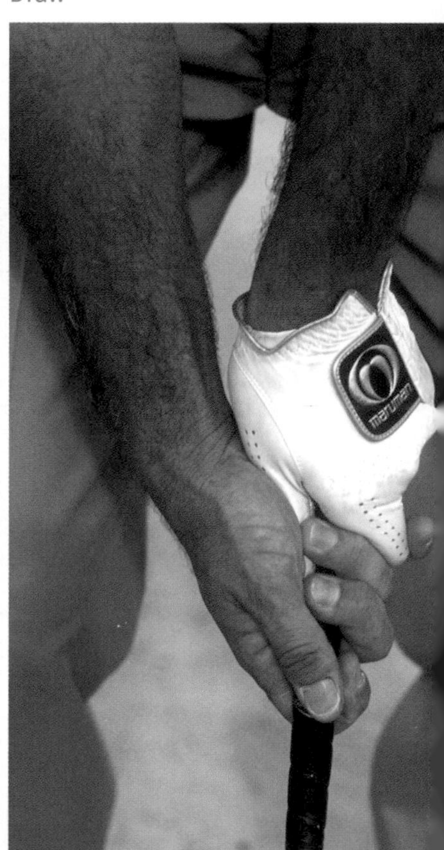

3.46c

AN OPEN CLUBFACE CREATES CUTS, FADES, AND SLICES

Let's say you've hit your ball behind a big tree, and the best way to get back into the game is to play around the left side of it. The easiest way to produce a slice every time is by simply aiming left and hitting the ball with an open clubface. The problem with this shot (a slice) is that many golfers don't allow enough room for the ball to start to the right of their swing line (they expect the shot to fly straight first, then slice).

A serious slice can be seen in Figure 3.47. Notice how I aim way left of the big tree, to assure that my ball doesn't hit it. This "start-to-the-right-then-slice-more-to-the-right" shot is invaluable to a good Damage Control game, and it's simple to hit. But you must learn how far right the ball will start, and then how much it will slice, before you can aim your setup and swing and play it with confidence. I'll show you the drill that can teach you both things in Chapter 7.

A CLOSED CLUBFACE CREATES PULLS, DRAWS, AND HOOKS

Hooks are created with a glancing blow from a closed face through impact. The closed face starts the ball left, and then the spin makes it hook farther to the left from there. The same precautions apply to this shot, except in the opposite direction. Most golfers don't allow enough room for the left start off the clubface, and too often hit straight into the trouble they're trying to avoid.

A serious hook shot can be seen in Figure 3.48. See how far to the right I've set up, to allow for the initial launch to the left? This "start-left-then-hook-more-to-the-left" shot is also valuable for

Following pages: 3.47, 3.48

Damage Control. Again, you must learn how far left the ball will start, and how far it will hook, before you can use it on the course. A drill for learning both of these aspects of flight curvature will also be demonstrated in Chapter 7.

Let me give you a few words of caution here: It's important to find out which method of creating curved shots is the easiest for you and your swing. Which shot can you hit more consistently—an intentional hook, or a slice? It's never wise to exacerbate your swing problems when in trouble. Always use the simplest technique available to get out of trouble and back into the game. Don't let your ego slip into the equation of trying overly difficult shots from bad lies.

3.5 The Good and Bad of Swing Shaping

Being able to change the shape of your swing is critical to playing with Damage Control. In a reasonably sized book we could never demonstrate and detail all of the swing shapes necessary to play from the almost infinite number of trouble shots you will encounter in your golfing future. But it isn't necessary anyway, because memorizing particular swings isn't what Damage Control is about. Understanding the principles of Swing Shaping is what you want to carry with you on the golf course, so for each trouble situation you find yourself in, you can create the best swing for your escape.

The key to success lies in understanding why and how to make swing changes. Once you comprehend which setup postures affect which body parts, actually making the swings you need becomes pretty easy. Golfers who have never experienced swinging and hitting shots in different and creative ways can really have fun learning this Damage Control skill. Creating different and effective swings is not difficult; it's just different.

First let me give you the bad news: Changing the shape of your swing requires several elements that are probably new to you. For example:

By . . .

- Gripping down on the shaft
- Leaning forward
- Changing the timing of your hand/wrist action

. . . you can change how much room your swing requires behind the ball.

By . . .

- Positioning your spine angle properly
- Rotating the appropriate part of your body (upper/lower)
- Keeping your arms connected to your chest

. . . you can execute powerful swings in very flat or upright planes.

By . . .

- Leaning so your spine is perpendicular to the ground
- Emphasizing your upper body and arm swing
- Learning to swing in balance, when balance is different than normal and difficult to maintain

. . . you can conquer the problems sloping terrains present.

By:

- Setting up with your clubface properly aimed at address
- Creating that face angle accurately through impact

. . . you can affect the starting direction and curvature of your ball, to avoid hitting trouble in your immediate vicinity.

But here's the good news: You don't have to remember *any* of the above details about Swing Shaping. In fact, once you understand and feel the fundamental principles of changing the shape of your swing, it's virtually impossible to forget them. With a little practice

(Chapter 7), it is absolutely reasonable for golfers of all skill levels to remember how it feels to execute swings of different shapes, and to hit trouble shots reasonably well.

And more good news: You don't have to be an expert swing shaper to play with Damage Control. You simply have to be adequate at it (Figure 3.49). The requirement of Swing Shaping is only to hit a good enough shot to get the ball back somewhere into the game on your first attempt. The shot doesn't have to be perfect. It just has to end up somewhere decent, in a safe lie. Then you can make a good shot to recover and possibly avoid losing a stroke.

If only the rest of the game were this easy!

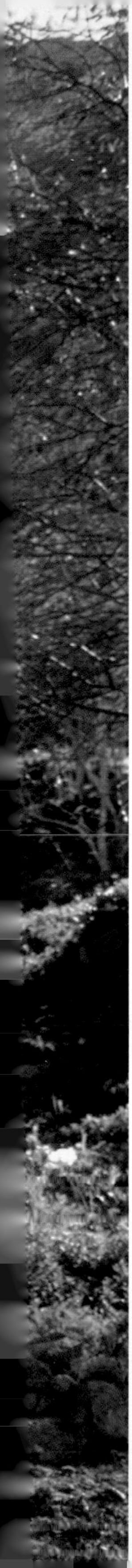

3.49

CHAPTER 4

Hand-Fire Feel

When Normal Swings Won't Work, Hand-Fire Feel Is Your Only Way Out

FOR MOST NORMAL GOLF SHOTS, the less tightness, tension, and grip pressure in your hands, the better. In fact, for the short game and putting, I recommend only enough grip pressure to keep the club from coming loose and flying away during the swing. However, this "hold-on-only" function for your hands doesn't always work when you're hitting escape shots from trouble.

Think about a ball lying down in a patch of knee-high grass. Imagine the feel in your hands, wrists, and forearms as you force your swing down and through the matted grass around the ball. Focus on the intensity of effort you would apply through impact to blast the ball up and all the way out of this mess. This effort, this fire in your hands and wrists that travels through to your forearms (and can even reach into your shoulders and torso), is the "Hand-Fire" of Damage Control.

Feeling the correct Hand-Fire for trouble shots is the third skill of Damage Control. While it's probably more difficult to describe than it is to feel, you shouldn't play without Hand-Fire feel. Because when normal swings won't work from trouble, turning on the correct Hand-Fire will be your only way out!

4.1 Understanding Hand-Fire

The total effort you expend in your hand action, your grip pressure, and the brute force you apply throughout your entire swing all combine to form your Hand-Fire for a given shot from trouble (Figure 4.1). Notice I said "total" effort. This includes the effort the shot takes from the backswing takeaway, down into and through impact, and all the way up to the finish of the swing. Your trouble swing Hand-Fire will usually total greater (on rare occasion, less) than the normal effort you expend through hand action and grip pressure for normal shots.

When trouble provides extra resistance to your swing, the intensity of your Hand-Fire must determine the speed, momentum, and force of your clubhead as it moves through impact with the ball, to handle it. A feel for the correct Hand-Fire is the feel for the correct energy, effort, and application of pressure and force through

4.1 The Hand-Fire equation

the impact zone. It is also important to note: I said *through* impact, not *to* impact: this is an important difference, and will be discussed below.

I know you can't physically feel the various degrees of Hand-Fire sitting in a chair reading this book. But if you examine the examples below in your mind's eye, you will begin to understand Hand-Fire, at least intellectually. Then, when you do our drills in your backyard (detailed in Chapter 7) and then get out on a course, you'll reap the benefit. By focusing on the feel in your hands through impact as you create different swings for different trouble shots, you will create and recognize your own way to measure Hand-Fire. That's the goal of this chapter: to get you to first recognize, and then later evaluate, your feel for the Hand-Fire needed to execute successful escape shots from trouble.

HAND ACTION

Wrists and Forearms: The combination of your wrist motion (cocking and uncocking) and forearm-rotation-controlled clubface manipulations is known as "hand action." Some amount of hand action occurs in all normal golf shots (putts don't need wrist or forearm action, but many golfers do employ them even in putting). What I mean by wrist cocking can be seen in Figure 4.2 and forearm rotation in Figure 4.3. A motion I don't recommend in normal golf swings is the wrist hinge (wrist collapse) shown in Figure 4.4.

4.2 Wrist cock

4.3 Forearm rotation

4.4 Wrist hinge

Hand action is not always intuitive. The hand action we need for Damage Control is hand action *above and beyond* that which occurs in normal shots from good lies. Damage Control often requires additional hand action to deliver the control required to create abnormal trajectory shots, or the power to blast balls out of the "stuff" of trouble lies. This can include action to control the clubhead path and face angle to be unique and different in some way from the hand action you use in normal golf shots.

Using extra power in their hand actions seems intuitive to golf professionals, but in many cases it is never even considered by amateurs. Many don't ever change the force or timing of their wrist cocks or forearm rotations to benefit their shots. They either don't think about it, or they don't know how to do it. Their hand actions always stay the same, even when they try to extricate balls from deep trouble. As you'll see in the photographs to follow, when Hand-Fire is demanded by the golf course, a player had better know how—and how much—to apply. Otherwise, escape attempts from trouble will be doomed to failure.

Normal hand action: To see an example of normal hand action, look at the late Payne Stewart chipping from the fringe on the PGA TOUR (Figure 4.5). Payne's hand action involved a slight wrist cock on his backswing, a slight recock on the follow-through, and a modest amount of forearm rotation through impact. His motion

4.5

was essentially perfect in both cases. Payne had a wonderful touch around the greens, and was one of the best chippers of the ball I have ever seen. 4.6

Another good example of normal hand action can be seen in the half-wedge swing of Lee Janzen's 40-yard shot from a good lie in light rough (Figure 4.6). Lee uses very quiet hands (which is a good thing when precision is required), and he would qualify as a golfer who has the perfect *normal* hand action. And for a great view of the perfect amount of forearm rotation in a 5-iron shot, look at a young Ben Crenshaw through impact in Figure 4.7.

4.7

Extra hand action: Certain situations on the course—especially trouble shots—require more than normal hand action. This point is paramount to your understanding of Hand-Fire. When you take a normal swing through impact, you get a normal shot reaction. If a normal shot reaction is not what you want, however, then something has to change the way your club passes through impact. That something is hand action.

In Figure 4.8, I'm hitting a knockdown 9-iron shot between two trees on the 14th hole at Pinehurst No. 2. Because I want the shot to stay low but also have lots of backspin, I'm keeping my hands ahead of the club through impact. I'm delaying the normal release of my forearms and hooding the clubface to keep the ball from flying to the right. I can feel that this extra hand action is different from the amount I would use for a normal shot from this distance.

A better example of increased hand action, in the form of greater

4.8

forearm rotation through impact, is shown by the great "escape artist," Seve Ballesteros, in Figure 4.9. Seve used his tremendous talent to produce extreme hand action through some of his shots. His escapes are legendary. A rather mundane shot for him, here he is shown hooking a wedge shot around the tree that's blocking his vision of the hole (it's not easy to make a wedge shot hook).

4.9

Instead of rolling the hands over through impact to produce a dramatic hook, however, a player sometimes needs to use Hand-Fire to control a club to do exactly the opposite. By this I mean manipulation of the club to *not* turn over. This means holding the clubface open as it passes through impact to block the normal rotation of clubface closure as it impacts the ball. Unquestionably, one of the most creative and talented professionals to ever play the game is Phil Mickelson (Figure 4.10). In both of these shots, Phil holds the clubface open well past impact, until after he has launched his shot.

One more example of strong hand action is the sequence of Gary Player shown in Figure 4.11. Notice his wrists immediately after impact. Even though his hands have not continued to move

4.10

through and past their impact position (as they do in his normal swing motion), he has completed his post-impact (finished swing) wrist recock action. This hand action requires both strength and tremendous timing to effectively produce a high and spinning shot from downhill sloping sand, one of the most difficult shots in the game.

4.11

GRIP PRESSURE

Grip pressure is in the hands. It resides mainly in the fingers with a little involvement of the palms. If you rated it on a scale from zero to ten, zero would be not holding the club and ten would be squeezing it as hard as you possibly can. For normal golf shots, grip pressure increases with rising clubhead speed to counter greater outward forces generated by higher swing speeds. Golfers instinctively increase their grip pressure as they swing faster to keep the club from flying out of their hands and down the fairway.

Rating grip pressure numerically is not necessary, but you should recognize that grip pressure for normal shots should be generally low. If you think about just holding onto the club for putting, chipping, pitching, and finesse wedge shots around the greens, you're about right. As the shot distance increases, the grip pressure must also increase. Keeping your grip pressure as low as possible will give you better sensitivity for delicate touch and feel shots, but less ability to apply power to a shot when it's needed.

Pros have soft hands. Having soft hands means having light grip pressure, and you can see this if you get close enough to watch some of the world's best players as they play. A great example of soft-hands grip pressure is Fred Couples hitting a cut-lob shot from a perfect lie to a tight pin placement (Figure 4.12) less than 10 yards away. Fred does absolutely nothing with the pressure in his hands through this shot, except hold onto the club lightly (it sometimes looks as if he might actually let go of the club as it swings through impact). Freddie demonstrates how he thinks of the effort involved

4.12

in this shot with his hand toss and one-arm swing (Figure 4.13), both of which accomplish the same ball trajectory with his soft hands throughout. I don't see Freddie adding any effort to his normal soft-hand action when he hits this shot, and I can't imagine anyone doing it better.

4.13

Of course, you can imagine how this light grip pressure would have to change drastically if his ball were sitting all the way at the bottom of a tall Bermuda grass lie and he had to rip through the grass to produce the shot.

The same soft hands can be seen in the three-quarter wedge swing of Steve Elkington in Figure 4.14. Because Elk's shot carry distance is longer than Freddie's lob shot, I'm sure he held onto the club with a little more pressure in his fingers and hands. As you can see, however, he is not squeezing the club, and he certainly doesn't have a death grip on it. He doesn't exert any excess pressure, which helps him achieve his excellent distance control and touch in these shots.

4.14

As shots get longer or meet more resistance, grip pressure increases. Increased outward forces are generated as longer clubs are swung faster on longer shots. Correspondingly, the grip pressure necessary to hold onto the club also increases for these shots. It shouldn't get too high, though, even on long and somewhat difficult shots. You can see this in the 7-iron grip of Phil Mickelson (Figure 4.15)—his left hand is almost off the club through impact, and it's clear he's just holding on with it. The good news here is that this hands-off approach—he's using a grip pressure of no more than "firm" intensity—means that Phil is not manipulating the clubface through impact. Paul Azinger (Figure 4.16) also exhibits a firm grip as he prepares to blast a buried ball from sand.

4.15

4.16
Ryder Cup captain Paul Azinger faces a buried lie at East Lake.

Death grips don't cut it. One last thought about grip pressure: If you use a super-tight death grip and excessive wrist tension in your normal game for normal shots, it will cause touch and feel problems. You don't want that. I'm suggesting increased grip pressure (and other increased Hand-Fire contributions) only when playing Damage Control shots from trouble, where optimum touch is not a requirement. If you have a problem with excessive grip pressure in your normal game, take care of it as part of a normal game improvement program with lessons from your local PGA Golf Professional.

BRUTE FORCE

As a man who specializes in teaching the short game, finesse shots, and putting, I almost cringe when it comes time to talk about the use of brute force in the golf swing. When our research shows that it's necessary, however, I've got to do it.

"Through" . . . not "to": Brute force is the extra effort and power a golfer must provide (from the body, hands, and arms) to create the speed, power, and stability his clubhead needs to pass through the extraordinary resistance sometimes encountered around a golf ball. In addition to providing active hands and strong grip pressure, brute force is often required to power a club through the water, grass, bushes, or whatever trouble the ball is in. While you may not have thought about it, I'm sure you've experienced it.

In a normal sand shot, you need to move some sand forward along with the ball, so you use enough Hand-Fire to provide extra speed for your clubhead into and through impact. This shot, however, doesn't require any significant brute force. But when you need to cut through long grass behind the ball so that your club can get to the ball with significant clubhead speed, you'll find yourself using brute force. It may also be needed to continue moving the club through all the resistance past impact to make sure the ball gets out of the trouble. The operative word here is *through*: If your clubhead just gets *to* impact and stops there, the likelihood of the ball getting out of trouble isn't very high.

Where brute force comes from: Brute force is necessary whenever your ball is sitting down in water, sand, heavy grass, weeds, mud—anything heavy, thick, or sticky—that slows your clubhead as it approaches or leaves the zone of impact. Your body must sometimes play a part in supplying brute force by providing a stable foundation from which to launch these extra-powerful swings. To support brute force in a swing, a strong base is required to either push with, or push against.

When a ball comes in high and hard and lands in wet or heavy sand, you can get the kind of lie shown in Figure 4.17. To get this ball up and onto the green, a clubface angle that will dig deeply enough to get below the ball (Figure 4.18) is required. The problem is that when the leading edge of a club digs into sand, the club can neither bounce off the sand and keep the sand divot shallow, nor maintain its speed through the impact zone. Thus all the wet, heavy sand around the ball, along with the ball itself, must be moved out of the bunker with brute force (Figure 4.19). This means that the club must be powered by a significant effort from

4.17.

4.18

4.19

the hands, wrists, and forearms pushing against a solid core and base. If your wrists and forearms are not up to providing this force (and this is especially a problem for many women), the chances of escaping the trouble are severely diminished. Look at what happens to this same shot if I make a normal swing effort with no Hand-Fire (Figure 4.20). What a disaster!

4.2 The Intensity of Hand-Fire

When the three factors that create Hand-Fire (hand action, grip pressure, and brute force) are combined, they determine the overall intensity of any trouble shot. At the Pelz Golf Institute we tried to estimate the Hand-Fire intensity involved in a shot by rating it on some kind of metric or scale. But we realized golfers can learn it more easily by relating it to a "feel."

Some extremely delicate shots onto fast and/or downhill greens require below-normal Hand-Fire. When a shot requires only a little extra grip pressure to keep the club stable through some light rough, the amount of Hand-Fire needed is low. When faster-than-normal wrist action and forearm rotation is added to an increased grip pressure, the Hand-Fire intensity goes up. And when brute force must be added to the mix, the Hand-Fire goes up still further.

What about when you need to bludgeon a club through tall, thick, wet grass, and the ball is sitting down in water? In some cases the requirement for Hand-Fire can run all the way up to (or even exceed) the maximum a golfer can deliver. You might be well advised to take a drop with a one-stroke penalty when this happens!

4.20

NORMAL SWINGS

To get an initial sense of what Hand-Fire feels like, I suggest you pick up one of your wedges and make some swings with me. Start with the normal three-quarter wedge swing that I'm making in Figure 4.21. I normally swing through to a full finish in this swing, but you can see my wrists recock when my hands reach shoulder height on the follow-through. Make a few of these swings (complete your finish) and put your mind's eye on the effort made by your hands, wrists, and forearms. Tell yourself that this is your normal amount of Hand-Fire for a three-quarter wedge swing.

4.21

4.22

Low Hand-Fire wrist cock: Next make a shorter backswing, but this time with a quicker-than-normal wrist cock. The faster you complete your wrist cock in your backswing, the later you'll uncock your wrists in the downswing, and the earlier you'll recock them in your follow-through (after impact), as I demonstrate in Figure 4.22. The more quickly you execute your wrist-cocking motion, the more you must use Hand-Fire to accomplish it. This swing motion qualifies as a low intensity of Hand-Fire.

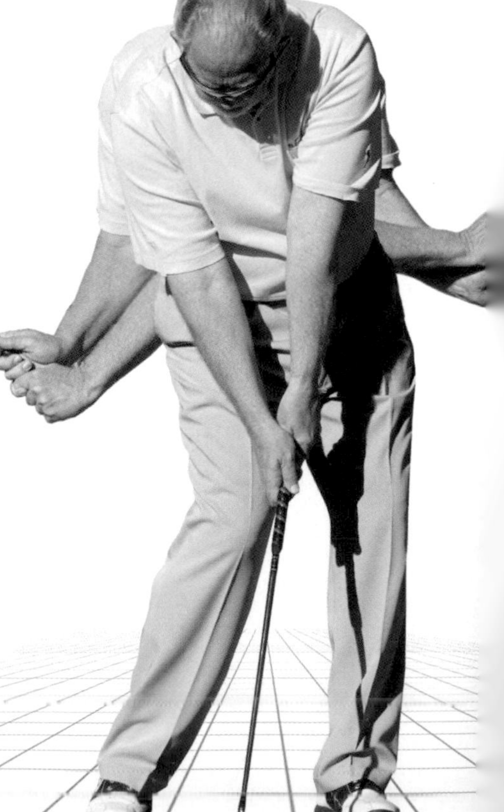

Forearm rotation: Now go back to your normal three-quarter wedge swing and think about the rotation action of your forearms (as shown in Figure 4.23). We are now making normal forearm release motions using the normal amount of Hand-Fire required for our normal three-quarter wedge swing. This is how normal Hand-Fire feels for your normal wedge shot forearm rotation.

4.23

If you examine Figure 4.24 carefully, you'll notice I'm now using a modest amount of additional Hand-Fire to rotate my forearms more quickly through the impact zone (note: my hands are closer to impact when I rotate my forearms, as compared to normal). Try this quicker-than-normal forearm rotation for yourself, and feel the added amount of Hand-Fire you feel.

4.24

Internalize the feel. Try both of these motions (the wrist cock and the forearm release) alternately with your normal swing motions and see if you can feel the differences. If you can feel them, the differences will be in the low-intensity range of Hand-Fire effort, and you will both see and feel its effect on your swing and clubhead motion.

If you're not getting the feel of Hand-Fire yet, don't worry. When you see enough real swings involving higher values of Hand-Fire (these will come later in this book), and then go to a golf course and make these swings yourself, you'll immediately feel what we mean.

MODERATE HAND-FIRE INTENSITY

Good lies in light rough usually don't require anything more than the normal Hand-Fire you use for the same club from a good fairway lie. However, when a ball is sitting slightly down in the grass, especially if the grass is higher than light, i.e., 1½ inches rough, then there's a need for a little extra Hand-Fire.

Modest Hand-Fire: The Hand-Fire used to create abnormal clubface behavior is usually less than the effort required to cut through stuff around the golf ball, especially when your ball lies in serious trouble. As a simple reference for you, I feel like I simulate a feel of modest Hand-Fire when I swing with a one-pound weight on my clubhead (Figure 4.25). This is about the same intensity of feel as the one I get when I'm making a block or cut-shot swing, holding the face open through and past impact, to curve the ball to the right. Whether it is a cut-shot swing, or a one-pound-weight swing, the feel of Hand-Fire is about the same to me, in terms of the effort required. Now try to imagine and feel this effort as you make a cut-shot swing (you'll need this swing sometime in the future, I guarantee it). 4.25

A little smoke: Look at a greenside swing of Vijay Singh (Figure 4.26) when he's faced with a ball sitting down in 2-inch Bermuda grass. This photograph was taken just five steps off the practice green at East Lake Golf Club in Atlanta, home of the PGA TOUR Championship. Notice his hand-action intensity and the motion of the clubhead immediately after impact. Now imagine how this shot might turn out if he had used only the normal light grip pressure required to pitch a shot 7 yards from a perfect lie. His club would have probably stopped cold when it encountered the sticky resistance from this grass. I think you can see (and perhaps imagine a bit) the feel of a little smoke in Vijay's Hand-Fire.

4.26

Almost any ball sitting in 3-inch or longer bluegrass or 2-inch Bermuda grass rough, especially if the grass is wet, will require serious Hand-Fire smoke to produce consistent shot results. Similarly, if one were to find their ball sitting half-down in a furrow of sand, or in casual water (with the bottom of the ball in the water, and no good drop area available), these conditions would also provide resistance to the clubhead through impact, and would require a little smoke.

I can simulate the feel of "smoke-level" Hand-Fire when I shove a box full of books across the carpet (4.27). This action involves a feeling of pressure up the back of my left hand, in both wrist joints, up my arms, and into my shoulders. Try something like this until you feel the pressure of slight resistance in your arms; this is what a little smoke in your Hand-Fire should feel like.

4.27

Smoldering hands from U.S. Open rough: The 1999 U.S. Open at Pinehurst No. 2 had what I believe is the perfect-length Bermuda grass rough to test the skill of golfers. At 4 to 4½ inches, most Bermuda grass rough (Figure 4.28) will let a golf ball sink to the bottom, while still giving the golfer a good view of the ball. This leads golfers to believe they can get a good strike on the ball and get it to the green. The difficulty of this shot is that it requires a smoldering amount of Hand-Fire to extricate the ball, but also enough touch to play for the appropriate amount of bounce and roll to stop the ball on the green once it gets there (shots have minimal backspin from this lie).

4.28

Similarly, a ball sitting in a "fried-egg" lie or more than halfway down in an unraked footprint in the sand (Figure 4.29) requires smoldering Hand-Fire. Smoldering hands are needed to carry the clubhead into and through the sand with enough speed to move the ball 10 yards up and onto the green (Figure 4.30). In this case, the problem of not enough backspin often causes this shot to be very difficult to stop close to the pin (the ball must land in the rough or fringe to kill its speed, because it will *not* have much backspin on it).

4.29

4.30

SERIOUS HAND-FIRE

Even stronger Hand-Fire is necessary to extract a ball from even worse rough conditions or when it's more deeply imbedded into the sand. When a ball finds its way into 6- to 8-inch rough, there's a good chance you might not get it out on the first swing. The same applies when a ball plugs into sand and most of the ball remains below the surface, or the ball is under water.

Imminent fire: When "imminent fire" power is required to extricate a ball from trouble, you know you are in a potentially serious—as in disaster-score = serious—situation. Several examples of this are similar to the lies in the previous section, but now the ball is buried completely below the surface of something wet, or heavy, or both (Figure 4.31). In this example, my ball was completely buried in heavy sand, and I used serious Hand-Fire to chop down into the sand. The sand not only went in several directions at impact, it completely stopped the motion of my club, arms, and body.

4.31

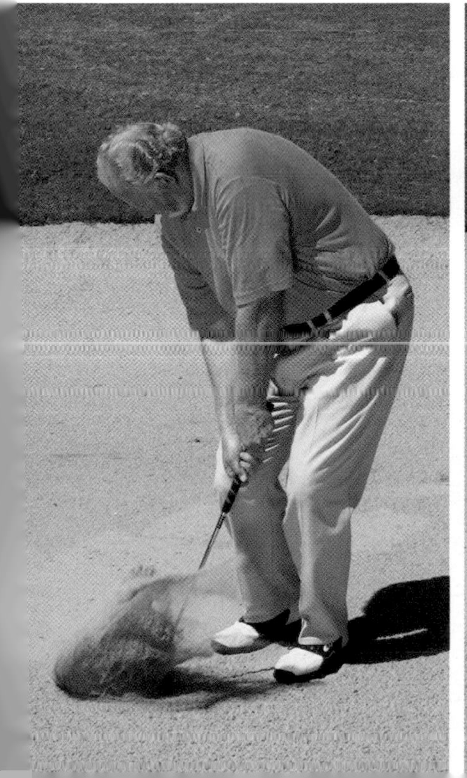

4.32

Another example of imminent firepower is the effort that Tom Sieckmann has put into his "clubhead-toe-in-first" escape from a completely buried lie in Figure 4.32. If you look closely at the photos after impact, you can see serious firepower in Tom's forearms and hands.

Open flames: Open-flame Hand-Fire from a strong player can blast through a surprising amount of long wet grass, sand, dirt, sticks, bushes, branches, water, and anything else in the way of a successful escape shot. Of course, it would be best to not get into these impossible lies in the first place. But when you do, open flames are required.

The need for open-flame Hand-Fire occurs after you've driven the ball into the lip of a fairway sand bunker and it has plugged all the way under the sand on a severe upslope. Moving this much sand will require open-flame Hand-Fire effort to get the ball out (Figure 4.33). (Note: When preparing to supply open-flame Hand-Fire in this situation, don't forget the extra effort required to turn your body and weight through impact—and uphill!)

4.33

4.34
Without an "open flame" trim slap at the sand, Azinger would never have been able to pop this shot up and out of its buried lie.

Another example of open flames Hand-Fire intensity can be seen in the image of Paul Azinger blasting a ball from a greenside bunker with water close behind the green (Figure 4.34). As you can imagine from this photograph, without strong hand action at impact, this ball would never have popped up and out of the sand.

Blast furnace: There are untold numbers of water hazards in the world of golf, many of which have soft, muddy transition edges that trap golf balls. You can see the ball, you know you can hit it, but the question is: Can you extricate it from the mud and water in your first try? These shots are tempting but very dangerous to try.

Partially submerged balls in water and muck present an interesting dilemma for golfers. This shot encourages one to lay the clubface partially open so that the bottom of the club splashes and bounces off the water, which will prevent the club from digging in too deeply but will still keep the clubhead speed up. But the clubface also needs to be closed enough to allow enough penetration for the clubface to make contact with the ball. Solid club-to-ball contact is necessary to power the ball up and out of the goop (Figure 4.35). (Believe me, I didn't want to hit any more of these shots for this book).

4.35

4.36

Ultimate Hand-Fire: Are you interested in the feel of ultimate Hand-Fire? It includes a lot of brute force. Try pushing your club against something really solid from your impact position, like I'm doing in Figure 4.36. Don't swing into this; just lay your club on it and then push it to feel the force. This might be similar to what it feels like to cut through wet, 8-inch-high U.S. Open rough to get to a ball that's sitting on the ground—you never honestly know if you can get your club through it or not!

When a ball is completely submerged in water it can be successfully blasted out with a square club face. This face angle allows the club to cut down into the water. Success for this shot depends upon your ability to create a very high swing speed before entering the water, then to apply enough Hand-Fire (which takes plentiful wrist and forearm strength) to maintain clubhead velocity through and after impact. Such power is demonstrated in the full-out blast by Masters champion Craig Stadler (Figure 4.37a–c).

Similar swing speeds and Hand-Fire strength are needed to bludgeon balls out of the foot-high wet bluegrass rough, weeds, and liquid-fertilized grasses used around fairways in important tournaments today. When the pros encounter such trouble, they use their well-conditioned wrists and forearms to apply the maximum amount of Hand-Fire needed to blast their ball back into the game.

4.37a–c

4.38a

Masters champion Craig Stadler blasting from water.

4.38b

4.38c

4.3 Learning Hand-Fire Feel Is Essential

The reason for showing this much Hand-Fire action to you is not to encourage you to use it. Rather, it's my belief that seeing photographs of players successfully getting out of the worst kinds of trouble can help you get your mind around the concept of Hand-Fire, the third skill of Damage Control. Knowing the feel of both the minimum and maximum amounts of Hand-Fire will help you refine your usage of the technique in your own game.

The lessons of this chapter on Hand-Fire feel are simple. The speed and quickness with which you 1) cock, uncock, and recock your wrists; 2) rotate your forearms; and 3) manipulate your hands through your swing, determine your hand action. Your grip pressure is also an important component of your Hand-Fire, and it must be changed from trouble shot to trouble shot. Additionally, there is the application of brute force when you need to bludgeon your way through stuff around your ball in a seriously troubled lie.

To play with Damage Control, you need to apply Hand-Fire to control and manipulate the club to curve your ball around—or extricate it from—whatever trouble you find on the course. Don't think that the application of Hand-Fire runs counter to the methods used to teach a normal swing. Believe me, we don't want you to add Hand-Fire to your normal game. It must be strictly limited to Damage Control situations, where normal swings won't work!

You must understand that you can't hit a ball out of water with a normal swing using normal effort and grip pressure; you can't get a ball out of tall grass or deep sand (Figure 4.38) with a nice, smooth finesse swing; and you can't adjust your shot trajectories away from normal without applying Hand-Fire somewhere in your swing.

4.38

CHAPTER 5

Red-Flag Touch

BEAUTIFUL SWING! NICE SHOT, but . . . but . . . *Oh! Too bad!*

There is nothing more discouraging than standing with thousands of people watching your perfectly executed escape shot land just like you wanted it to in the center of the green, only to see it bounce and roll over the back, down the hill, and into the water. This is especially agonizing when it leads to a disastrous score and ruins your round.

The fourth skill of Damage Control is Red-Flag Touch. This skill involves having a little red flag attached to your temple, connected directly through to your brain. It works this way: When you're preparing to play from trouble and your red flag pops up, it issues a brain alert: Look out; you're in danger and you're looking at a dangerous landing zone. If this escape shot lands in that red-flag landing zone, it might not stop until it finds even worse trouble.

When your red flag pops up, you are in Red-Flag danger. Be alert and focused. Plan and play smartly. Be careful; do NOT hit this shot out of the frying pan and into the fire!

5.1 The Meaning of Red Flags

RED-FLAG CONDITIONS

There are many conditions found in golf from which trouble can lead to even worse trouble. Red-Flag conditions can take many forms, and they're especially destructive when your shot into them must be played from a trouble lie, which will negatively affect both backspin and trajectory control. These conditions can be very difficult-looking places that obviously have the potential to send a ball off into serious trouble, or very innocuous-looking surfaces such as super-firm and super-fast greens that slope gently off into water.

RED-FLAG STATUS

Red-Flag status initiates when you find yourself in a lie bad enough to prevent you from predicting your shot pattern with confidence, and you're in the vicinity of severe fire trouble (Figure 5.1). In this example, the fork in the broken tree branch prevents the club from hitting the ball cleanly if you attempt to play toward the green, and will probably send the ball off in some unknown direction after impact if you do so. Obviously the creek bed between you and the green creates a high probability of adding a penalty shot or two (and who knows what else?) to your score in this situation.

Whenever there's a chance that your escape shot—even if it's made with a reasonably well-executed swing—might end up in another frying-pan lie, or worse, a red flag should go up in your brain. You are in Red-Flag status, and you should play this shot with an extra amount of care and attention, combined with a conservative enough approach to avoid a disastrous result.

RED-FLAG TRAJECTORIES

The trajectories of shots from trouble are more difficult to control, and they miss their desired flight path more frequently and by greater amounts than normal shots. Probably more than half of all trouble shots come out higher and softer, with significantly less energy than planned. The rest (very few come out perfectly) come out hotter, with lower trajectories than expected. Both results cause serious problems, because in trouble scenarios you never know which one is coming next.

If you're standing over a ball in trouble, and for whatever reason you feel that you might skull the shot or hit it fat, your red flag should pop up and send the alert: Back off and reconsider the swing you are about to make. There may be something wrong with your setup that requires you to do something to better control how high or hard this shot will fly. Or you may need to re-verify your ball position or reconsider your target selection. Remember, your red flag is telling you: "There's *something* wrong, so be careful. We can't afford a really bad performance here—we are in Red-Flag territory!"

RED-FLAG BACKSPIN

The more debris that comes between your ball and the clubface through impact, the less backspin your shot will have. The more obstacles that bother your swing and make you change its shape to avoid a collision with the club, the less likely you are to hit the shot solidly. For both these reasons, escape shots very often don't have good backspin.

When your lie is somewhere between clean and nesty, it's very tough to predict what kind of backspin your shot will have. Will the shot come out of a grassy lie at the bottom end of the backspin spectrum, with essentially zero spin (Figure 5.2a)? Or will it come out almost normally from the almost clean lie, with normal backspin (Figure 5.2b)? From all such lies, your red flag should pop up. Be careful, because this ball may run forever after it lands, or at least until it runs into some kind of trouble. Do you really want to play this shot directly at the flagstick and take on the risk involved?

5.2a Red Lie
5.2b White Lie

RED-FLAG LANDING ZONES

Red-Flag landing areas can be greens, hard and fast fairways, closely mown mounds, tree groves with overhanging limbs, steep banks, closely shaven gentle slopes—the list can go on forever. Red-Flag areas are any landing spots that reject balls into disasters. As you will see in the following sections, red flags can be flown for many seemingly innocuous situations if "fire" lies, severe penalties, and disaster scores lie nearby.

The firmness and speed of landing areas, especially when gently sloping surfaces are present, are probably the most innocent looking of all the Red-Flag conditions golfers commonly face. They catch golfers unaware as they escort well-executed and otherwise well-planned shots right into serious trouble.

5.2 Red Flags for Surface Conditions

Golf is played on many surfaces, and the conditions of most of them vary with weather and time. The grass on the green grows, gets mowed, and gets rolled. Thatch below the grass surface is compacted and aerated. Fairway and rough grasses grow and get cut, moisture absorbs and evaporates, sand compacts and gets raked, tree limbs extend and get trimmed, and water levels rise and fall. Around the world, even on any given course, the conditions under which we play the game are virtually never the same two days in a row. We see these surfaces all the time, think nothing of them normally, and enjoy playing the game on them day in and day out.

As surface conditions change, most remain reasonably benign and are simply considered "part of the game" for the day. There are some conditions that are normal when shots hit from good lies land there, but that become real problems when shots hit from troubled lies land on them. As I said earlier, any surface that causes a significantly high percentage of shots to scoot into serious trouble and penalty situations should be classified as a Red-Flag surface condition.

SUPER-SOFT

Have you ever lost a ball in the middle of the fairway? You probably haven't, unless your shot flew into a wet, low-lying, super-soft area and plugged below the surface. Because this is seldom the case, we don't worry much about it. I want to assure you, however, that it happens (I have lost many balls in such conditions because I enjoy playing in the rain).

When you do play into such an area, a Red-Flag alert should pop-up to remind you to keep all shots hit into this area on a low trajectory. This will help keep them from plugging down into the surface and disappearing from sight.

FIRM AND HARD

When green complexes are surrounded by trouble and green surfaces are so firm that pitch-marks disappear, a red flag should pop up. When approaches and greens are so firm that balls bounce three feet or more into the air after impact, red flags should also go up. These conditions make all chipping, pitching, and wedge shots more difficult to play, even for well-struck shots from good lies. Firm greens and approaches give no quarter to trouble shots coming in with no backspin, and this is good reason to issue a red-flag warning.

When a fairway becomes as hard as an airport runway, it can be very difficult to keep your drive on the short grass. Firm fairways let balls run on until they're stopped by the higher grasses of the rough. When this happens, the course is said to be playing hard and fast, and if the rough is also long and penal, scoring over the entire round will run higher than normal. But these conditions shouldn't elicit a red flag unless they lie immediately beside water or other fire-lie conditions. Firm fairways themselves don't cause disaster holes. At worst, shots run into the rough next to them, and you should be able to play your ball back to the fairway without serious damage.

BACKSPIN MAY NOT SAVE YOU

Only high-backspin shots with steep landing angles have a chance to stop on very firm and fast greens. Normal soft greens allow balls to penetrate the surface of the green. This penetration leaves a pitch-mark and helps stop the forward momentum of the ball, after which backspin can more readily take effect.

But escape shots rarely have much backspin. When your shot from trouble faces a hard green, a good choice may be to play a bump-and-run type shot short of the green, or to play to a position that leaves the next shot somewhere below the flagstick, which would make the next chip and/or putt an easier uphill shot.

Remember, it's not always easy to put enough backspin on the ball to fly it to a firm green and get it stopped somewhere near the flagstick—even from good lies on level terrain—and it's especially difficult from a trouble lie. You should also be aware that backspin becomes effective only after a ball establishes roll contact with the surface of a green. Even shots endowed with plentiful backspin will bounce hard several times on firm greens before establishing roll contact, and only then will they begin to slow down.

Your takeaway from all this is: Be aware of the moisture content and surface firmness of the greens on which you're playing. When you play on greens that don't leave pitch-marks, beware of playing shots into them from trouble lies. Get your red flags up on all trouble shots under these conditions, and *plan* on shots not stopping as fast as normal.

5.3 Red Flags for Slopes

One of the greatest golf courses in the world is Pinehurst No. 2 in North Carolina. The design contains more hidden Red-Flag landing areas on and around the greens than any course I've ever seen. The areas surrounding many of the greens are contoured to allow all but the best-struck shots to dribble off and away from the putting surface into extremely difficult recovery positions. No. 2's greens aren't surrounded by water, canyons, or obvious disaster-pit jungles, and most don't even appear to be elevated, so most golfers don't put up their red-flag warning. But these landing areas for incoming shots create more 7s, 8s, and 9s on scorecards than you could imagine (Figure 5.3).

This design masterpiece was the creation of Donald Ross, who lived by, played, and studied the course for more than twenty years. I can imagine Ross, a good player himself, standing on the greens in the evening looking back at the fairways and roughs, planning how to create dangerous but benign-looking landing areas. I'm sure he enjoyed watching golfers who were blissfully unaware of what was about to happen fly, bounce, and roll balls into disaster scores around those greens.

5.3

GROUND-SLOPE EFFECTS

Most golfers don't understand how slope can affect the bounce and roll of a ball. Stay with me for a minute here. I'm going to get just a little bit technical, but you *need* to understand how slopes affect your game. And you especially need this for Damage Control, because these effects are magnified when they're combined with shots hit from trouble.

Slopes affect balls rolling uphill and downhill differently. It is not the case that what you lose rolling uphill equals what you gain rolling downhill, as your intuition might tell you. To see what I mean, look at the example of how a ball with a given reference speed rolls 13 feet on level ground (Figure 5.4). If you tilt the ground like the back of the green at Bethpage Black #15 (shown in Figure 5.5) and roll this same ball at the same speed up the slope, it will roll only 7 feet (less than 50 percent shorter). But when you then turn and roll the same ball with the same speed down the same slope, it will roll 42 feet (more than 300 percent farther)!

5.4 Green speed= 13 feet

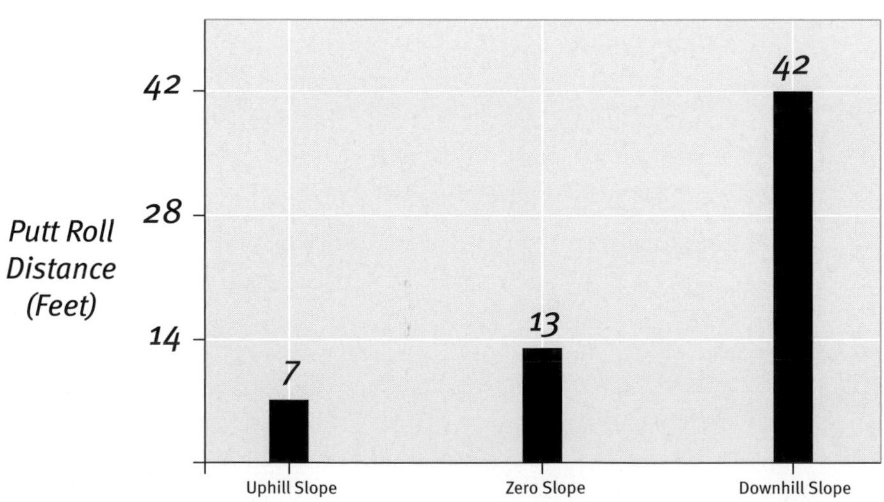

SLOPE ROLL RULES

The rules for putts rolling on sloped greens are:

1. Balls gain more distance rolling down a hill than they lose rolling up.
2. The faster the green speed, the greater the difference between up- and downhill roll distances.

5.5

This rule creates a dangerous situation when a golfer prepares to putt down a slope. Without realizing that the green is in effect extra-fast when they putt downhill, they often don't engage their red-flags, and three-putt as a result of running their first putt 10 feet past the hole. When greens are really fast, and trouble lies are waiting above the hole, these green slopes become Red-Flag surfaces.

BOUNCING OFF AN UPSLOPE

A ball bouncing on a slope is a different problem. To understand how a slope effects the bounce of a ball, first look at an illustration of a ball bouncing off level ground (assume hard ground, so bounce is expected). When a drive lands on a level (flat) fairway at a 45-degree angle, it bounces forward at the same angle of 45 degrees (both angles are measured from a line perpendicular to the ground) as seen in Figure 5.6.

This rule sounds a little complicated, but you can easily see the results by looking at Figure 5.7. If the same incoming drive as in Figure 5.6 lands on the 23-degree upslope of a mound in the fairway (instead of on level ground), it will bounce straight up in the air and stop. Can you believe this? Only a 23-degree mound in the fairway can stop an incoming drive which lands on it, dead in its tracks?

It's true. Every upslope you ever land a shot on will affect the angle at which your ball bounces by twice the upslope angle. This is why your drives stop so short when they land on even small upslopes. And the same effect controls every shot you try to bounce into an upslope in front of a green.

SLOPE BOUNCE RULE

The rules for a ball bouncing off a slope are:

1. The angle of incidence equals the angle of reflection.
2. For every 1 degree of slope change, the bounce angle changes by 2 degrees.

5.6

Incoming
(Angle of Incidence)

Outgoing
(Angle of Reflection)

45° *45°*

45° *45°*

Level Level

Level Ground

5.7

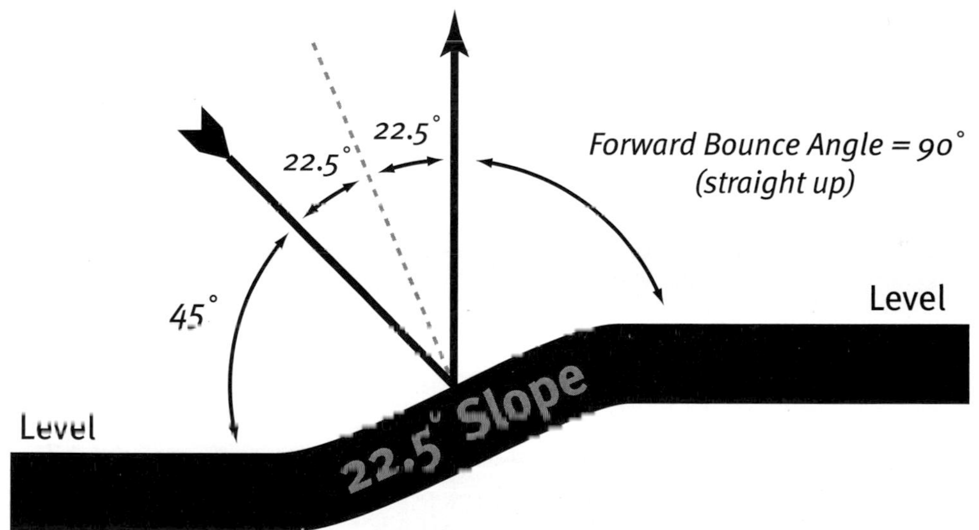

DOWNSLOPES ARE WORSE THAN UPSLOPES

But the other side to this story is how *far* a ball bounces and then rolls off a downslope. The same rule of bounce applies, but in this case the angle of the downslope doubles the resulting bounce angle in the opposite direction. It creates a bounce angle with the horizontal that's *twice* as low. This is why your wedge shots, after landing on a 23-degree downslope, bounce straight forward and

5.8

then roll over the green and into the back bunker or creek. It's also the reason that some of your drives go unexpectedly long off the tee: They've landed on a local area downslope in the fairway and have rolled twice as far as normal.

Unfortunately, this phenomenon controls what happens when your short-game shots land on firm, downslopes on greens. It's the reason why balls bouncing off downslopes kick way farther forward than golfers expect them to. This effect gets even worse when a slope running away from the incoming shot direction encounters a trouble shot, which has little or no backspin. In this case, the down slope becomes a Red-Flag landing area. Just imagine that a low-spinning ball from trouble lands on a firm downslope. The result looks like a scared rabbit—the ball runs as fast as it can and doesn't stop until it finds a briar patch to hide in!

The slope on the left side of the 8th green at Pinehurst No. 2 is a good example of a Red-Flag landing area. The last 12 feet on this side of the green slope down to the steep hill beside the green, and this combination creates problems for shots coming in from either side of the green. You can see the result of a shot from the bottom of the hill with a putter up the Red-Flag slope to the pin in Figure 5.8. Also imagine what pitch or bunker shots are like from the other (right) side of the green. From there players see a flagstick on top of a gentle knoll, and just past the pin the slope starts running straight away and down the hill to where I'm standing. Honestly, I've seen PGA TOUR pros write "10" on their scorecard because of this Red-Flag green and side slope!

FIRM DOWNSLOPES CAN BE RED-FLAG SPECIALS

Almost all downslopes near trouble cause serious problems for golfers. And golf courses have mounds with downslopes all over them. But when a downslope is firm and has trouble, water, or a valley below it in play, the problems can multiply to gigantic proportions.

For example, it's a Red-Flag special when you find yourself putting from behind the flagstick on the 9th green at Augusta National, like the great Japanese player Isao Aoki did a number of years ago in the Masters Tournament (Figure 5.9). Of course the green was very firm and extremely fast, and the back-to-front slope here is about as serious as it ever gets in golf. Even with his incredible talent and touch, I watched as he almost made his putt, then walked beside his ball and watched it gently, slowly, inexorably roll down to and off the front edge of the green, and then 70 more yards down the fairway to the bottom of the hill (from where he had earlier played his second shot).

5.9

A different version of this problem occurs when the layup area for the second shot of a par-5 hole slopes gently down into a pond. This situation becomes a Red-Flag area when the fairway turf is dry and firm. A similar phenomenon (the ball running too far) can occur on any green near trouble that slopes away from a golfer's incoming long-iron (low-trajectory) shot. Such holes become extremely difficult when the greens get firm, and this is the reason you don't see many of these types of holes in the game today.

DISASTERS AT VALDERRAMA #17 (536 YARDS, PAR-5)

Most greens are designed to slope toward incoming shots to help golfers get their balls stopped on the green surface. A few with more significant slopes can become brutally difficult to play when they're also groomed to play firm and fast, and sloped toward water. Such a green is the 17th at Valderrama Golf Club, host of the 2000 World Golf Championship (Figure 5.10). If you saw Tiger Woods score 7 on the hole, after hitting 7 almost perfect shots, you understand how a fast green sloped down to water can be considered a Red-Flag opportunity for disasters.

VALDERRAMA

5.10

A number of other players encountered disasters at this hole, validating its all-world Red-Flag status:

1999 WGC-American Express Championship (Final Round)

- Tiger Woods made an 8 and still won in a playoff.
- Bogeys (6) for Sergio Garcia and Stewart Cink cost them $41,000 each in earnings.
- Tom Lehman made an 8 on his way to a final-round 80.
- Colin Montgomerie, Mike Weir, John Huston, Steve Pate, and Jeff Maggert made 7s.
- Notah Begay III and Brent Geiberger made 8s.
- Loren Roberts, Thomas Bjorn, and Craig Spence made 9s.
- David Frost made 10.

Other disasters that week:

- Bob Estes made 7 in rounds 1 and 3 and still finished T11.
- ►►SIDENOTE: Nick Price (T4) made par on the hole in all 4 rounds.
- 2000 WGC-American Express Championship:
- Two back of eventual winner, Mike Weir, Tiger Woods makes 7 at #17 in the final round and loses by 4 shots. Woods found the water three times (in rounds 1, 2 and 4).
- Nick Price, one shot out of the lead, makes 8 (two balls in the water) in the final round to eventually lose by 4 shots to Mike Weir.
- Eventual winner Mike Weir makes a triple-bogey 8 in the second round. (He eagled in round 1, birdied in round 3, and made par in the final round.)
- Mark Calcavecchia and Hidemichi Tanaka also fell out of contention with double-bogey 7s.
- Despite disaster scores, the hole averaged 4.817, fourth easiest during the tournament, further emphasizing the importance of Red-Flag awareness.

5.4 Red Flags for Things You Don't Often Try

Any time you get into a situation you have never tried to play from before (and certainly never practiced from) you may have trouble executing the shot successfully. When poor execution of a new shot can get you into serious trouble, it should cause a Red-Flag alert.

There are places on most golf courses where players seldom hit shots. In these situations, you are now armed with the skills of Setupology and Swing Shaping. Take enough practice swings so that you feel you can repeat your swing with confidence. Remember, you can have bad golf holes, but we are trying to remove the disaster holes from your game.

There are also times when you simply must avoid three-putting, even when the percentages say you will probably have difficulty doing so. In golf, the stroke between two putts and three can sometimes seems to count for much more than it really should. A three-putt can change the momentum of your round and turn a good hole into a disaster. *Not* three-putting can also save you from stress on the next hole and keep you from hitting "three-putt aftereffect" shots into trouble. Not three-putting can help keep your Damage Control Mentality (Chapter 6) intact.

CUT-LOBS, BUMP-AND-RUNS, HIGH-BACKSPIN PINCH SHOTS

I've been urging golfers to play around with, and have fun practicing, the cut-lob shot for the last thirty years. It's a shot that's required often, but many golfers still don't play it and most never practice it. If this description fits you, a cut-lob shot probably warrants your Red-Flag attention. If you practice it a few times (we have a new way for you to try this without threatening the health of fellow

5.11

golfers in Chapter 7), you'll find it actually has a nice margin of error. The harder you hit the shot the higher it flies, but the distance it carries doesn't change that much (Figure 5.11).

Bump-and-run shots are easy to hit, but difficult to judge. Early in my career I was watching and admiring the bump-and-run work of my good friend Ben Crenshaw (Figure 5.12). I asked him how he had become so good at the shot, because I didn't see any special technique in his hands or swing. To quote Ben (as he smiled at me in his own quiet and uniquely honest way): "I've done it a lot!"

Since then I've thought about what he said, and added a thought. Only fifty years ago greens rolled at about the same green-speeds as fairways roll today. This should make bump-and-running almost like putting back then, and look how well they used to putt. My conclusion? Ben was exactly on target. Practice this shot enough and you can get good at it too. Then you can take the red flag off it!

5.12

Pinching a ball to get maximum backspin is a shot most golfers don't have and don't know how to get. (Of course, they haven't practiced it—no one practices what they don't know how to practice.) The primary requirements for creating spin are a glancing blow, clean contact between the clubface and ball, great grooves in your clubface, and acceleration past impact. From trouble lies, few golfers can produce any, let alone all, of these.

I caution you against using it, and suggest you put a red flag on it, because it probably won't work from trouble anyway.

It's risky to use a glancing blow from a bad lie, because there is usually too much stuff around the ball to make clean contact. Even if you could accomplish both clean contact and a glancing strike, how many golfers have great grooves and accelerate their clubs past impact? Not many. I hope you get the message: Your red flag should pop up any time backspin is required to stop a shot from trouble.

RED FLAGS FOR ABRUPT TERRACES AND LEVEL CHANGES

Pelz Golf Institute research shows that putts from 20 to 25 feet in length that traverse an abrupt level change (terrace) of more than 6 inches are ten times less likely to be holed, and three times more likely to be three-putted, than level putts of the same length. Our testing also shows that golfers make more than twice as many putts up or down the same elevation changes if the transition slope is smooth instead of abrupt. It's clear that golfers don't read the break or speed of terraced greens very well (Figure 5.13).

Serious practice is needed to develop touch for the effects of terraces on greens. There is no doubt: sharp terraces deserve a small amount of Red-Flag attention whenever you putt up or down over

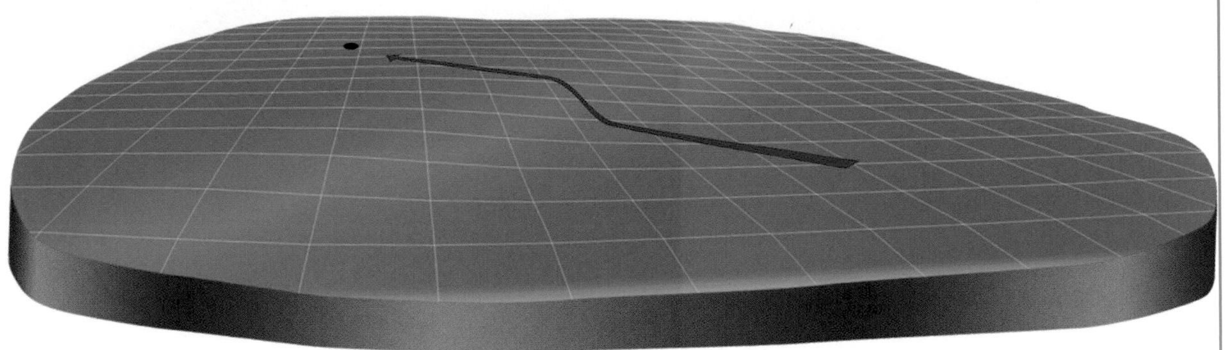

5.13

them (they don't usually cause disasters, but they can definitely result in lost strokes). The sharper the terrace and the greater the elevation it traverses, the more dangerous it is (Figure 5.14).

Terrace Effects

1. Putts traversing a level change (terrace) of more than 6 inches are ten times less likely to be made than level putts of the same distance (in the 20- to 25-foot range).
2. Putts over the same terrace are three times more likely to be three-putted than level putts in the same length range.

5.14

LONGER SHOTS THAN WHAT YOU PRACTICE

The longer the putt, the more likely it is to be left short of the cup. It's not as if golfers can't get their putts to the hole if they want to—they have plenty of strength and power to get them there, but they still don't (as shown in Figure 5.15). This data comes from mid-handicap (15 to 25) players, but data for the pros shows the same trend (pros just don't leave the putts as far short).

5.15

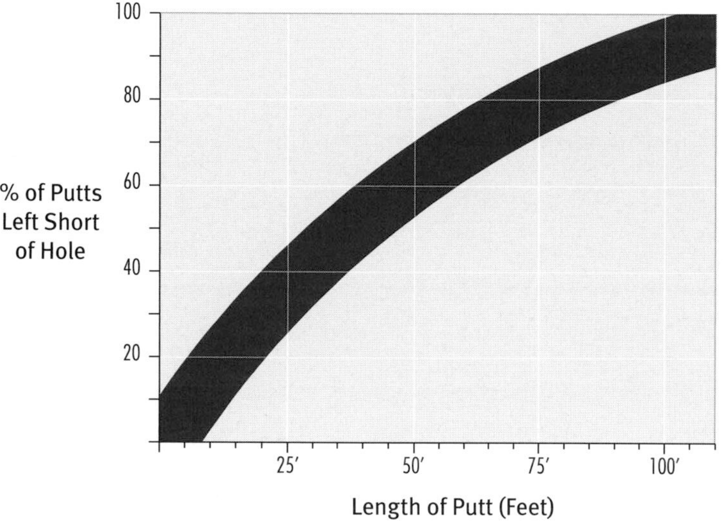

The same effect is true for long chip shots—the longer the shot, the greater the chance that the shot will be left short.There is a good reason for both phenomena: When golfers plan the length and intensity of their swing, they almost always assume they'll hit the shot solidly. Unfortunately, the longer the swing, the less solidly they actually hit these shots.

Imagine, then, how often players leave extra-long chips and putts short when these shots are longer than any they've ever tried before. It approaches 100 percent. (Despite the fact that I know this, look what happened to me at the 18th green at the Whistling

Straits course in Kohler, Wisconsin, before the 2004 PGA Championship (Figure 5.16).

I should point out that you're probably looking at the wrong putt, my second attempt at a 206-foot putt, which happened to luck its way into the hole. (Note: They tell me it's the longest putt ever holed on television. If you know of a longer one, please e-mail the details to us at comments@pelzgolf.com). Now look closer, and you'll see my first try: I left it no less than 50 feet short of the hole.

A first putt of 50 feet is a long putt. But to leave a second putt of 50 feet is unheard of. And yes, even though I understood the high probability of leaving a long putt short, I still left my first putt 50 feet short—in front of a worldwide TV audience on the Golf Channel! I had never tried a putt that long before, and I had absolutely no idea how hard to hit it. The conclusion: Longer shots than you have ever tried before need a Red-Flag alert. You'll need all the Red-Flag touch you can muster, every time you face one.

5.16

5.5 Red Flags for Fast Green Speeds

The rolling speed of a ball on a green is an important and dynamic part of the game of golf. The faster the green speed, the more a putt will break as it rolls to the hole, the farther a ball will roll before it stops, and the more Red-Flag touch it takes to control the stopping point of your chips and pitches, especially from trouble lies.

The worldwide metric for green speed is the distance (in feet and inches) that a golf ball will roll on a perfectly flat green surface, given the initial USGA reference speed from a Stimpmeter (old standard) or a Pelzmeter (new standard—same reference speed). When a green allows a ball to roll an average of 8 feet, 10 feet or 12 feet after being released with this reference speed, the green is said to have a green speed of 8, 10, or 12 feet respectively.

DOWNHILL SHOTS GET A RED FLAG WHEN GREEN SPEED EXCEEDS 10 FEET

Downhill chips, pitches, and putts are always more difficult to roll accurately to the hole than similar uphill shots. This is because a ball gains speed rolling down a hill and it is harder to get it to stop. This causes mistakes in putt starting speeds to be emphasized more for shots going downhill than those going up. The result: A golfer's speed mistakes are magnified on downhill shots and minimized on uphill shots.

When you face a downhill shot, especially on a green with a green speed of 10 feet or greater, be on the alert: Forget about your line and focus all of your attention on giving the ball the proper speed to stop near the hole.

DIFFICULTY INCREASES EXPONENTIALLY AT GREEN-SPEEDS ABOVE 11 FEET

Faster is not necessarily better, but faster is always more difficult on sloping green surfaces. Modern greens keep getting faster, and when the green speed exceeds 11 feet, ordinarily simple shots on mild slopes get really dangerous and warrant red flags.

As an example of where difficulty begins to explode, I can show you a test I ran at Pinehurst No. 2 before the 1999 U.S. Open. Pinehurst has a great grounds crew under the direction of Robert Farren and Paul Jett (GCSAA) who allowed me to roll shots and test the greens on several occasions. In May, the 9th green was a perfect pussycat for chipping and putting, and I chipped ten shots in a row from the spot shown in Figure 5.17, within 2 feet of the pin. The green-speed at the time measured 10 feet, 6 inches.

Then, about three weeks later, just before the tournament, I chipped three balls from the same spot to the same pin for a *GOLF Magazine* article. All three chips were measured to have landed within three inches of the same spot on the green . . . but look where they ended up after the green-speed had increased to 11 feet, 8 inches (#1-white by the hole, #2-red in the sand, and #3-yellow

5.17

rolled back off the green behind where I hit it from). At the slower green speed, I thought the chip was an easy shot. Only after the green speed increased to 11 feet, 8 inches did I notice the crest at the top of the slope (see dotted orange area) that separated the shot results into three different categories. Note: the green speeds were kept at 12 feet for the tournament, so imagine how much of a Red-Flag touch the pros had to play with, to score below par the way they did.

SUPER-FAST GREEN SPEEDS ABOVE 12 FEET

Any green with a speed of more than 12 feet is essentially a Red-Flag terror. Because no green is truly flat (water must drain off for the health of the grass), even mildly sloping greens become difficult to deal with at that speed, especially when you're playing from trouble.

5.18

A super-fast green can make pitching, chipping, and putting reasonable and beautiful (fast greens tend to be smooth, allowing a ball to roll in a pure arc), as long as they slope gently. Add a small amount of additional slope plus contours and undulations, however, and they become very difficult for pros and terrifying for amateurs (or anyone who doesn't have Red-Flag touch).

On the 16th hole at the Cordillera Mountain Course at a speed of 12 feet, 6 inches, it was difficult to stop this putt from rolling off the green (Figure 5.18). I had to grip down on the putter shaft to decrease the power I gave the ball, before

I could get it to stop. Precision speed control becomes so very important when green-speeds exceed 13 feet, because at these speeds putts become almost impossible to stop on downhill slopes.

I need to make a counterpoint here. You need to understand that super-fast greens can be okay if they're handled properly. Craig Currier (GCSAA) had his green speeds at 14 feet at Beth Page Black on Long Island, New York, for the last round of the 2002 U. S. Open. (Note: I'm sure of this speed, because Eddie and I were part of the greens crew and we measured all 18 greens every morning and evening for Craig, Figure 5.19.)

This is a terrifyingly fast speed, yet not a single player in the field of the world's best players complained about the greens being too fast. There were zero complaints because Craig had all his greens rolling at the same speed, and this green speed was appropriate (difficult, but possible) for the gentle slopes and not-too-wild contours of Beth Page Black.

5.19

RED-FLAG CONDITIONS CREATE RED-FLAG SHOT PATTERNS

Red-flag conditions (of slope, green speed, surface firmness, and environmental conditions) adversely affect normal shot patterns. Look at a generic 7-iron shot pattern to a generic green (represented by the black dotted line in Figure 5.20).

Now look what happens in Figure 5.21 when the same quality of shot (from the same normal lie) flies into and lands on Red-Flag conditions. Even when shots are launched by good swings, the size of the shot pattern (represented by the orange dotted line) becomes enlarged significantly due to ball run-out.

However, when lies are bad and escape swings are less than perfect, balls launched into these conditions on poor trajectories with low backspin create shot patterns that are way larger than a golfer's expectations. At the far end of this spectrum, when the lie is so bad that you have no clue how or where the ball will go when you hit it, and you're hitting into a Red-Flag landing area, you're looking at the ultimate Red-Flag shot-pattern situation (represented by the dotted red line in Figure 5.22).

5.20

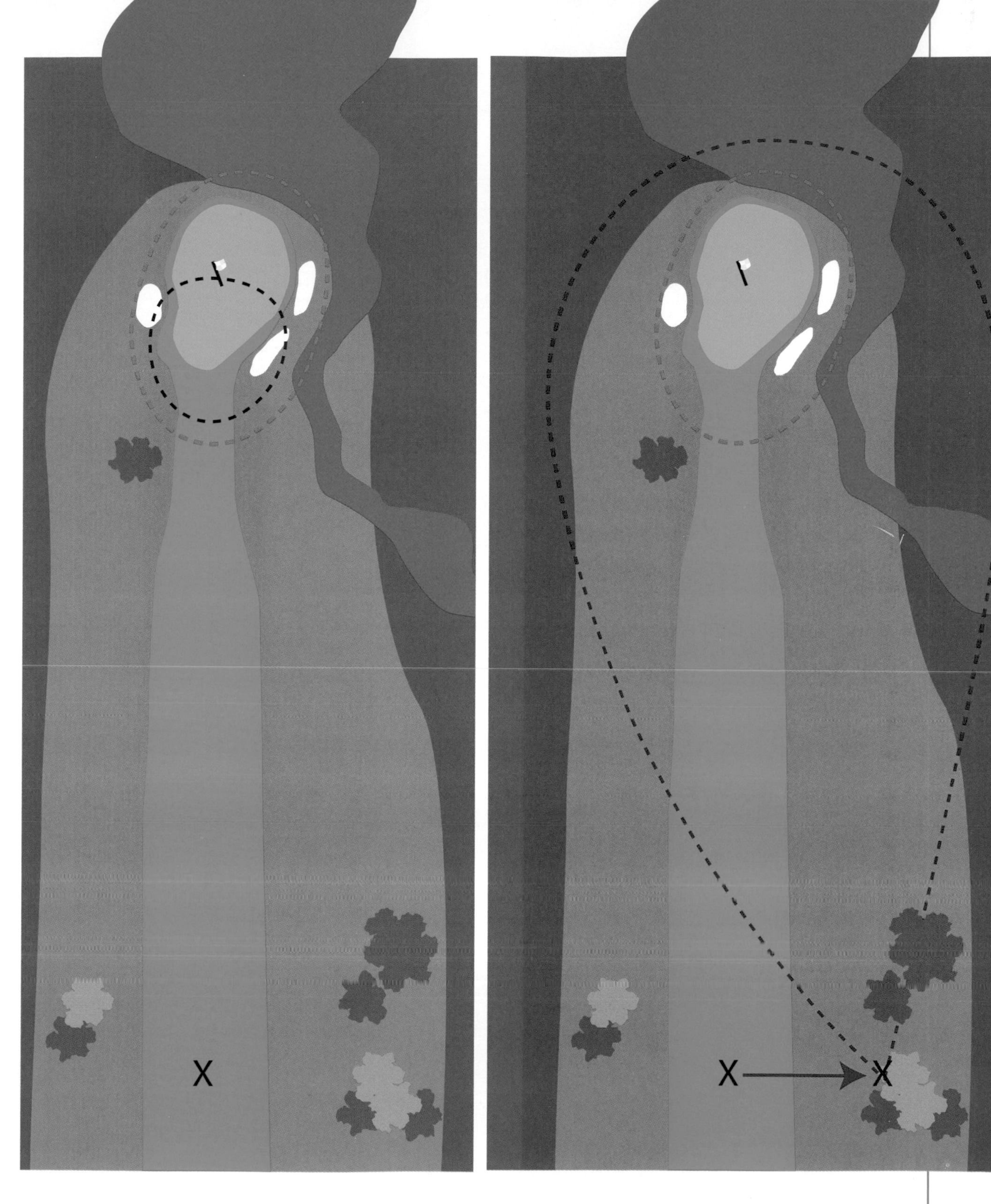

5.21

5.22

5.6 Ultimate Red Flags for Combinations

If there were ever a need for an ultimate red flag, it would be when you're faced with the combination of firm and fast conditions, a sloping and undulating golf course, and trouble all around. When these attributes are all combined in landing areas for incoming shots from trouble lies, the results are nothing short of consistent disaster scoring, unless you play with the ultimate amount of Red-Flag touch.

THE COMBINATION (FIRM, FAST, UNDULATING, AND PLENTIFUL TROUBLE)—PERFECT FOR MAJOR TOURNAMENT TESTS

The Masters Tournament has the formula down perfectly. They provide players with the ultimate challenge (weather permitting): fast fairways; firm, fast, undulating greens with copious slopes; sloping fairways and approaches to greens; and trees, flower beds, and water. They tailor the course to provide great difficulty from the center of every fairway, and next-to-impossible Red-Flag difficulty from trouble left and right: difficult. . . but possible!

A chip shot that Ernie Els faced during the last round of the 2004 Masters illustrates Augusta National's Red-Flag perfection. Els missed the 9th green about mid-green to the right, with a right front pin position. Attempting to pitch close from this position is a Red-Flag special, with the ball odds-on to roll well past the hole or, if he tried to play the shot to the flagstick, even off the green and some 70 yards down the fairway. Ernie pulled it off, however, playing 25 feet of break on a 30-foot shot hit at perfect speed. He hit an essentially perfect pitch with incredible Red-Flag touch, in what I would estimate was a one-in-a-hundred-shot performance (I'll never forget it).

Pinehurst No. 2 also gets it right for major tournament week, creating typical Red-Flag conditions behind the 3rd (Figure 5.23), 9th, 14th, and 15th greens, and to the left of the 8th and the right of the 18th green. And they make all of these areas so easy to hit into. Simply by playing from the 4-inch Bermuda rough to any back pin position and hitting a very good shot (not great, just very good), a player can find his ball dribbling through Red-Flag conditions into a fire lie in a heartbeat.

5.23

Shinnecock Hills Horror Stories

Red-Flag conditions can turn into impossible conditions. When a golf course becomes too hard and fast for the slope of its terrain, balls cannot be stopped from rolling off the greens, and even Red-Flag touch is not good enough to deal with it. It's certainly no fun to compete if conditions are neither fair nor possible. Such a situation occurred during the third and fourth rounds of the 2004 U.S. Open Championship. On those two days Shinnecock Hills, one of the very best golf courses in the world, became an unfair place to play the game.

The course played beautifully for the first two rounds, but then a few greens dried out and some became unfair, and unputtable, on Saturday. Then the wind blew throughout Saturday night. After being cut and prepared Sunday morning, several greens were so fast by 11:00 AM that balls would not stay on them. Tournament officials were forced to either stop play or water the greens intermittently between groups, which they did. That's right—they actually watered greens before some groups but not others during U.S. Open Championship play, which is incredibly unfair.

Shinnecock Hills is a great golf course, and I'm not denigrating it—I love the course. I mention these conditions because they happened, they may happen again, and knowing about it may motivate you to develop your Red-Flag touch for the future. You need to be able to recognize and differentiate between normal, difficult, and Red-Flag conditions. And by realizing what lies just beyond super-Red-Flag conditions (the unfair and the impossible), it may help you optimize your Red-Flag touch.

SHINNECOCK HILLS #10 GREEN (Figure 5.24)

A number of the world's best players who putted from behind the cup on the 10th hole at Shinnecock Hills on Sunday rolled their balls about 60 yards down the hill in front of the green. The green was so firm and fast that there was no fair place for a hole location on the putting surface.

5.24

= 60 yards

RED FLAGS ARE GOOD THINGS

The development and internalization of Red-Flag touch in a golfer has two components. One is the acquisition of a Red-Flag awareness in your brain that will alert you to Red-Flag conditions on the course. This component focuses your mind on the evaluation and prediction of what will happen to your trouble shots when they land in Red-Flag conditions. Being aware of what happens to your shots *after your swing execution* will become part of your Red-Flag touch, and will help you to play with heightened mental energy when you're in trouble.

The other part is developing the appropriate knowledge, based on the results of Red-Flag situational experience, to know what kind of shot, trajectory, and spin you need to try for in Red-Flag situations. Once you internalize this knowledge, it will allow you to better understand the kind of escape shots you want to play and how to play them. Learning this requires you to develop the five skills of Damage Control, use them in Damage Control practice, and finally experience the intricacies of using Red-Flag touch on the course.

You know, if golf was easy, it wouldn't be as much fun as it is! Red-Flag conditions are great for the game. They challenge you, punish you, and, thank heaven, occasionally reward you. The great courses of the world aren't just the most beautiful courses. They are also the places that make our red flags pop up most often. We all enjoy playing well under Red-Flag conditions. In this regard, I can't imagine the feeling Retief Goosen must have enjoyed after conquering Shinnecock Hills to win the 2004 U.S. Open.

5.7 The Meaning of Red-Flag Touch

After reading this chapter's descriptions of many (but certainly not all) of the various forms of Red-Flag dangers that exist, I think you probably have a pretty good idea of what having Red-Flag touch means. Red-Flag touch is entirely different from the first three physical skills of Damage Control (Setupology, Swing Shaping, and Hand-Fire feel) detailed in previous chapters. Those three all deal with how and what you do as you set up and execute escape swings from trouble.

Red-Flag touch is totally different and totally experiential. It's about 1) having the sensitivity and awareness to realize when your shot from trouble could land in a red flag area; 2) understanding the danger this represents; and 3) having the experience to know how to play extra carefully, to avoid playing from out of the frying pan and into the fire.

Red-Flag touch involves understanding and planning for what's going to happen after you launch an escape shot: how far it will fly, where it'll land, how it might bounce, and most importantly, where it'll stop. To acquire Red-Flag touch and internalize it into your game, you must combine acute observational awareness of Red-Flag landing areas with trouble-shot experience to allow you to avoid their consequences. The result will allow you to visualize how trouble shots will react to the Red-Flag conditions into which you must sometimes play them, and you'll be able to execute a shot that will end up in a safe lie despite the surrounding danger.

As you learn to watch out for firm and fast landing areas, slopes that control the direction and distance your shots travel, and green speeds that can approach the impossible level, you'll be learning Red-Flag touch. You'll be employing Red-Flag touch when you realize that your next shot, even if you execute it perfectly, may bounce and roll into trouble. And when you kick your imagination into a new place to deal with such conditions, you'll find that the game takes on new excitement and new meaning.

When your Red-Flag touch is good enough to handle a shot from the right rough to a left side pin location, with a 12 foot green-speed, on the 18th hole of the TPC Sawgrass (in Jacksonville, Florida—Figure 5.25) without encountering disaster, you will have added a whole new dimension to your game. It's thrilling to develop and use Red-Flag touch; and once you do it, you'll have another skill in your Damage Control arsenal!

5.25

CHAPTER 6

Damage Control Mentality

TO PLAY WITH DAMAGE CONTROL you need to learn five skills. The first four have been detailed in the four previous chapters. Learning to use those four skills within the Code of Damage Control is the fifth skill, the skill of playing with a *Damage Control Mentality*.

Setupology, Swing Shaping, and Hand-Fire feel are the physical skills necessary to execute escape shots. Red-Flag touch is the experiential skill of knowing how trouble shots will behave after they're launched. Damage Control Mentality is different from all of these: It's a completely mental skill that combines the ability to obtain the information needed to plan successful shots from trouble with the unemotional analysis and

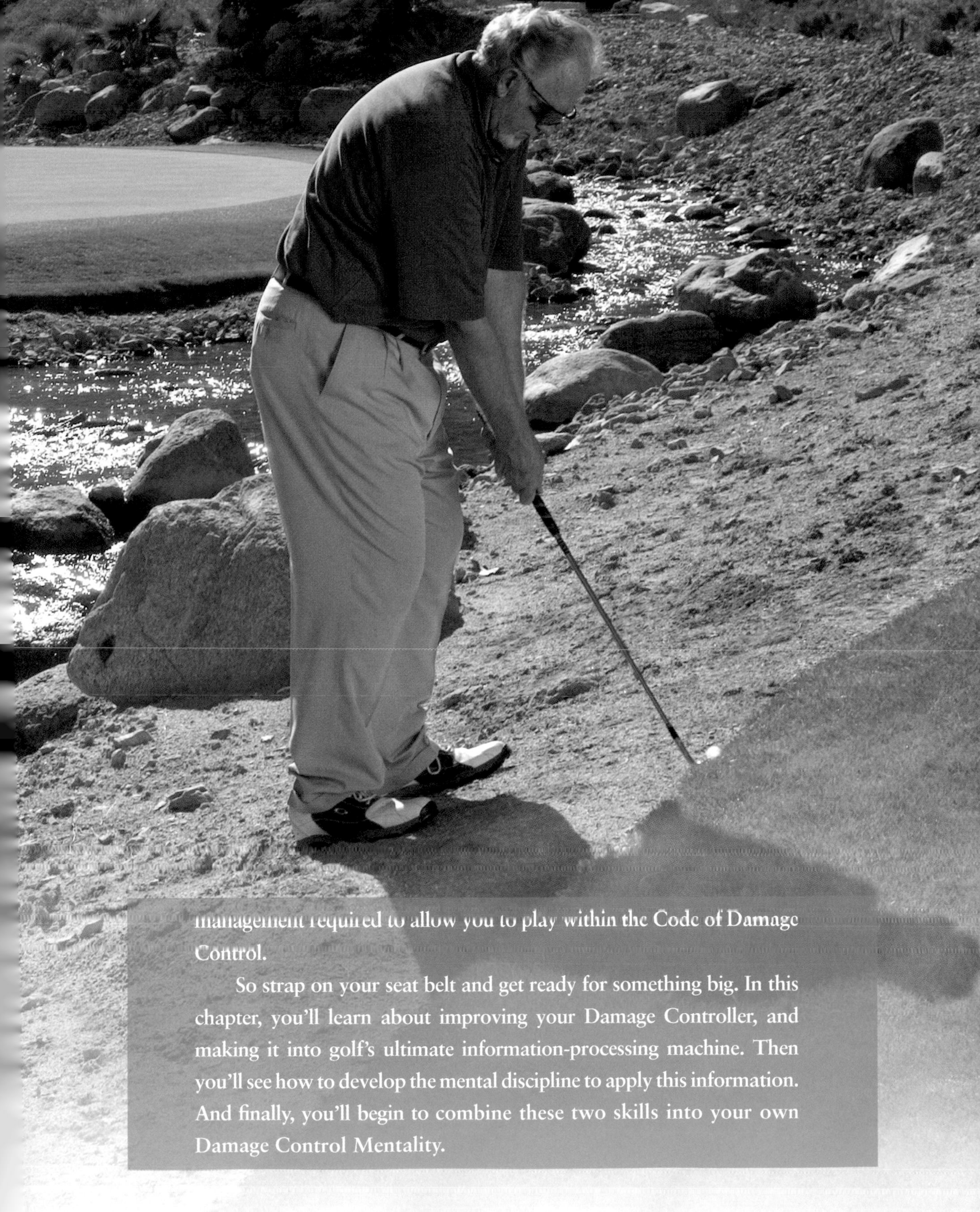

management required to allow you to play within the Code of Damage Control.

So strap on your seat belt and get ready for something big. In this chapter, you'll learn about improving your Damage Controller, and making it into golf's ultimate information-processing machine. Then you'll see how to develop the mental discipline to apply this information. And finally, you'll begin to combine these two skills into your own Damage Control Mentality.

6.1 How Your Damage Controller Works

The human brain is capable of being an incredibly efficient information-gathering and -processing system. It incorporates the visual operations of a camera, the sophisticated analysis of a software program, and the storage operation of a massive memory chip. It also can perform calculations of extreme complexity, and has a vast understanding of balls, roll, backspin, slopes, swing forces, energy transfer, aerodynamics, and physics. It is better and smarter than any man-made computer will ever be. We all have this kind of capability in our heads, even if we don't think about it or use all of its potential. The problem facing golfers is that they need to bring their mental firepower into focus and train it to be effective when they're in trouble on the golf course.

6.1

In Chapter 1.3 we described how we want you to compartmentalize (for the sake of learning to play with Damage Control) your golf brain into two parts: the one you use for normal play; and the one you use to play from trouble. By doing this, you're allowing the Damage Controller part of your brain (Figure 6.1) to concentrate on measuring, estimating, and evaluating your trouble situations in an efficient and focused way, and to analyze, create, imagine, and make decisions and predictions for your trouble shots. At the Pelz Golf Institute we have worked for years to understand how PGA TOUR pros think and play from trouble. In the following pages we will show you what we have learned, and how you can use it to improve your Damage Controller, a process that's vital to helping you to learn to play with Damage Control.

THE THINKING PROCESS

In a schematic diagram of the functions that your Damage Controller must accomplish (Figure 6.2), we've prioritized three fundamental steps of planning an escape from trouble:

1. In the "Lie" step, you evaluate the lie of a ball and its surroundings to determine a club and swing for a shot that can be played from these conditions.
2. In the "Skill" step, you determine the shot pattern you expect to produce from your club and shot choice, based on your skill level.
3. In the "Target" step, you calculate the probability of success for the shot by visually projecting your shot pattern onto various target areas.

I'm sure you've never thought about having a Damage Controller section of your brain before, or even about how you think during a round of golf. But don't worry, most other golfers haven't either. Even the pros haven't thought about the thinking process they use when they play from trouble. They've just practiced it and done it so often that they do it very well. We've studied this and committed it to the written page so that you can understand the ability you need to acquire to successfully play from trouble. Understanding *what* you need to learn always makes *learning* it much easier.

6.2

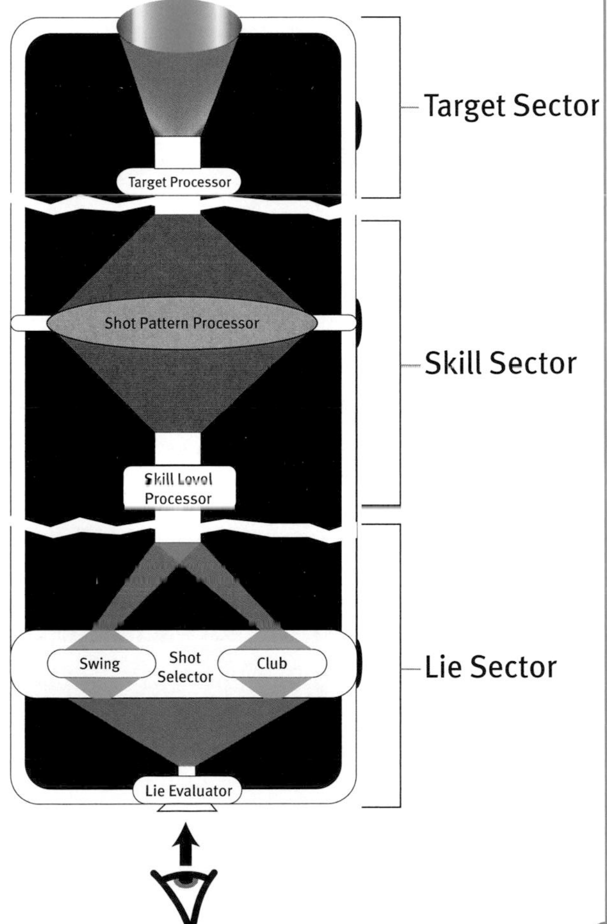

This information is not particularly complex or difficult to understand, but it has to flow in the correct logical sequence and be used a few times before you can become comfortable with it. This is important, because your Damage Controller has to be reasonably accurate when you face shots from trouble. Why? Because as you know by now, the penalties for not getting things right from trouble are often huge.

STEP 1: SEEING AND ANALYZING LIE CONDITIONS

Degree of Difficulty	#	Color
Safe	1 2 3	(green circle)
Marginal	4 5	(yellow circle)
Frying-Pan Trouble	6 7	(orange circle)
Fire Trouble	8 9 10	(red circle)

6.3

When you find a ball that's landed in trouble, you must first evaluate the condition of its lie. After looking at the conditions close to the ball, you must then examine the surrounding area. You must make an initial estimation of what kind of club-to-ball contact can be made. You're also evaluating the kind of swing that can be made under the conditions (bushes, tree limbs, etc.) present around the ball. With this information you create a prioritized list of shots that can be played from this lie. You're also analyzing and assigning a difficulty to the lie (you might base this, for example, on some internal "lie-difficulty" color scale or number rating from 1 to 10, as shown in Figure 6.3). To see how your Damage Controller might view a typical frying-pan lie, look at the close-up of a ball and the area immediately behind it in Figure 6.4. In this case, it looks like good clean contact can be made with the ball. Then as you back out, you see a tree trunk that might get in the way of your swing (Figure 6.5). It takes just a brief instant for you to "think" and estimate a recommended shot and its difficulty rating (as shown in

6.4 RIGHT

6.5 OPPOSITE

Figure 6.6, sand wedge, upright ½-swing, difficulty = 6). The estimation of a shot's difficulty (rating) helps you to be aware of how likely you will be to succeed or fail in pulling off the shot.

6.6

STEP 2: CALCULATING SHOT PATTERNS BASED ON SKILL LEVEL

After determining your shot, your memories of how you've played such shots in the past will help create a shot pattern that you're likely to produce from this situation. You should be able to see its size and shape as if it were on a generic open fairway (see light area in Figure 6.7). Please note: Your shot patterns will be completely unique to your own skill patterns.

6.7

It is important to honestly incorporate your own skill set into this process, to accurately predict the likely size and shape of the shot pattern you will produce from the lie in question. As you look around at the different swings and shots you might play, your Damage Controller should show you a corresponding shot pattern for each shot considered.

STEP 3: CHOOSING A TARGET BASED ON ODDS AND STATISTICS

The process of choosing the optimum target at which to aim a shot is as important as picking the correct shot to play from a troubled lie. When you look around to evaluate different targets (Figure 6.8), your Damage Controller will visualize your shot patterns overlaid onto the actual course in play, with a superimposed color spectrum indicating the relative percentage of shots that will end up in each of the lie categories (green=safe, yellow=marginal, orange=frying-pan, red=fire). A simultaneous calculation of the predicted percentage chance of the shot ending up in a safe (green) lie should also occur.

6.8

As before, if you don't like your initial target or its odds of success, you can look for other target options. For the frying-pan lie you've been analyzing, if you choose the flagstick as your target, your chance of the shot ending up in a safe lie on the green is only 20 percent (Target #1, Figure 6.9). That's a 1-in-5 chance of success, with a large number of shots ending up in the sand, hitting tree limbs, or running over the green into trouble. These results are indicated by the small amount of green (safe) lies and large percentage of yellow, orange and red trouble lies predicted by your Damage Controller. For purpose of illustration, the predicted safe percentage number of 20 percent is also displayed on the right of the screen by the color spectrum.

6.9
Target #1

Obviously, when you choose a difficult shot to a dangerous target, your chances of success will not be high. But look at what happens when you pick a safer target area out to the right, 40 yards short of the green (Target #2, Figure 6.10). Your success rate for a shot into a safe lie in the fairway jumps to 92 percent. When you choose this target from this lie, about the only way you can get your next shot into trouble is to shank it.

6.10
Target #2

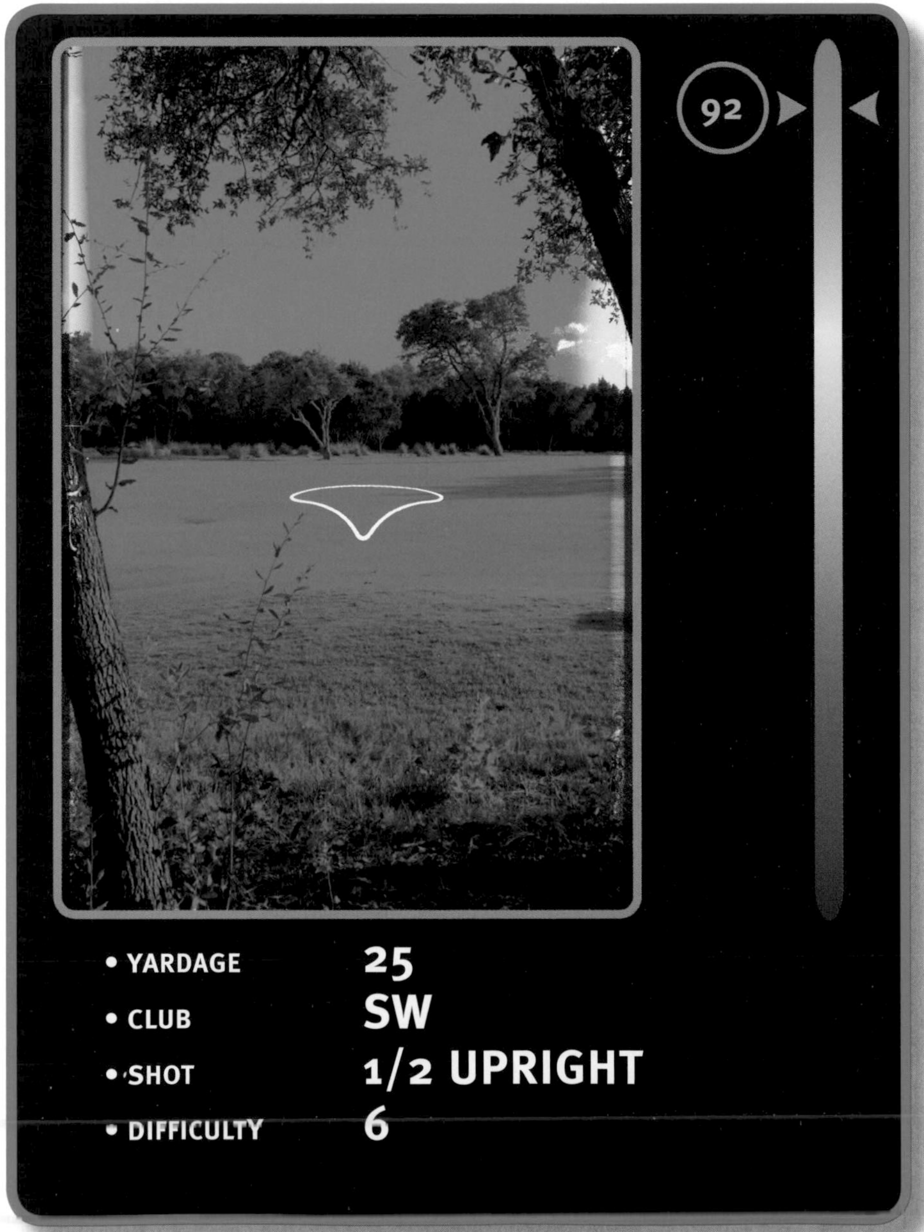

THE RISK/REWARD OF TARGET SELECTION

For a better understanding of the risk/reward analysis for different target selections when using your Damage Controller, spend a few minutes evaluating the next five figures.

Imagine you are a 12-handicapper whose drive leaked into the right rough. Notice your ball just left of bottom center (Figure 6.11, red arrow). You see your lie isn't too bad, with only the edge of a bush at the right edge of your direct line to the flagstick. The green is shaped like an inverted L, bending around the sand and closer to you on the front left. The hole is farther away (120 yards) on the back right, and serious trouble is everywhere: short, right, and long of the flagstick (a pond is right *and* behind the green).

6.11
Ball

You can hit a full 9-iron at the flagstick, or play a sand wedge out to the left somewhere; the farther left, the safer. Should you play aggressively? Or should you lay up left? If you chip almost straight out left, you'll be completely safe, but it will cost you a full stroke and you need badly to save par. Let's see what the Damage Controller process says about selecting your target before playing this next shot.

Figure 6.12
If you go for the pin, you have a full 9-iron from 120 yards. This shot rates 7 on the difficulty scale, and you'll probably end up wet, sandy, or worse eight out of ten times.

Play 10 yards left of the flag?

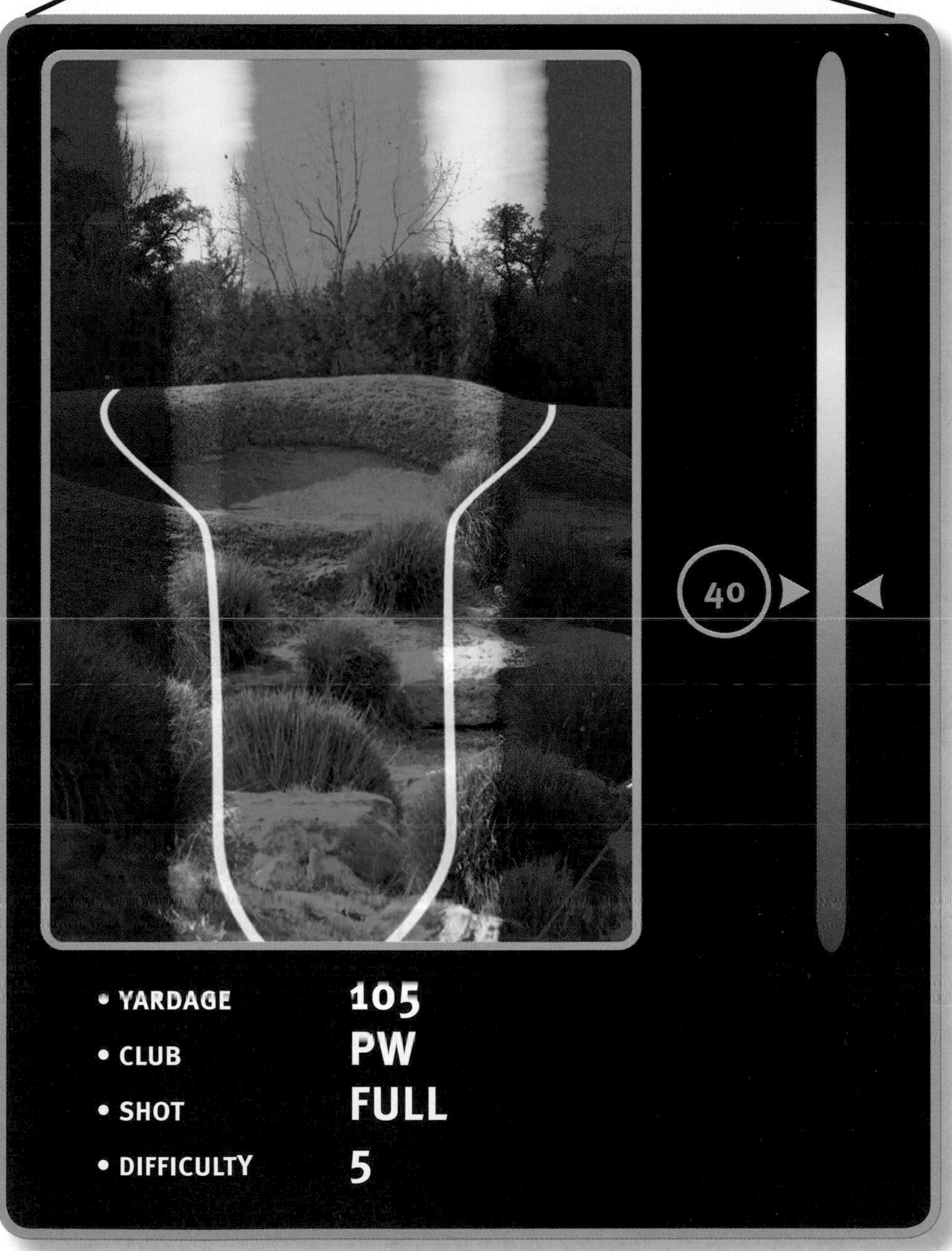

Figure 6.13
Going for the middle of the green is better, but you still must hit a full pitching wedge at least 105 yards (average difficulty). Your chance of being in the sand or worse is about 60 percent.

To front of green (20 yards left)?

Figure 6.14
Aiming for the front edge of the green leaves you a three-quarter-swing pitching wedge (80 yards) plus a little margin for error. This shot is easier (4) and your chances of ending up in trouble are lower (40 percent: if your shot leaks right, you're still in trouble).

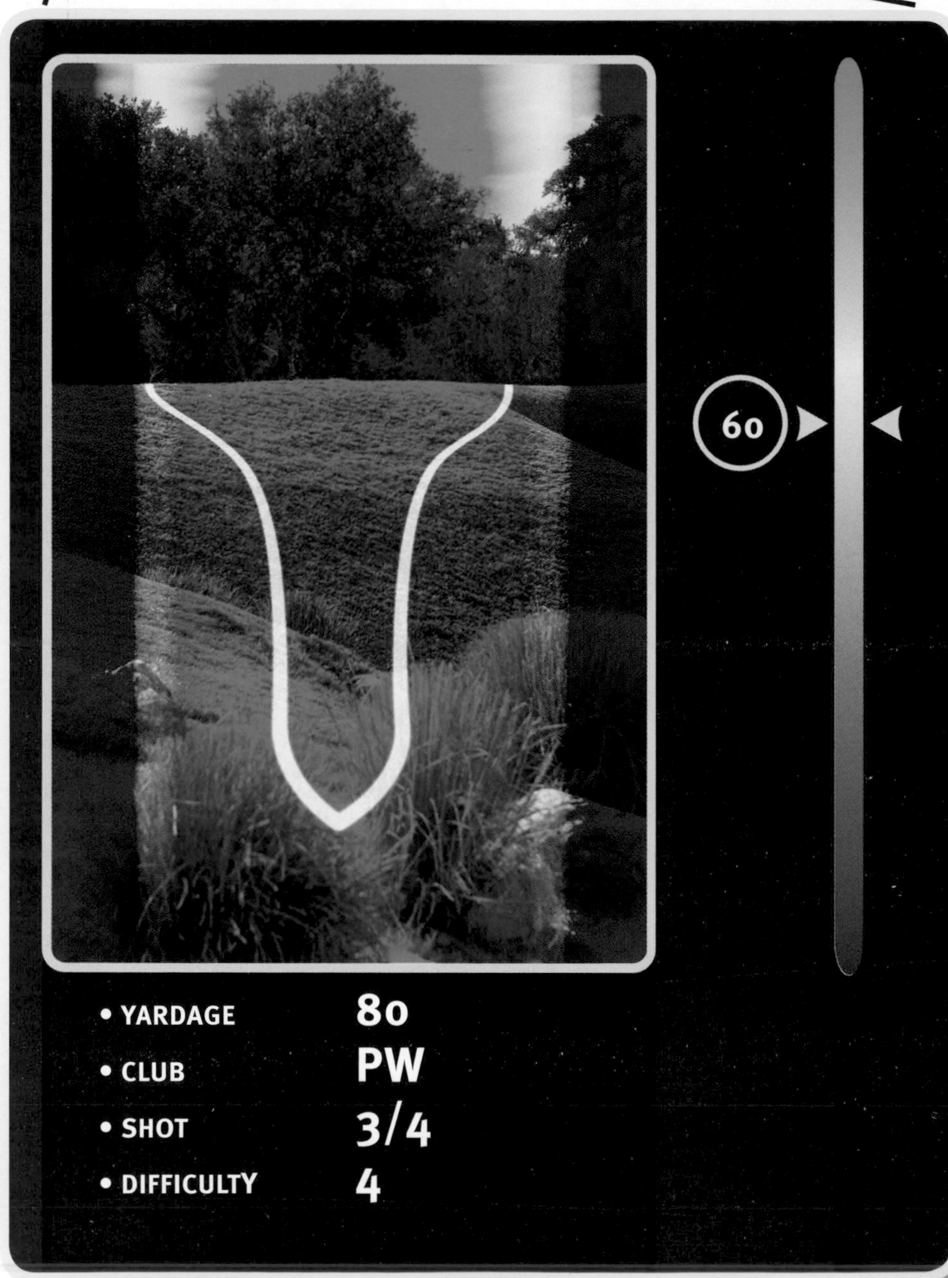

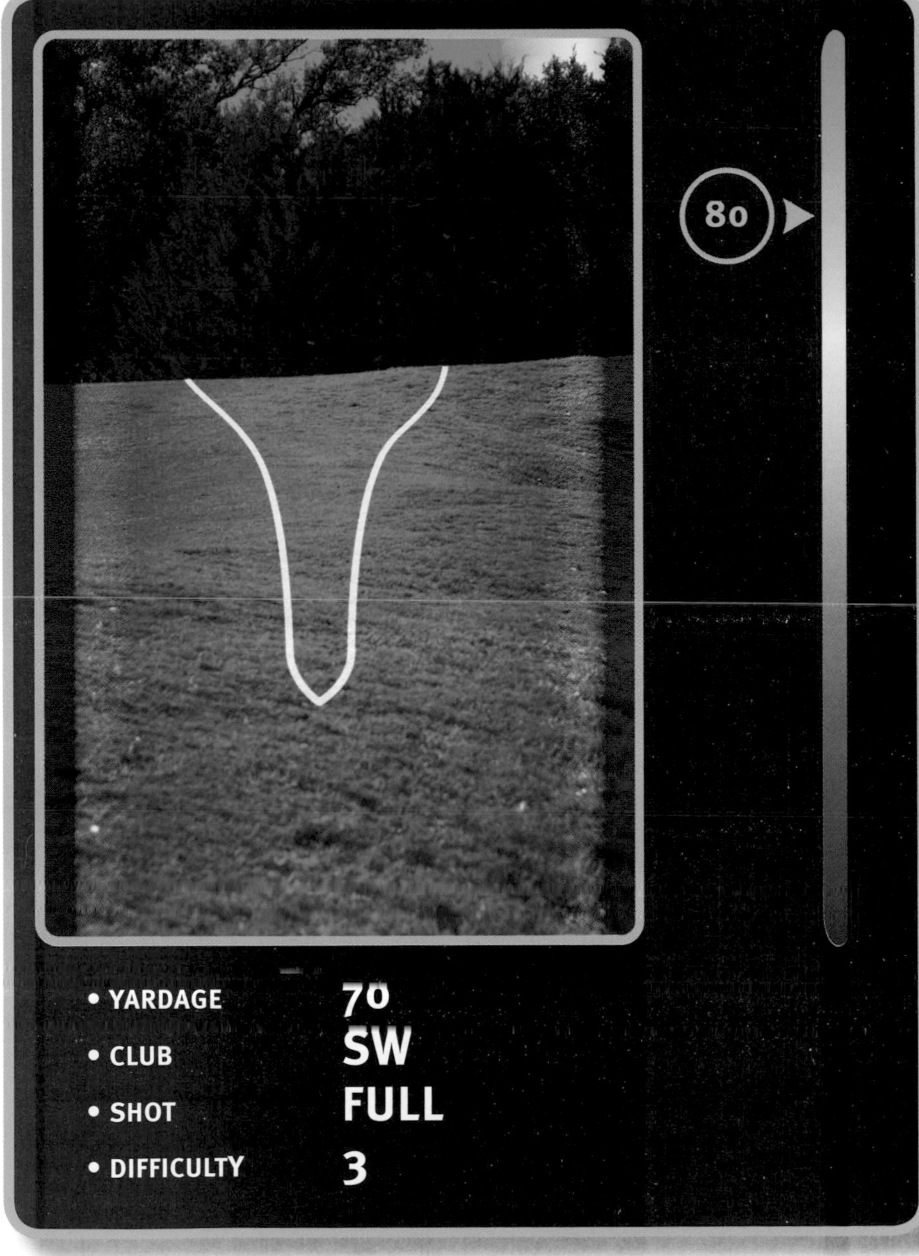

Play just short of green left?

Figure 6.15

Hitting an easy sand wedge out short and left of the green is almost completely (80 percent) safe, but puts the par-save burden on your short game. You'll need either a good chip or a good putt, but you almost certainly won't ruin the round with an 8 on the hole.

Notice that for these four figures, each one had the same lie, the same golfer, and the same skill level. The only thing that changed between the four was the target you selected. This should give you a feel for how target selection works: you take into account the shot difficulty with your relative chances of success for the target choices available. You have the final information you need to choose your own destiny—to play, or not to play—with Damage Control.

THE ULTIMATE INFORMATION

Your Damage Controller must take in information, process it, and present probable results to you. Your brain doesn't swing clubs and it doesn't hit shots; your body does. But the swing possibilities, the patterns into which shots are likely to fly, and the odds of success versus failure comprise the information you need to make intelligent decisions about what shot to hit and where to aim it. These decisions, combined with your ability to swing and hit shots, determine how well you'll play from trouble. Your Damage Controller decisions are an integral part of your Damage Control performance and scoring.

This is the information great players process and use when they play. They have been the model for our study and the development of the concept of Damage Controller thinking. Our goal is to help you understand what you need to make good decisions, to play successful shots from trouble, and to avoid disaster holes.

NO ONE IS PERFECT, NOT EVEN THE PROS

Your Damage Controller will never be perfect. It can provide the relative odds of success for a shot and target within the Code of Damage Control. It can predict results within reasonable tolerances, but will never be 100 percent perfect, because it deals with humans who are not 100 percent perfect. To give you an example: I was watching Johnny Miller, U.S. Open winner and perhaps the best iron player ever. He was playing his second shot to the 16th green while leading a tournament at Pebble Beach. After a perfect drive, from a perfect lie, he hit a perfect shank deep into the weeds behind a tree way right of the green. Even though the odds of Johnny playing that shot safely were in excess of 99.99 percent, he shanked it. His body performed a "one-in-ten-thousand" bad move. It happens.

Always remember: Some golfers are awesome, but everyone is human, and no human is perfect.

6.2 Two Parts of Damage Control Mentality

Having the skill to gather and analyze the information needed to play from trouble (playing with a great Damage Controller) is one component of a Damage Control Mentality. Having the mental ability and emotional control to use this information properly is the other. Combining both these skills is what gives a golfer a Damage Control Mentality.

PLAYING WITH YOUR DAMAGE CONTROLLER

You now understand how your Damage Controller works and the information it provides. Let's assume for the rest of this section that you've developed your Damage Controller perfectly and stored numerous trouble shot patterns in your brain. The question is: Do you have the emotional control on the golf course to use the information it will give you?

If you do, this is what would happen: By playing all trouble shots with the clubs, swings, and 90 percent safe targets with Damage Controller vision, in only 5 percent of those cases would you again end up in frying-pan or fire lies. If you then played *those* trouble shots according to a Damage-Controller approach, you would experience having a disaster hole only once in every few hundred trouble situations.

This means that instead of encountering two or three disaster holes every round (as you currently do), you would experience perhaps one disaster every fifteen or so rounds. Wouldn't that make playing from trouble simple? Just find your ball, and let your Damage Controller tell you where to aim. Voila—no more disaster scores. This sounds easy, but it's not. As in so many aspects of life, saying things is easy, but doing them is something else.

TAKE A LEAP . . . GET A SKILL

Having information and using it are two different things. To play with Damage Control you need to trust your Damage Controller and your imagination. You must believe your decisions are good and that you'll be successful in your escape attempts. I say this because I have seen that even in the world's best players, doubt and indecision are killers of success. If you can't commit and believe you will succeed, you *will not* succeed.

This sometimes requires a leap of faith plus the ability to handle human emotions not related to logic. No computer programs can be written and no logic systems can be developed to accomplish this move. This leap can act as a bridge, connecting your information with its useful application.

KNOWLEDGE ALONE DOES NO GOOD

The fact is, sharing your Damage Controller information with other golfers will do absolutely no good. I've tried it. It doesn't work, because the skills of Damage Control are missing in most amateurs. It's not that they aren't intelligent enough to have them. It's a problem of either:

1. Not having the physical or experiential Damage Control skills
2. Never being trained to evaluate the risk/reward odds of a shot from trouble, or
3. Simply succumbing to their emotions, the pressures of the moment, or ego.

Most golfers never imagine the realities of what their shot patterns might look like, have never considered their probabilities of reward versus risk when aiming at a target, and seldom if ever let statistics affect their judgment when it comes to hitting a golf shot!

A typical example of poor judgment occurs when a golfer in frying-pan trouble wants badly to save par. This golfer thinks: 1) I could hit a wedge out to a safe area 20 yards short of the green (Figure 6.16, green path), or 2) I can fly an 8-iron onto the green if I catch it really well (Figure 6.16, red path).

6.16

He knows intellectually that the safe route is probably the smarter, higher-percentage play. It requires only a reasonable pitch from short of the green, plus a 5- or 10-foot putt to save par. But he also knows emotionally that it is possible for him to hit that 8-iron shot onto the green. He really wants this par, and he knows "it would be great" if he got the 8-iron shot onto the green and two-putted for par.

In this situation, most golfers go for it nine times out of ten. And in those nine times they make one par, two bogeys, three doubles and three triple-bogeys.

PLAYING THE PERCENTAGES

Let's look at the scores statistically on this play. Playing safe, the golfer scores five bogeys and five pars (he'll make a good chip or a good putt half the time). If he goes for the pin, he scores one par, two bogeys, three double-bogeys and four triple-bogeys. The average scores are tabulated in Figure 6.17.

Scoring Percentages

- 10 times "Damage Control": Average score = 4.5
- 10 times "Go For It": Average score = 6.0

6.17

So which way would you play? Would you go for the "great shot" accolades from your friends one time out of ten, but pay off your bets to them after the other nine rounds, or would you play the smart percentages? The data from our study clearly demonstrate that golfers are emotional beings—they go for it most of the time.

USING GOOD JUDGMENT

It's like learning about a diet that will keep weight off, which also sounds like something you can actually live with and accomplish: Before you can benefit from it, you've got to commit to trying it! I don't want you to commit to Damage Control because Dave Pelz says it works. I want you to commit to it because you understand what our research is telling you about your game, because you recognize the frequency of disaster scores in your past play, and because you *believe* that Damage Control will improve your ability to shoot lower scores.

Learning to use good judgment in your game involves knowledge. You must understand that if it's better on average, then it's also better more often than it is worse. You must recognize how the targets you choose from trouble, and the odds of success for shots hit to them, determine your scores. You must believe in the statistics that say you'll score better by escaping before you recover from trouble than you will by trying hero shots.

MY SOLUTION: PLAY A SECOND BALL UNTIL YOU BELIEVE

If you sometimes have an insanely strong desire to try risky or dangerous shots, I have an idea for you. Play your real ball with Damage Control first, then try hitting the dangerous shot with a second ball just for the thrill of it. This way, if you hit the shot successfully, it's fun. If it fails, it doesn't ruin your score.

Playing with a second ball in your pocket is also beneficial to your future, because you'll subconsciously learn how often your "hero" shots turn out to collect the risk penalty, instead of the reward you were looking for (and remember—to collect the reward after hitting a great shot from trouble, you still have to putt well to take advantage of it).

THE CODE OF DAMAGE CONTROL

Once you have the five skills of Damage Control in your arsenal, you must apply those skills within the Code of Damage Control (Figure 6.18)whenever your ball finds trouble.

The Code of Damage Control

- Escape before recovery.
- Play the "probably will" shot, not the "possibly can" shot.
- Use the 90-percent-safe rule for target selection.
- Be honest in your evaluation of shot-pattern size.
- Never make a second mistake immediately following a first one.
- Never hit anything close to you.
- Verify ball position before you try to hit the shot.
- Before gambling, make sure the gamble has a much higher probability of payoff than penalty.
- Keep the damage to less than one stroke.

6.18

Escape before you recover. If you escape on the first shot more than 90 percent of the time, then get up and down 40 to 60 percent of the time, you're losing on average only a little more than half a shot per encounter with trouble. These are not unrealistic numbers (many of the PGA TOUR players I coach achieve better than this), and this is why your first focus from trouble must be to *escape*.

Play the "probably will" shot, not the "possibly can" shot. You'll probably hit one of the shots out of your shot pattern each time you play from trouble. If, however, you consistently try shots that you possibly-can-but-probably-won't hit, you will continue to suffer disaster scores and holes regularly, almost every round you play.

Use the 90 percent rule. If 90 percent of your shots from trouble end up in safe lies, you can control the damage to your scores. It means (by a simple progression of statistics and percentages) that you will encounter a disaster hole only once every fifteen or twenty rounds, instead of several times in each round, as so many golfers do.

Learn the size and shape of your shot patterns. This is easy to accomplish (Chapter 7) by creating "quick-view" shot patterns, which give you snapshots of your real skill and shot patterns from particular lies. By playing Damage Control practice rounds and accumulating multiple quick-view shot patterns, you'll learn the realities of your trouble game.

Never make a second mistake immediately following a first one. Even following the 90 percent rule, 10 percent of your escape shots from trouble are going to end up in marginal, frying-pan, or fire trouble. Assuming that 5 percent end up in frying-pan or fire lies, these are the shots you cannot afford to hit poorly. For the 5 percent of times this happens to you, become *extra* conservative and use the simplest of shots to a super-safe target on your second escape attempt. In other words, if you don't escape on the first try, make absolutely certain you do on the second.

TROUBLE COMES IN THREES

Many of the golfers in our disaster score study said their worst three swings of the day came in succession (leading to their three disaster scores). They frequently referred to a "bad things come in threes" superstition as an excuse. The truth is that it's easy to make one bad swing followed by another because:

1. Trouble lies and stances are by their nature more difficult than normal lies.
2. Golfers tend to be mad or embarrassed after making a bad swing and don't concentrate on their new trouble lie.
3. Golfers sometimes flub the next one because they're rushing to "get out of here quickly."

Always buckle down after a bad shot gets you into, or fails to get you out of, trouble. Don't try a risky recovery shot to save face or to avoid any possibility of losing an additional stroke; instead, play safely out with a good swing and accept that you might lose another stroke (or not, if you recover well).

The rule is: Never try to make a perfect swing after a bad one. Instead, just make a reasonably good swing to a safe target, then try to recover and one-putt.

Never hit anything close to you. When you hit a rock or a tree or anything close to where you're hitting from, the ball has a lot of energy and can bounce anywhere. It may hit you (two-shot penalty, plus potential injury), rebound into the water (another one-shot penalty), careen out of bounds (two-shot penalty), or bounce deeper into the rough, causing you to score who knows what.

Verify good ball position. Don't swing at a trouble shot until you know where your swing arc will bottom out. A Damage Control pre-shot routine that includes this verification is detailed in Chapter 7; don't miss it (learn it and never play from trouble without it).

Before gambling, make sure the gamble has a much higher probability of payoff than penalty. For gambling shots from trouble, there are always two questions to be answered: 1) If you choose a 50 percent safe target, how many of the 50 percent of shots that succeed in making it to safety will allow you to sink the following putt? If you don't make the putt, you may as well have just played safely and scored the same thing. 2) Will those one-putts be a greater savings than the loss of strokes encountered by the 50 percent of the shots which didn't find safety? (Note: I used a 50 percent safe target choice in this example. For any trouble shot you face, answer these two questions using the safety percentage for the target you actually choose to hit to.)

Keep damage to less than one stroke. Believe in averages, statistics, odds, and percentages. All of Damage Control comes down to escaping to a position better than you would have been in had you not hit into trouble in the first place. When you're in trouble, play conservatively and depend on good recovery play to save potential stroke loss. This virtually eliminates disaster holes from your scorecard and gives your short game the chance to make you a better player.

A DAMAGE CONTROL MENTALITY IS NOT THE SAME AS COURSE/GAME MANAGEMENT

Playing with a Damage Control Mentality is not about playing safe off the tee or from good lies in the fairway. It's about playing out of trouble as aggressively as you possibly can while staying within the Code of Damage Control (Figure 6.19). It means playing from trouble while avoiding additional trouble lies and without risking penalties.

6.19

Course management is different. Course management has to do with the way the golf course is designed and the strategy you choose to play it. Each hole was designed by a course architect with a specific play route in mind. "Sucker pin" positions and overly penal driving areas should be negotiated with care. This is good course management and is highly recommended, but it has nothing to do with a Damage Control Mentality. No matter how well you manage your way around the golf course, you will still get into trouble, and you'll need to minimize the scoring damage from there.

6.3 Developing Your Own

Let's take a quick status update here. You now know that the five skills of Damage Control are Setupology, Swing Shaping, Hand-Fire feel, Red-Flag touch, and Damage Control Mentality. You should also know that to achieve a Damage Control Mentality, you need to incorporate the two capabilities of 1) attaining information and 2) using it with intelligent judgment.

You've also seen how you must believe in and commit to using Damage Control to have a chance of developing a Damage Control Mentality. You understand and appreciate how critical it is to make good decisions when you're playing from trouble. And because of this magnitude of the consequences of making bad decisions, you can't afford to go forward in playing this game without optimizing the thinking in your Damage Controller.

THERE MUST BE A WAY

What you haven't yet learned is how to optimize the information gathering and analysis (thinking) in the Damage Controller part of your brain! This is something you must do, because no one can control scoring damage from trouble if they can't determine how bad their lie is, judge what swings are required, and know what shot patterns they are likely to generate from the situation. No one can minimize damage without an understanding of their percentages and the odds of success likely for their escape shots.

You must optimize the operations of your Damage Controller to attain a Damage Control Mentality. Although I've already mentioned several times that you will have to wait to develop and refine your physical skills of Damage Control until Chapter 7, I want to discuss how you can improve your Damage Controller skills now.

I have improved my own Damage Controller capability and I think you can too (because my brain is certainly nothing special). I've never been really wealthy, I don't have incredible physical talent, my mind is not the sharpest knife in the set, and I don't have any special skills that you don't have. Fundamentally then, this means that if I can do it . . . you can too. I know you can do it, especially if I give you a little help and tell you *how* to do it.

DIVIDE AND CONQUER

The secret to optimizing the Damage Controller part of your brain is to separate it from the "normal golf" part, so that there can be different thinking for different situations. This is why we use the analogy of a special Damage Controller partition in your brain, so that you can more easily allow yourself to think differently in different situations. Then, when your ball finds trouble, you can use the "trouble-thinking" part of your brain until you escape from trouble's clutches.

Now sit back for a minute and close your eyes. Place one hand on top of your head and concentrate. Press down on your brain (Figure 6.20) and tell yourself the following: I will forever hereafter designate one-quarter of a cubic inch of my brain matter to do my special Damage Controller work. And with your eyes still closed, commit to programming your Damage Controller for your own game and creating the information listed below for it in each trouble situation you encounter:

6.20

1. A clear vision of the lie and all trouble around it that could affect your swing or ball contact.
2. Your choice of club and swing (shot) that you believe will allow your ball to escape from the trouble.
3. The imagined shot pattern that you will produce from this situation.
4. What the final destination will be for the worst and best possible shots you might hit (worst first, then best).
5. A clear post-shot report (observation) of where the shot actually ends up.

YOU HAVE IT

That's it. Now open your eyes and smile. You now have an acknowledged Damage Controller section of your brain (Figure 6.21)! Your Damage Controller is ready to go, ready to begin gathering information, analyzing odds, and predicting results and shot patterns. It's ready to start improving!

6.21

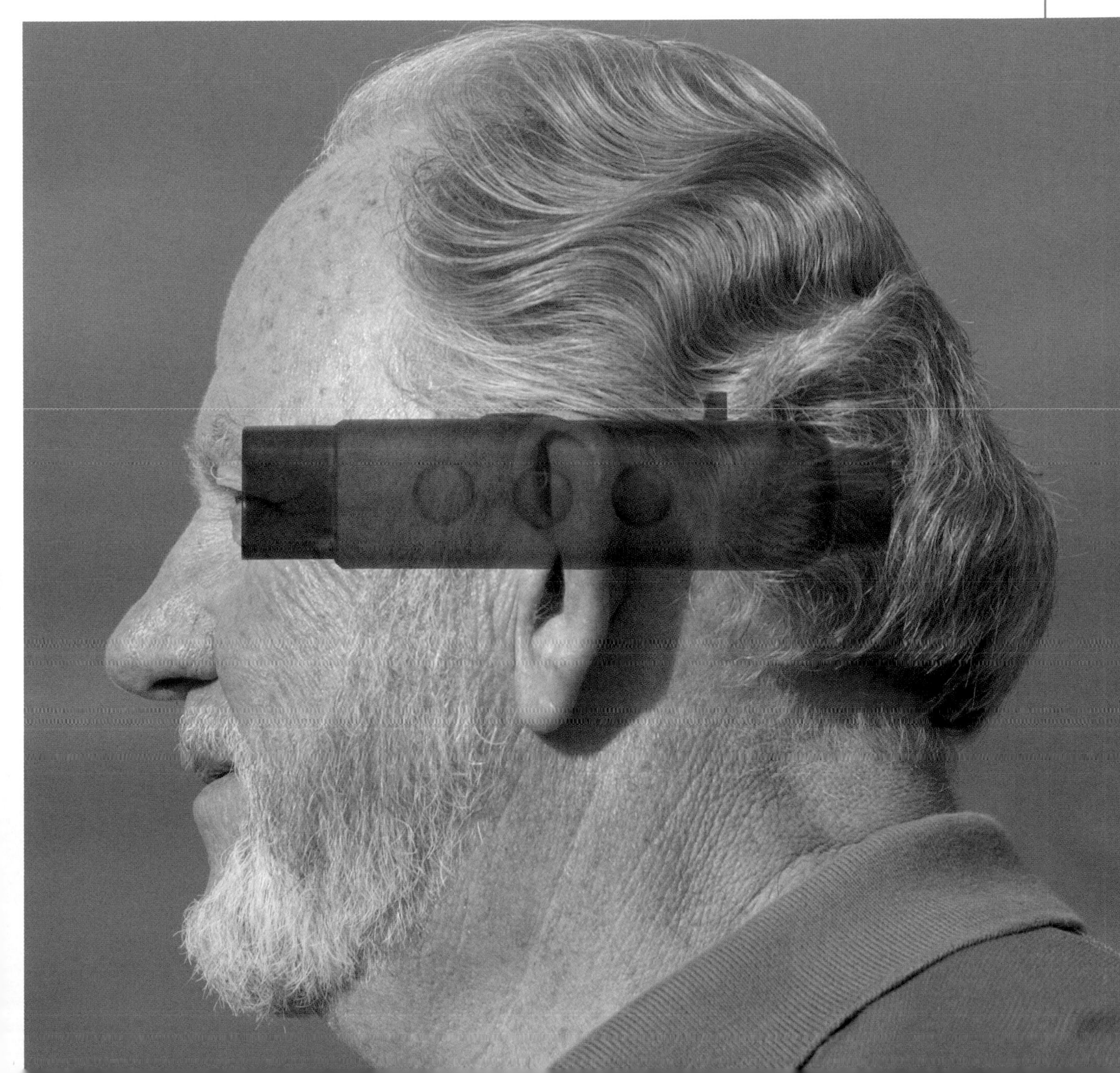

My friends Phil Mickelson, Vijay Singh, Steve Elkington, Mike Weir, Lee Janzen, Paul Azinger, Tom Kite, Andy North, and the late Payne Stewart all have or had Damage Controllers programmed full of skills, lie information, shot patterns, and probabilities specific to them. I know this because I've watched them play from trouble. And this is also one of the reasons that they all won major championships.

Yes, you have a Damage Controller in you; the only problem is that your Damage Controller skills (and those of most amateurs) aren't very useful or valuable because they've never been trained or optimized to help you play with Damage Control.

NOW YOU'VE GOT TO MAKE IT USEFUL

The cost of making your Damage Controller useful is real. There really will be a cost of time (reading this book), practice (in your backyard), and mental engagement (on the golf course during a few Damage Control practice rounds). It will take time to improve your Damage Controller thinking enough to be useful . . . but it will be worth it. It will allow you to play with Damage Control when it counts, on the course for the rest of your life. It will be worth your effort and more, because it will reward you many times over with lower scores and enjoyment of the game.

TAKE SOME TIME

I hope you're now close to having a real Damage Control Mentality. You've got your Damage Controller in your head, and I hope you've committed to developing and using intelligent judgment in your game on the course. You might feel that your Damage Controller is in dire need of some good input information, however, and you're probably right.

But don't worry. Your "in-trouble" brainpower will function and grow nicely from now on, because being *aware* of wanting to improve your Damage Controller is a giant step toward accomplishing it. As you train for the physical skills of Damage Control, you will learn how to make good escape swings. Then, as you begin to use those swings, you will begin to notice your shot patterns from trouble and store them in your fantastic memory bank.

When you get on the course, you will look at your trouble lies, with all that "stuff" around your ball, and begin to "see" your chances of successful escape. You will even look out and begin to imagine what your shot patterns might look like (Figure 6.22), as you evaluate different target options within the Code of Damage Control.

6.22

HOW CLEARLY WILL YOU "SEE"?

Will you see the color spectrum and the percentage numbers of my Damage Controller examples in your vision on the course? Probably not . . . *at least not at first*. But your brain (the Damage Controller part of it) will be aware of the essence of danger involved, and you'll start thinking about the probable odds of your successful escape. Then, after you've used this information to create a shot that escapes from the trouble you're in, and followed it with a good short-game recovery shot to avoid losing a stroke on the hole, you'll realize that you've just played with Damage Control.

6.4 Your Game Is . . . What It Is (For Now)

There is bad news and good news at this juncture. The bad news is that your normal game will never be good enough to keep you out of trouble, and you currently don't have the skills to avoid disaster holes. The good news is that you now know what you have to do to solve this problem: You must finish reading this book, do the drills suggested in Chapter 7, and then learn to use a Damage Control Mentality on the course.

More good news is that learning Damage Control is simple compared to learning the normal game of golf, which is what you've been trying to learn. Your previous game-improvement practice has always been devoted to improving your normal (safe lie) golf swing. Keep up this pursuit and I truly wish you improved (smaller) shot patterns from good lies in the future. But for today your shot patterns are what they are. Your deficiencies in the normal game won't be such a problem to you in the future, however, because you're getting close to having a new skill, which will enable you to play from trouble with Damage Control!

LEARNING DAMAGE CONTROL SKILLS WILL BE EASY

The concept of learning Damage Control is new, and you've probably never practiced hitting shots from uneven lies or making flat or upright swings. Although you've hit shots from trouble before, you probably weren't watching your results to learn about your shot-pattern shapes. You didn't know that all those shots were forming the shape of your shot patterns. Also, your setups, swings, and body motions were probably not yet skilled in the execution of escape shots. All of your previous practice making normal swings from level terrain has done nothing to help you learn to make Damage Control swings from trouble.

Functional Damage Control swings don't have to be all that good. They are far easier to learn than normal golf swings. And our program for learning Damage Control takes a different approach than taking normal lessons from schools or golf professionals.

This is all reasonable. After all, you've probably never once in your whole life taken the time to hit 10 shots from a trouble lie, just to see where they'd go and to get an idea of your shot pattern from that kind of trouble.

THREE STEPS TO LEARNING DAMAGE CONTROL

Learning Damage Control is like climbing a three-step ladder, because you need to take the steps in order. You can't go to the second level until you've conquered the first, or the third before the second. Let me take you through these three steps (Figure 6.23):

Three Steps of Learning Damage Control

- **Step 1:** Backyard swing practice to develop the physical skills of Damage Control with "Almost Golf" balls
- **Step 2:** On-course practice to determine shot patterns and Red-Flag touch
- **Step 3:** On-course programming of your Damage Control Mentality

6.23

Step 1 is to learn the first three skills of Damage Control (Setupology, Swing Shaping, Hand-Fire feel) by practicing in your own backyard. This practice will give you the feel of these skills, while also giving you an initial idea of what your shot patterns look like (details in Chapter 7). Simulated trouble lies and Almost Golf balls create a great learning environment with good feedback and at-home convenience, with no damage to property, lost strokes, or bad scores.

Step 2 is to learn Red-Flag touch and develop shot-pattern recognition in Damage Control practice rounds on your local golf course (Chapter 7 for details). These are rounds in which you don't keep score or hit shots off each tee. On each hole you simply go straight to the trouble areas you usually get into off the tee (or around the greens), throw down ten balls, and hit a ten-shot pattern of shots from where they lie.

Step 3 is to play a Damage Control "super-gamble" round on your local course, followed by a Damage Control "super-safe" round, both for score! These are normal rounds, except that in the super-gamble round, every time you play a shot from a trouble lie, you pick the super-gamble target (less than 20 percent safe odds). In the super-safe round you pick all 90 percent or greater super-safe targets. In other words, play these rounds with an overemphasis on Damage Control standards. Make sure you keep an honest tally of both of your final 18-hole scores, then compare your scores and see which one is lower.

EVALUATE THE DETAILS OF THESE ROUNDS

There should be no disaster holes or disaster scores on your scorecard for the super-safe round. There may be several, however, on your super-gamble round. Examine the holes where you encountered serious scoring trouble, and see how many times it was a bad swing versus a bad target selection that cost you strokes. Also examine how often your successful super-gamble recovery shots resulted in the reward of saving strokes.

There will be a balance point somewhere between playing with a super-safe versus a super-gamble mentality that is best for you based on your skill level. The goal is to find the point of balance for your game, enabling your Damage Controller to use it to manage your decisions and choices in future play.

Once you find your balance point, instead of the two or three disaster holes you used to encounter each round, you should soon be looking at only one really bad hole every fifteen or so rounds. This kind of improvement will come for sure, but only after you've developed the skills of Damage Control, including a Damage Control Mentality.

Soon an average of two to five strokes per round will have disappeared from your scorecard, just like I promised in the Introduction of this book.

WHAT'S NEXT?

You have now read the difficult parts of this book. If you intellectually understand Chapters 2 through 6 (the five skills of Damage Control), you should be ready to learn these skills both physically and mentally (and emotionally). This means reading Chapter 7, our "how-to" section.

First, in your own backyard, you will learn to stand, feel, swing, and see how the physical skills of Damage Control work. Then in Damage

Control practice rounds you will learn the procedures and shot patterns of playing with Damage Control, and develop Red-Flag touch. And by playing a few real rounds with emphasis on Damage Control standards, you'll refine your own Damage Control risk-reward system (Figure 6.24). It's exciting what all this can do for your scoring, but be patient. The backyard and golf course will wait. Reading Chapter 7 is your next move. 6.24

CHAPTER 7

Developing Damage Control Skills

YOU'VE READ THE CONCEPTS of Damage Control, seen the skills, and thought about the mentality. But intellectual understanding will only take you so far. It's time now to internalize the "feels" of Damage Control into your mind and body.

This can be accomplished in three steps. First, learn to physically make acceptable escape swings from trouble lies in your backyard. Then play practice rounds at your club to stimulate yourself mentally and to learn about your shot patterns and target-selection skills. And finally, play special Damage Control rounds with special rules, to optimize your ability to shoot lower scores.

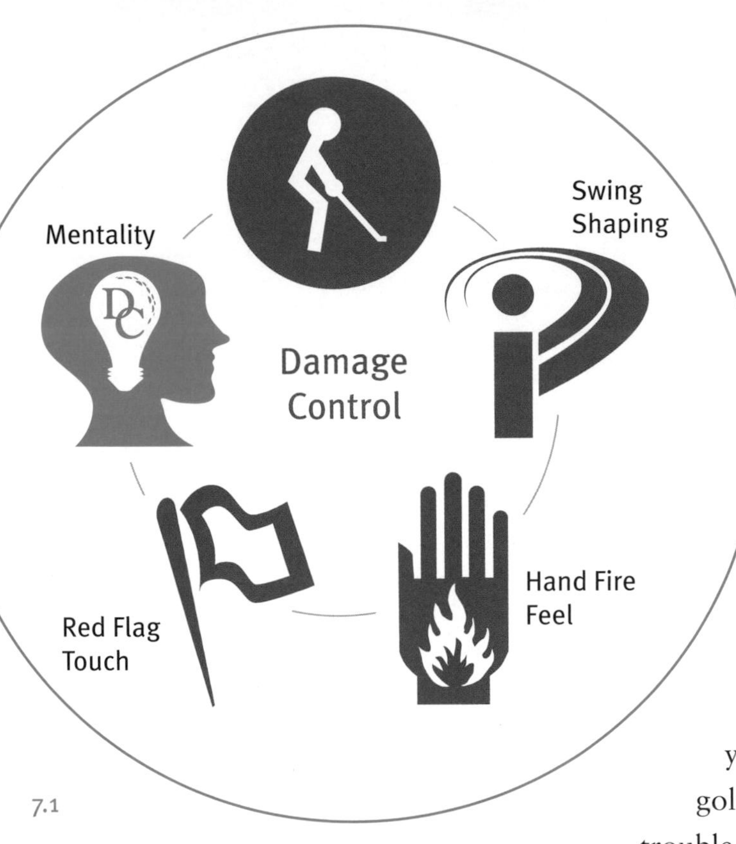

7.1

Once you accomplish these three steps you will be prepared to avoid disaster scores and lower your handicap by somewhere between two and five strokes. You will have become a Damage Control player (Figure 7.1). The only remaining effort will be for you to fine-tune your Damage Control Mentality over time, as you return to playing normal golf for score. How you handle trouble in these rounds will identify how your skills and target selections should be balanced to optimize your scoring in the future.

7.1 Getting Started

Yes, you read correctly: You can practice the drills of Setupology, Swing Shaping, and Hand-Fire feel by hitting special practice balls at home in your own backyard. It's convenient, effective, and won't damage any cars or break any windows, and it's the most efficient way to internalize the skills of Damage Control.

SELECT A DAMAGE CONTROL PRACTICE AREA

7.2

The first step in learning Damage Control is to find a space where you can swing safely and hit our special "Almost Golf" balls. These balls (Figure 7.2) are a product I have endorsed because I think they are so special. They're very light, have one-third the core rating, and fly only about a third the normal distances of a real ball. Molded with dimple patterns for good aerodynamics, they come off your clubs realistically, except they don't fly as far, break windows, dent cars, or hurt anybody.

Look at the side yard of our Pelz Golf Headquarters building in Austin, Texas (Figure 7.3). Do you have a space like this where you can swing in your backyard? If you have one, that's great. If you don't, try to find one nearby so it's convenient to practice and you don't have to waste time traveling back and forth.

When you're learning these new skills you shouldn't care at first where your shots go; you should care that you are learning to hit them solidly. In your backyard you can turn your attention inward and focus on the swings and feels of Damage Control, with no worries about lost strokes or score. I can't overemphasize how important this is to your long-term success in playing with Damage Control.

7.3

GATHER MATERIALS

You can't just go out back and start swinging, however. You need to set up learning aids first, to simulate the difficulties of trouble lies and swing obstacles on the golf course. The items you need are shown in Figure 7.4 along with a corresponding "shopping list." Don't worry; gathering up these items will not be a big deal—they're available at local Home Depot, Lowes, or other home improvement or sporting goods stores (except Almost Golf balls, which can be ordered from www.pelzgolf.com or www.almostgolf.com.

7.4

LIST OF MATERIALS

1. Target net (Dick's, Edwin Watts, PGA Tour Superstore)
2. Platform
   - Two 3' x 3' x ¾" plywood squares (Lowes, Home Depot)
   - Two 3' x 3' pieces of synthetic turf (SYNLAWN.com) to hit shots from on the platform
   - Heavy duty double-sided tape for attaching synthetic grass to wood platform (Home Depot, Lowes)
   - Two 10" gate hinges (or any heavy duty hinge or hasp, Home Depot, Lowes)
3. Two cinder blocks (Home Depot, Lowes)
4. Bag of play sand (Home Depot, Lowes)
5. Fake rock (to make: spray foam onto cardboard in a swirling motion, then wait three days to dry)
   - One can of foam insulation (Home Depot, Lowes)
   - One 1' x 2' piece of cardboard
6. Plastic bucket to hold water or sand (hardware store)
7. Boot tray, low lipped plastic tray or lid (Home Depot, Lowes)
8. Almost Golf balls: 10 (almostgolf.com, pelzgolf.com)
9. Fake tree and limb (Home Depot, Lowes, Target)
   - One 4'½" wooden dowel (one end sharpened)
   - One 5' pool noodle
   - One 5' x 1" diameter piece of pipe insulation
   - One 4' piece of heavy copper ground wire (as limb support)
10. Chair (simulating large obstacle)

WARNING SWINGING GOLF CLUBS CAN BE DANGEROUS

Practicing golf is just as dangerous as playing golf. You can slip from a platform, carpet, block, or chair, or swing and hit yourself or others; serious injury can occur. Equipment can be especially dangerous when wet. Please proceed with caution, at your own risk.

Please note: any of these items can be changed or substituted for per availability and your practice area needs.

Hand-Fire feel drills can have mulch, pine needles, peat moss, etc. added to water and/or sand when heavy resistance materials are required. Check our website (www.pelzgolf.com) in the future for further backyard practice area and equipment ideas and suggestions. We would also like to hear from you (email photos, plans, ideas, etc. to comments@pelzgolf.com) regarding the designs and construction of your Damage Control practice area and equipment.

NOTICE: DANGER WARNING . . . PRACTICE AT YOUR OWN RISK!

SET UP YOUR DAMAGE CONTROL LEARNING STATION

Remember: safety first! Make sure you've oriented your learning station so that no one can walk up behind you without your knowledge. Be especially careful around small children and pets. It's your responsibility to make sure no one ever gets hit or hurt by a swinging golf club. Whether at the golf course or at home, please be careful when swinging a club.

You should also be careful to hit the Almost Golf balls away from people, even though the balls probably won't hurt anyone seriously. These balls normally fly about a third the distance of a normal golf ball; that's not too far for a wedge shot, but if you're practicing with irons and woods, they can fly over a hundred yards (and scare or sting anyone hit).

Look again at our learning station at Pelz Golf with the learning aids in use (Figure 7.5). The backyard of my home is shown in Figure 7.6. As you can see, we have lots of room at Pelz Golf and can hit in virtually any direction. At home I have almost no space, no yard (only my SYNLawn putting green behind the pool), and must hit anything more than a pitch shot into the net. However, even this confined area is still a great place to practice and learn Damage Control techniques.

7.5

As you may have guessed, the authors of this book (me, my son Eddie, and Pelz Golf Institute staff member Joel Mendelman) are all enthusiastic students of the game (aka golf nuts). We all have Damage Control practice stations; mine is on my pool deck, Eddie's is in his yard (Figure 7.7), and Joel's is in his home (Figure 7.8). As you can see, Joel's setup doesn't take up much space, so we don't want to hear any excuses about you not having enough room to learn the skills of Damage Control!

7.6

7.7

7.8

7.2 How to Prepare for Shots from Trouble

The best way to optimize the way you play golf is to optimize your practice. The easy way to make this happen is to be smart enough to practice like you're going to play.

PRACTICE LIKE YOU PLAY

Every trouble shot you attempt is a new and unique experience. For each new trouble lie you encounter, you will set up in a slightly (sometimes radically) different way, with your body in a different position from the swings you normally make from safe lies on tees and level fairways. This is why it's important to have a consistent approach to understanding (both physically and intellectually) the specific demands of trouble shots.

Each Damage Control drill in your backyard (and every on-course trouble shot) should begin with the Damage Control setup routine. This routine must become a habit, a part of your game for now and in the future. The Damage Control setup routine we recommend proceeds through three steps as follows:

SETUP ROUTINE

Step 1: Take a stance about 10 to 12 inches from your ball and check your posture for stability and balance. Use the principles of Setupology (Chapter 2) to position yourself to make a solid and in-balance escape swing. Then run a preliminary check for swing-shape clearance and swing balance by executing a stutter-step (9 position) practice swing (Figure 7.9a-i).

7.9a

7.9b

7.9c

7.9d

7.9e

7.9f

7.9g

7.9h

7.9i

Focus on feeling how your body balance interacts with the lie and terrain of this trouble shot as you move slowly through the nine positions of the stutter-step swing. Also notice how much you will need to modify your swing shape away from normal to minimize contact with any surrounding obstacles.

Step 2: Repeat the stutter-step swing positions, but use a gradually increasing tempo and change your focus to the shape of the swing you'll need to make. Check all obstacles for ample swing clearance as you make this second swing in slow motion, through the same nine positions of swing #1. During the slow-motion swing, concentrate on feeling your body move.

Next move slightly closer to the ball (same setup and stance) and take another swing at about three-quarter speed, somewhat faster than swing #2. Again feel your body move and your balance requirements as you make the swing. Keep your focus on feel as you also begin to notice where the clubhead brushes the ground (bottoms out).

Step 3: Check for final feel and correct ball position with a full speed "preview" swing. This gives you the exact feel and balance of the real swing you're about to make, from as close to the ball as you feel comfortable (the closer the better without hitting or moving the ball). If you like this swing, look down before you move your feet and examine the exact position of where your divot occurred.

Would that swing have made clean ball contact, or would it have hit the ground behind the ball (as in Figure 7.10)? If it would have produced a "fat" shot, move forward and take another swing, until your practice swing makes a perfectly placed divot (Figure 7.11).

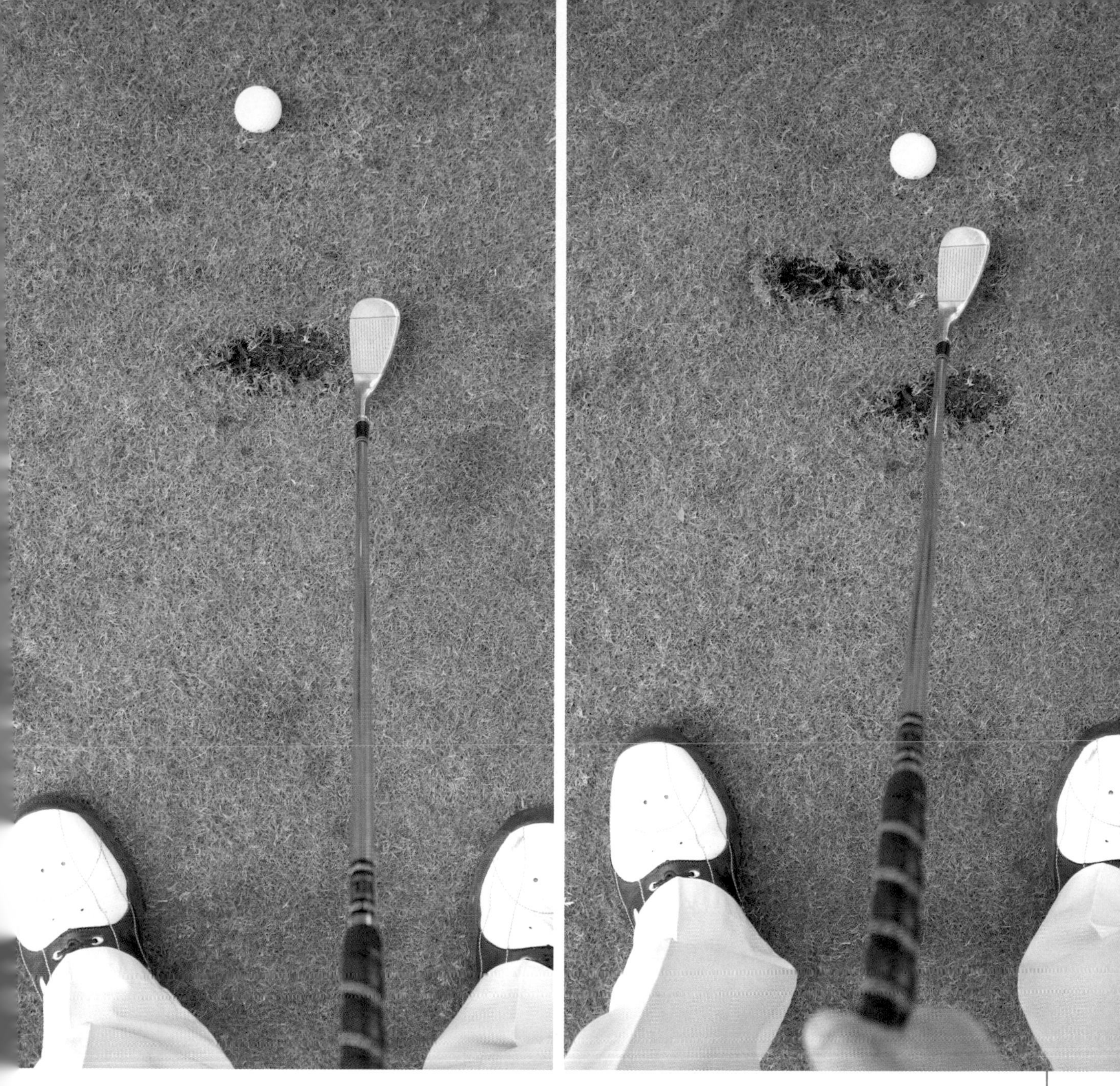

7.10

7.11

Now you're ready to move in and hit the real shot. (Note: If your preview swing is not going to make a visible divot, you can still notice where your club starts to brush the grass [or whatever the ball is sitting in]. Always make sure your ball is positioned to be hit before anything else of significance.)

PERFECT SETUPS HELP

A key to executing successful escape shots is to make a good, solid swing that makes clean, solid contact with the ball. And a key to doing that is to start the swing from a perfectly adjusted setup position for the trouble you're in. When you verify the perfect ball location for your shot, as judged by the location of your preview-swing divot (for the slope, stance, and swing obstacles you face), you've met an important requirement for this success.

IN CASE THERE'S NO SPACE

A second version of the setup routine must be used when obstacles restrict any swings other than those made from exactly the same position you need to play from. In this case, follow the exact same stutter-step and preview-swing concept, except execute all four swings from your real address position over the real ball. No other swing position would accurately duplicate the swing restrictions you are about to encounter. You must be careful not to move the ball or break any branches in any of these swings, and it is very difficult to make real speed swings under such conditions. In these cases, make slow-motion backswings and follow-throughs as realistically as possible, even if they must be made separately. Remember, the purpose of the pre-shot routine is to show your brain what you want to do, and how it will feel, before you have to do it for real.

When a Damage Control setup routine is successful, it provides the feel of the swing you can make in the space available, the balance you'll need, and the perfect ball position for solid shot execution. Then you can duplicate the preview swing and execute the successful escape shot you have planned with confidence.

Use this setup routine during your backyard practice so it becomes a habit as you're learning the skills of Damage Control. When it becomes familiar and natural to you, and you repeat it before trouble shots on the course, it will make executing these shots easier and more successful.

7.3 Take It to Your Backyard

Every golfer has their own unique physical problems, so consider your own specific limitations and proceed cautiously. Take it slowly. Stretch and warm up before any practice session, and be careful not to injure your back. Don't swing and hit anything hard, brittle, or dangerous (Notice: We have used foam blobs to simulate rocks in the practice drills below).

Damage Control is a new concept. It involves new postures, positions and skills that you've never practiced before. Don't overdo it. Proceed wisely and *at your own risk*.

DRILL ADVICE

1. **Don't worry about making bad swings.** Your bad swings and learning errors don't ruin any scores in your backyard.
2. **Pay attention to your shot patterns, even with the Almost Golf practice balls.** You can learn about your scatter directions; real balls on the course will give you different distance and size patterns, but they will be similar to the shot-pattern shape of the Almost Golf balls. Hit groups of ten shots at a time. Pay special attention to the shot-pattern created by your first group of ten versus your second group of ten. The first is usually your worst. Improvement will come with repetition and familiarity.
3. **Pay attention to ball flight.** Pay particular attention to your ball launch characteristics, ball-flight starting direction, and the in-flight curvature of your shots after impact. Note: Wind has a greater effect on Almost Golf balls than it does on real balls because the practice balls are so light. Therefore, the feedback they provide will not be good in windy conditions.
4. **Have fun learning the skills of Damage Control.** Remember, you're not keeping score and you don't have to hit Damage Control shots perfectly for them to be successful. Each drill should be approached in a relaxed fashion and with a sense of adventure. You'll be attempting shots that you may have rarely (if ever) encountered before, so have fun with them and don't worry about your results. These drills have not only been created for your instruction but also for your enjoyment. Enjoy and swing away!

Backyard Drills

DRILL 1: OBSTACLE OFF HEEL OF CLUB (Figure 7.12a–b)

Materials needed: Almost Golf balls, foam rock obstacle

Step 1: Take your normal address position and feel how you might shank the ball or hit the obstacle.

Step 2: Start your setup routine using spine-angle Setupology, crowd into the ball (move closer at address), bend over at the waist, and grip down on the shaft.

Step 3: Complete your routine to feel an upright swing and reduced swing power.

Step 4: Execute ten shots and observe the resulting shot pattern.

Points of emphasis:

- Create a more upright swing plane.
- Swing power is reduced because the shaft is shortened (you've gripped down).
- You should still be able to make an almost full shoulder turn with reasonable power.

7.12a

7.12b

DRILL 2: OBSTACLE OFF TOE OF CLUB (Figure 7.13a–c)

Materials needed: Almost Golf balls, foam rock

Step 1: Take your normal address position and feel how normal impact might hit the obstacle.

Step 2: Start your setup routine using Setupology; set up slightly farther from the obstacle and play the ball off the toe of the club.

Step 3: Complete your routine and imagine the reduced power of the shot.

Step 4: Execute ten shots and observe the resulting shot pattern.

Points of emphasis:

- Expect a 25 percent loss in power due to toe impact.
- Try open- and closed-face swings to gain confidence in swinging close to an object and to understand shot curvature.

7.13a

7.13b–c

DRILL 3: OBSTACLE IN FRONT OF BALL (Figure 7.14a–c)

Materials needed: Platform, Almost Golf balls, foam rock

Step 1: Take your normal address position and feel how your follow-through would hit the rock.

Step 2: Start your setup routine using spine-lean Setupology, play the ball back in your stance, and lean forward.

Step 3: Feel reduced power of setup and how the ground will stop the club before you hit the rock.

Step 4: Execute ten shots and observe the resulting shot pattern.

Points of emphasis:

- Take a club with more loft.
- Open the clubface to provide an extra margin of loft.
- Aim left of the target and release grip pressure as you reach impact.

7.14a

7.14b TOP

7.14c BOTTOM

DRILL 4: OBSTACLES CLOSE BEHIND BALL (Figure 7.15a–c)

Materials needed: Platform (standing on end in a V), Almost Golf balls

Step 1: Take your normal address position and feel how you would have no backswing.

Step 2: Start your setup routine using normal Setupology, but face the platform with a closed clubface and set the ball more toward the toe of club than normal.

Step 3: Complete your routine to feel a normal swing parallel to the platform.

Step 4: Execute ten shots hitting ball with closed (aimed left) clubface off toe of club, and observe low shot trajectories and shot pattern.

Points of emphasis:

- Use a club with lots of extra loft (to compensate for closing clubface).
- Shots will roll a long way because of zero backspin.
- Visualize a trajectory starting to the left, then hooking.

7.15a

7.15b RIGHT TOP

7.15c RIGHT BOTTOM

DRILL 5: OBSTACLES AHEAD OF YOU (RESTRICTED FOLLOW-THROUGH) (Figure 7.16)

Materials needed: Platform, Almost Golf balls, foam tree

Step 1: Take your normal address position and feel how you would hit the limb with a full follow-through.

Step 2: Start your setup routine using normal Setupology.

Step 3: Complete your routine to find (and feel) the limit of your follow-through.

Step 4: Execute ten shots and observe the resulting shot pattern.

Points of emphasis:

- Try different heights for the tree limb.
- Try different distances from the limb.
- Learn how much extra room you require in your follow-through, because stopping the club is always harder than expected.

7.16

DRILL 6: OBSTACLE ABOUT 33" BEHIND BALL (Figure 7.17a–c)

Materials needed: Platform, Almost Golf balls, foam tree

Step 1: Take your normal address position and feel how you would hit the tree limb with your normal backswing.

Step 2: Start your setup routine using normal Setupology.

Step 3: Before initiating backswing, pre-cock wrists fully, move clubhead up toward your head then make stutter-step swing. Verify club clearance in all positions, including downswing.

Step 4: Execute ten shots and observe the resulting shot pattern.

7.17a

LEFT

Points of emphasis:

- Try it first with a wedge, then a 7-iron, then a 4-iron.
- This swing will become more comfortable over time.
- Backswing radius varies with the golfer's physique, club length, and terrain; try this shot from several different slopes.

7.17b

RIGHT TOP

7.17c

RIGHT BOTTOM

DRILL 7: OBSTACLE ABOUT 36" BEHIND BALL (Figure 7.18)

Materials needed: Platform, Almost Golf balls, foam tree

Step 1: Take your normal address position and feel how your normal backswing hits the tree limb.

Step 2: Start your setup routine using normal Setupology, grip down on the shaft, and feel the club miss the tree.

Step 3: Complete your routine to verify swing clearance.

Step 4: Execute ten shots and observe the resulting shot pattern.

Points of emphasis:

- Any club you shorten will produce less carry distance than normal.
- Your swing arc will have a smaller radius by the amount you grip down.

7.18

DRILL 8: OBSTACLE 38" BEHIND BALL (Figure 7.19a–b)

Materials needed: Platform, Almost Golf balls, foam tree

Step 1: Take your normal address position and feel how you would hit the tree limb with your normal backswing.

Step 2: Start your setup routine using Setupology, and play the ball back in your stance.

Step 3: Complete your routine to feel swing clearance and the balance requirements of the swing.

Step 4: Execute ten shots and observe the resulting shot pattern.

Points of emphasis:

- Your club will have less effective loft.
- The shot will fly lower than normal.
- The swing radius of the clubhead will be normal, so distance will still be strong.

7.19a

7.19b

DRILL 9: OBSTACLES ABOVE YOUR HEAD (REQUIRING A FLAT SWING) (Figure 7.20a–b)

Materials needed: Platform, Almost Golf balls, foam tree

Step 1: Take your normal address position and feel how you would hit the tree limb in your backswing.

Step 2: Start your setup routine using spine-(trunk) angle Setupology by squatting down at address.

Step 3: Complete your routine to feel how low you need to squat (or go to knees) for swing clearance.

Step 4: Execute ten shots and observe the resulting shot pattern.

Points of emphasis:

- It is more difficult to rotate when squatting, so power will be limited.
- The lower the limb, the flatter your swing plane must be.
- Lower the height of the limb until it forces you to your knees. You'll be surprised at the power you can still generate.

7.20a

7.20b

DRILL 10: BACKSWING LIMITATIONS REQUIRING AN UPRIGHT SWING PLANE (Figure 7.21a–b)

Materials needed: Almost Golf balls, foam tree

Step 1: Take your normal address position and feel how you would hit the tree with a normal swing plane.

Step 2: Start your setup routine using spine-angle Setupology, move closer to the ball, bend over more, grip down on the club (or use a shorter club), and feel your swing plane missing the tree.

Step 3: Complete your routine to feel your surprisingly powerful shoulder turn.

Step 4: Execute ten shots and observe the resulting shot pattern.

Points of emphasis:

- The more you bend over, the more upright the swing plane will be.
- You need to use a shorter club the more you bend over.

7.21a

7.21b

DRILL 11: BALL SITTING UP ABOVE GROUND (Figure 7.22)

Materials needed: Platform (standing in an inverted-V shape), Almost Golf balls, foam rock, long tee

Step 1: Start your setup routine using spine-angle (standing vertical) Setupology with the club 3 inches above the ball.

Step 2: Complete your routine to feel how heavy the club feels during the swing.

Step 3: Execute ten shots and observe the resulting shot pattern.

Points of emphasis:

- Try hitting shots at different heights to see the effect of club loft directing ball to the left.
- The more horizontal your swing and the farther away from your body the ball, the heavier the club will feel.
- A heavier club feel increases the tendency to hit below (under) the ball.
- The higher the ball, the flatter your swing and the more vertical your spine needs to be.

7.22

DRILL 12: FADING THE BALL AROUND A TREE (Figure 7.23a–b)

Materials needed: Platform, Almost Golf balls, foam tree

Step 1: Take your normal address position and feel how you would hit the tree with a normal shot trajectory.

Step 2: Start your setup routine using normal Setupology, aim two steps left of the tree, and open the clubface slightly.

Step 3: Complete your routine to visualize swinging along the setup line and the ball fading around the tree.

Step 4: Execute ten shots and observe the resulting shot pattern.

Points of emphasis:

- Start with short shots and slow swing speed.
- As tempo and distance increase, notice that the shots start on the same line, but that curvature increases.
- Opening the clubface starts the ball farther right, curves it more, and launches it higher with more backspin.

7.23a

7.23b

DRILL 13: DRAWING THE BALL AROUND AN OBSTACLE

(Figure 7.24a–b)

Materials needed: Platform, Almost Golf balls, foam tree

Step 1: Take your normal address position and feel how you would hit the tree with a normal shot trajectory.

Step 2: Start your setup routine using normal Setupology, but aim two steps right of the tree and close the clubface slightly.

Step 3: Complete your routine and visualize the ball drawing around tree.

Step 4: Execute ten shots and observe resulting shot pattern.

Points of emphasis:

- Start with short shots (slow swing speeds) and then gradually increase swing tempo (notice that shots start on the same line, but curve more).
- Try aiming farther right and closing clubface more.
- Visualize the shot trajectory prior to shot execution (focus on learning how closing the clubface starts the shot farther left and creates more hook, a lower trajectory, and less spin).

7.24a

7.24b

DRILL 14: SIDEHILL TERRAIN, BALL ABOVE FEET

(Figure 7.25)

Materials needed: Platform, cinder-blocks, Almost Golf balls

Step 1: Take your normal address position and feel how the club is too long and how the clubface aims left.

Step 2: Start your setup routine using spine-angle Setupology (stand more vertically), grip down on the shaft, aim right of the target.

Step 3: Complete your routine to feel normal hand (non-blocking) action.

Step 4: Execute ten shots and observe the resulting shot pattern.

Points of emphasis:

- Start with a half swing, then repeat ten-shot sessions with a full swing.
- Try sessions with different slope heights.
- Try sessions with different club lofts.
- Learn correlation: The greater the slope and club loft, the more right you must aim.

7.25

DRILL 15: SIDEHILL TERRAIN, BALL BELOW FEET

(Figure 7.26a–b)

Materials needed: Platform, cinder blocks, Almost Golf balls

Step 1: Take your normal address position and feel that the club is too short.

Step 2: Start your setup routine using spine-angle Setupology, retain your normal spine angle to the ground, and squat down to reach the ball.

Step 3: Complete your routine to feel limited rotation and strain on balance.

Step 4: Execute ten shots and observe the resulting shot pattern.

Points of emphasis:

- The heel of the club hits the platform, the toe does not.
- Try different slopes, different shot distances.
- Aim directly at target (notice that the clubface does not aim right of target).

7.26a

7.26b

DRILL 16: DOWNHILL TERRAIN, FRONT FOOT BELOW BACK

(Figure 7.27a–b)

Materials needed: Platform, cinder blocks, Almost Golf balls

Step 1: Take your normal address position (vertical spine); feel how your swing and the club bottom-out behind the ball, which would result in a fat shot.

Step 2: Start your setup routine using spine-lean and stance-width Setupology, play the ball back in your stance, lean forward to get your spine perpendicular to the slope, widen your stance for balance.

Step 3: Complete your routine to feel limited body rotation, pressure on your leading leg, imbalance on your follow-through, and to verify divot location.

Step 4: Execute ten shots (walk through each after impact) and observe resulting shot pattern.

Points of emphasis:

- Decreased effective loft and lower launch angle will make the ball bounce and roll farther than normal, especially on shorter shots.
- Learning exact divot location for ball position is paramount.
- Complete your swing past impact before walking through to catch your balance.

7.27a

7.27b

DRILL 17: UPHILL TERRAIN, FRONT FOOT ABOVE BACK

(Figure 7.28a–b)

Materials needed: Platform, cinder blocks, Almost Golf balls

Step 1: Take your normal address position and feel how the club would dig into the ground after impact, possibly hurting your wrist.

Step 2: Start your setup routine using spine-lean and stance-width Setupology, lean back, get your spine perpendicular to the slope, and widen your stance for balance.

Step 3: Complete pre-shot routine to feel gravity fighting rotation through impact, pressure on your back leg, and the need to fall back to catch your balance after your follow-through.

Step 4: Execute ten shots, step back to catch balance after each swing, observe the resulting shot pattern.

Points of emphasis:

- Notice how increased effective loft launches shots higher and shorter (use a less lofted club to compensate).
- Focus on turning through impact before stepping back after impact to catch balance.

7.28a LEFT

7.28b RIGHT

DRILL 18: BACKHAND SWING (Figure 7.29a–b)

Materials needed: Platform, foam tree, Almost Golf balls

Step 1: Start your setup routine with a backhand Setupology. Play the ball about 3 inches out in front of your toe line, put your free hand on your shoulder (to anchor pivot point during swing), and keep the clubface perpendicular to the target line.

Step 2: Complete your routine and feel surprising power; verify divot location.

Step 3: Move in and execute ten shots, then observe the shot pattern.

7.29a LEFT

7.29b RIGHT

Points of emphasis:

- Grip the club with your arm hanging straight down under your shoulder.
- Place your finger on the shaft for added control of the clubface.
- Experiment with different clubs (for loft and distance changes).

DRILL 19: OPPOSITE-WAY SWINGS (Figure 7.30a–b)

Materials needed: Platform, foam tree, Almost Golf balls

Step 1: Start your setup routine with normal Setupology, but take an opposite-from-normal grip and turn the club (use a 5-iron for this drill) upside down (toe down).

Step 2: Complete your preview swing with a feel of smooth, accelerating motion.

Step 3: Focus on repeating the preview-swing motion and feel to make solid contact with the ball.

Step 4: Move in and execute ten shots, then observe the shot pattern.

Points of emphasis:

- Take special notice of club loft versus shot height and direction.
- Opposite-way swings require many repetitions to eliminate the awkward feel.
- Try different clubs to find optimum trajectory for distance, then find the optimum club to produce lofted shots.

7.30a

7.30b

DRILL 20: HAND-FIRE FEEL: DEAD HANDS (Figure 7.31)

Materials needed: Platform, foam tree, Almost Golf balls

Step 1: Use the lowest possible grip pressure, zero hand action, and zero brute force.

Step 2: Swing ten times without, then ten times with, Almost Golf ball.

Step 3: Learn the feel of how lightly you can grip the club and swing without slippage.

Points of emphasis:

- Put your mind's eye in your hands.
- Focus on the feel of "Death Hands."

7.31

DRILL 21: HAND-FIRE FEEL: WRIST COCK VS. WRIST HINGE

(Figure 7.32–7.33)

Step 1: Gradually cock your wrists to full cock at top of half backswing.

Step 2: Swing through the impact zone with smooth acceleration and to a full cock at half finish.

Step 3: Repeat the swing motion with your eyes closed to feel the wrist cock.

Step 4: Now try hinging your wrists to verify feel of what NOT to do.

Points of emphasis:

- Keep mind's eye in hands.
- Feel wrist cock in backswing and follow through as good.
- Feel wrist hinge as bad.

7.32

7.33

DRILL 22: HAND-FIRE FEEL: FOREARM ROTATION (Figure 7.34)

Step 1: Swing ten times without and ten times with an Almost Golf ball, overexaggerating the rolling over of your forearms.

Step 2: Hit shots while slowing down, then speeding up forearm rotation.

Step 3: Learn how forearm-rotation tempo is critical to shot direction—impact with clubface open-right; with clubface closed-left.

7.34

DRILL 23: HAND-FIRE FEEL: BRUTE FORCE (Figure 7.35)

Step 1: Set club into cement block as if to lift cement blocks as shown.

Step 2: Exert light pressure to feel the beginnings of brute force in your forearms and wrists.

Step 3: Exert more pressure to feel the demands in your arms and shoulders; ultimately, with maximum force, you should feel brute force into your chest and torso.

7.35

DRILL 24: A LITTLE SMOKE FOR A FRIED-EGG LIE (Figure 7.36a–b)

Materials needed: Tray, sand, Almost Golf balls

Step 1: In 2-inch- deep sand in tray, swirl ball in circles to create a fried-egg lie.
Step 2: Start your setup routine with normal bunker Setupology.
Step 3: Complete your preview swing (above ball), feeling more Hand-Fire than normal
Step 4: Move in and execute ten shots, then observe shot pattern.

Points of emphasis:

- Slap sand through impact to apply Hand-Fire to fried-egg lie.
- Never preview your divot in a hazard on course (it's a penalty to touch sand before impact).
- Ball position should be slightly forward, your clubface semi-open; aggressive acceleration is critical.

7.36a

7.36b

DRILL 25: SMOLDERING HAND-FIRE FOR BURIED LIE IN WET SAND (Figure 7.37a–b)

Materials needed: Tray, sand, water, bucket, Almost Golf balls

Step 1: Make some wet sand in the bucket, then pile the wet sand 3 inches deep in tray and create a buried lie.

Step 2: Start your setup routine with Setupology (position ball 1 inch forward of stance center, close the clubface).

Step 3: Complete your preview swing with a feel for applying brute force through impact.

Step 4: Move in and execute ten shots, then observe the shot pattern.

Points of emphasis:

- Ample hand, forearm, and wrist strength are required to prevent wrist breakdown after impact.
- Learn correlation of shot length to follow-through (long follow-through = long shot, short follow-through = short shot).
- Shot carry distance will be shorter, trajectory lower than normal.
- Expect zero backspin and extra-long roll-out on green.

7.37a

7.37b

DRILL 26: BLAST FURNACE FROM PACKED MUD OR WATER

(Figure 7.38a–b)

Materials needed: Tray, sand, cedar mulch, bucket, water, Almost Golf balls

Step 1: Wet or mix the sand, mulch, and water in the bucket, then pile 4 inches deep and create a buried lie.

Step 2: Start your setup routine with Setupology (ball position in the center of your stance, clubface toed in).

Step 3: Complete your preview swing prepared to supply maximum Hand-Fire.

Step 4: Move in and execute ten shots, then observe shot pattern.

Point of emphasis:

BE CAREFUL: This shot requires strength. There is a **potential for injury**. Approach the shot wisely—if you doubt whether you can get the ball out when you're on the course, take an unplayable lie.

7.38a

7.38b

DOUBLE-UP, TRIPLE-UP, COMBINATIONS OF PROBLEMS!

With the drills in this chapter, we've addressed a number of problems that you'll encounter on the golf course, and how to practice them in your backyard. To experience and develop all of the swings suggested will take you a number of practice sessions, but if you do them, the results will be fundamental and meaningful to your game. Having said this, there is an additional and elevated level of Damage Control that you can achieve in your game.

Additional competence (and still lower scores) will come from developing the ability to hit shots from trouble lies that involve multiple difficulty factors. You've seen, for example, how we recommend handling a lie from behind a rock, or under a tree limb, or on a downslope. Now try to imagine how you might hit a shot with the ball above your feet, a tree in your backswing (Figure 7.39), and maybe a large rock in front of the ball, all at the same time.

The shots and skills of Damage Control are virtually endless. You can practice as many combinations of problems as you like in your own backyard, but you'll never exhaust all the possibilities. You can set your platform high or low at any angle, move your phony tree limbs or rocks to any position, and lean or tilt your spine to as many angles as you can imagine. You will still not encounter a swing that some golfer hasn't needed on a golf course somewhere before.

7.39

BACKYARD FUN

We've detailed lots of new concepts, shots, skills, and backyard practice drills so far, and I know they can help you improve your game consistently. I want to emphasize another point, however, that doesn't directly relate to scoring: **KEEP IT FUN!**

Keep your backyard practice sessions fun by hitting funky shots from funky lies, and try miracle escape shots—all with your Almost Golf balls. How high can you loft shots? Over the house (Figure 7.40)? How low can you go? See and stretch your golf-skill boundaries. And have fun while you learn. The more fun it is, the more you'll do it, and the more it'll help your game!

Friendly competition is the best way to stay focused during practice sessions—it makes you try harder to hit every shot better to win the game. Play games with your family, your kids, or your friends. Create difficult lie conditions, pick targets—the closest to the target wins the point!

7.40

7.4 Take It to the Course

At this point it's time for another quick status check. Earlier we showed you how to set up a practice facility and develop the skills of Setupology, Swing Shaping, and Hand-Fire feel at home in your backyard. Let's assume that you're going to do the drills we've suggested and hopefully learn to make the swings and hit reasonable shots from those circumstances. In fact, let's assume you're going to get really good at these first three skills of Damage Control.

It will then be time to play Damage Control *practice-rounds* with real balls, to real targets—that is, to "take it to the course." Once you've learned to make the necessary swings to hit shots from trouble, you'll need to learn where those shots are going to fly, and how they're going to react once they get there. In other words, you need to learn your shot patterns, and you need some Red-Flag touch.

FIND TROUBLE AND PLAY FROM IT

The Damage Control practice round is a really fun round to play. There is no score involved, no specified number of holes or shots to hit, and no "rules of play."

The point of the round is to locate the trouble spots that you normally get yourself into on the full 18-hole layout of your course, and then learn to play from there. I recommend doing this in the early morning or early evening, when the course is relatively empty (so you won't bother those trying to keep serious score).

Here's how a Damage Control practice round is played: Go to the first tee but don't hit a shot. Look out and identify the trouble you normally drive your ball into. Then drive your cart straight there and throw ten balls into it. Make sure all the balls are in some kind of trouble, then choose a target and hit all ten as you would if you were really playing. You have to hit all shots according to the Damage Control principles you've learned in your backyard. Then look at your shot pattern and soak in some knowledge.

KEEP MOVING

This is a snapshot of what your shot pattern looks like from that trouble. It's only ten shots, so it's not your ultimate shot pattern. It's a quick look, an initial indication, of what your shot pattern really looks like from that kind of trouble.

Just look at the pattern, then pick up your balls and move on. Don't get hung up on the accuracy or inaccuracy of anything here. Just pick up the ten balls, get in your cart, and drive to the worst trouble you can find around the first green, and throw your ten balls there. Then repeat your "escape-from-trouble" scenario again: Choose your trouble spot, select a target; hit ten escape shots; observe your shot pattern, pick up your balls, and move on to the next hole.

KEEP YOUR FOCUS

Move around the course in your Damage Control practice round—play all 18 holes if you have the time—devoting your entire attention to finding and playing Damage Control shots from trouble. (Note: Make sure you don't hold up any play.) And remember that you're looking for all kinds of trouble: high grass, sand with deep lips, severe slopes, water edges, steep banks, shots from the rough on slopes over water (Figure 7.41), low-hanging tree limbs, or fences. Consider anything that's given you trouble in the past or that you think may do so in the future.

Don't forget: no scoring, no putting out, no normal-game shots—just relax and have fun. This is a Damage Control practice

round; you're looking at shot patterns and watching how shots 7.41
behave with little or no backspin, to develop your Red-Flag touch. You're also refining your Damage Control Setupology, Swing Shaping and Hand-Fire feel at the same time.

ESTABLISH "QUICK-VIEW" SHOT PATTERNS

After you play ten shots to establish a "quick view" of a shot pattern, look at it but don't stress over it. Respect it because it has meaning. If your pattern is poor, recognize that and make a mental note to practice from this lie in your next backyard session. But don't stay there all day hitting shots until you get them to be perfect. Don't overanalyze or treat any particular trouble area as being overly important. Remember, there are an infinite number of them, and you only hit ten shots from that particular one.

The primary objective is to train your brain to imagine where your trouble shots are most likely to go. If you could hit a million

7.42

shots from every trouble lie imaginable, your Damage Controller vision would know what your shot pattern is in each case. But ten shots at a time will give you an idea (Figure 7.42).

Exercise your brain. Teach it to imagine. Project an image in your mind's eye, then hit ten shots and see the result. Compare your estimate with reality. Learn, study, grow, and stretch: This is the way poor players become better and good players become great. Prepare yourself for the situations you expect to get into and the results you expect to see as you're getting out. As you develop the skills of shot-pattern recognition and Red-Flag touch, you'll find that the rest of your Damage Control skills will coalesce and improve, and your confidence from trouble situations will soar.

DO NOT KEEP SCORE

While practicing funky shots from funky lies, try some miracle escape shots. Use old balls for really dangerous shots when you don't have much chance of success. Have fun while you learn. Before you hit the shot, imagine the shot trajectory and how the ball will react after it lands. Then execute and see; is it what you expected? It's okay to try shots that aren't likely to succeed, because knowing the reality of your chances will help your target selection in the future.

Again, I remind you: Don't hold up play. I don't want to get you (or me) into trouble with your golf professional, fellow members, or the course ranger. Other golfers might think you're a little crazy, or they'll just be irritated by your practice on the course. I've been told many times to practice only in designated areas, never on the course. But you can't practice Damage Control on perfectly flat driving-range tees, or from perfect fairway lies. You have to do it from real trouble on the course.

Let me ask one more favor. When you're practicing Damage Control on course, please fix every pitch-mark you make on a green. If you're practicing from a grassy creek bank and happen to fly eight out of your ten shots onto the green, please fix all eight of those marks. Your fellow members will appreciate your efforts, the condition of the greens and your putting will benefit, and you'll be much less likely to get in trouble for your Damage Control practice.

PICK YOUR "TOP THREE"

After you've been doing this for a while, pick the three most likely areas to cause you trouble on the entire course and hit twenty-five escape shots from each. Make your selection after looking at every hole for its maximum trouble, and then combining that information

7.43

with the way you tend to miss shots (Figure 7.43). If your bad shots are slices to the right, pay special attention to the trouble on the right side of the fairway. This evaluation will give you a better look at your true shot-pattern size, and will help you to be better prepared for the trouble you're most likely to face in your next round.

FOCUS ON RED-FLAG TOUCH

Be sure to pick some trouble spots near true Red-Flag landing areas, because launching good escape shots from trouble is only the first part of the equation. When a well-struck escape shot lands on the downhill slope of a firm green and rolls into water, you still have to count the disaster score. It doesn't matter that you executed a good swing and played the shot exactly the way you wanted to (Figure 7. 44).

The best way to train your Red-Flag touch is to see enough well-struck shots end up perfectly, even though others may end up in trouble. This will teach you what caused the difference. Don't hesitate to find extremely difficult trouble spots and hit shots from them repeatedly, even if your shots turn out disastrously. From this kind of practice, you'll find that there's usually a statistically best play. It may not be a 100 percent solution, but if it's the best solution for a given situation, you need to know what it is. That's the one you want to play from that spot in a tournament.

There are at least a few Red-Flag landing areas on essentially every course, and you need to learn to deal with the ones that affect your scores the most often. You should also realize there are areas on courses around the world that have much more severe and disastrous consequences than those you normally play from. And it's important to note that the penalties for misjudgments in Red-Flag touch are magnified as the greens get firmer and faster every year. For this reason you should play at least a couple of Damage Control rounds every year to keep your Red-Flag touch sharp.

7.44

And don't worry about getting "too good" at this. As you become a better player, you can always keep things interesting by finding courses that present more difficult challenges.

7.5 Try It In Your Game

After you've played several Damage Control practice rounds, you need to go back to playing normal golf. Having learned to set up, shape your swings, use your hands, estimate shot patterns, and recognize Red-Flag areas when you find yourself in trouble, your game will be better. You'll avoid most disasters and shoot somewhat lower scores right off the bat.

There is still one final step you can take, however, to optimize the effect of Damage Control on your game. That is to optimize the part of your Damage Control Mentality that makes shot choices and target selections, so that they optimally fit with the talent and skill level of the rest of your game. We suggest doing this by playing two very special Damage Control rounds on two consecutive days (so the state of your game will be reasonably constant for both rounds).

BE A "SUPER-GAMBLER"

Some golfers hesitate to devote a round of golf to an experiment, because the round might otherwise be the best round of their life. Knowing how remote the chance of this is, I suggest you devote two special rounds for the express purpose of optimizing your Damage Control Mentality. The chance of you then having a career best round will dramatically improve.

The first experimental round should be played with your Damage Control attitude set at the "extremely aggressive" end of the decision spectrum. We call this a Super-Gambler round. It means that you play every shot with the flagstick as your target. No matter what's in your way, no matter how close a creek or a tree limb or an out-of-bounds stake is, you go for the flag (Figure 7.45).

7.45

This round takes no extra time and no extra effort—you simply need to be focused and aware of the choices you're making on every shot. No matter what trouble you might get into, you just keep firing at the flag, all day long. No matter how narrow the fairway, go for it with a driver. Assume you'll hit a perfect shot every time you swing, no matter what the consequences may be if you don't.

That's it, that's all you do in your Super-Gambler round besides keep score. Don't worry about anything—just play as hard as you can, let it fly, and see how you score.

PLAY A "SUPER-SAFE" DAMAGE CONTROL ROUND

The next day, completely change your attitude. Play your Damage Control round from the other end of the decision spectrum: Make every decision on every shot using a Super-Safe mentality.

Don't try to do anything special or take any chances or gambles. Keep your focus all the way around the course on playing safe (choose all shots to targets that are 95 percent or more safe), just to see and feel the difference from the previous day's strategy. Then see how this mentality affects your score.

THERE IS A BALANCE

I have yet to see a golfer who has played their best when playing every trouble shot Super-Safe. Likewise, I have never seen a golfer who played their best while gambling to the max every time. Everyone has a balance point in their aggression scale that is best for their overall scoring capability, and it always lies somewhere between the completely safe (0 percent gamble) and full-out, 100 percent gambling ends of the spectrum.

Where this balance point is for any particular golfer depends on their Damage Control skills. It can also change as the situation or need for a particular result changes. Although it's all still new to us, from the results we've seen so far this balance point doesn't change nearly as much as golfers expect it to.

FIND YOUR OWN BALANCE POINT

The point of devoting two special rounds to explore the extremes of Damage Control decisions is to see where the limits of aggression versus safety take your scores. As you analyze these two rounds after completion, you can begin to move toward striking a balance within your own game, so you'll know how aggressively you should play to score your best. Did you waste a few strokes when you were playing too safe? You probably did. Did you waste several strokes by playing too aggressively? Again, you probably did.

For every golfer there is an optimum amount of aggression they should use when choosing targets from trouble lies. If you're a numbers person, you'll want to put a number on how aggressively you should play. For others a number will bother them, and they'll be better off just "feeling" their way through this issue of aggressiveness.

Personally, I've settled on a low aggression level—I prefer to play to targets that I believe are in the 75 percent safety range. When I play from trouble at this level, I hit my best shots and my short game allows me to score my best.

You must base your level of aggressiveness on the state of your physical and mental Damage Control skills, with consideration given to how strong your short game and putting are. Are they at least good enough to save strokes 50 percent of the time when you put them in a position to do so?

GO LOWER YOUR SCORES

So there you have it. This is our concept of Damage Control: five skills that will help you avoid disaster scores and disaster holes. You can learn the three skills of Setupology, Swing Shaping, and Hand-Fire feel in your backyard. You can play Damage Control practice rounds and refine those three skills while you learn what your shot patterns look like and develop your Red-Flag Touch. Then you can play special Super-Gambler and Super-Safe rounds, with your attention focused on optimizing your percentages and feeding your Damage Control Mentality.

Obviously, you can work in your backyard as often as you want. It will probably take you several Damage Control practice rounds to get a good feel for your shot patterns and Red-Flag Touch. And within a few months of normal play you should feel as though you're honing in on an optimum Damage Control Mentality for your game and skill level.

Your scores should improve gradually during this time, and once you begin playing with an aggression level that fits your game, your scores will begin to drop consistently to a new level. That's our goal . . . I hope you'll make it yours.

HELP US HELP OTHERS

Two quick thoughts here before you finish:

1. **When you watch PGA TOUR or LPGA Tour pros on television, observe how they play (and execute) shots from trouble.** With a focus toward optimizing your own Damage Control game, you can learn a few tricks of the trade from the experts.

2. **As you practice and develop your own version of Damage Control in your backyard or on the course, please feel free to send us** photos and descriptions of the new swings and learning aids you develop, plus any new Damage Control playing suggestions or evaluations you may happen to create along the way (send these to comments@pelzgolf.com).

The reason I ask for this is that the concept of Damage Control is new, and we don't have all the answers. I'm sure we all have much to learn. I invite you to visit our Web site (www.pelzgolf.com) or my blog (www.pelzgolf.com) for the latest in Damage Control from our research and your feedback. I'll blog about new developments as they come in over time, and I'll post frequent updates on my Twitter account at dave_pelz.

I thank you in advance for your help, and I know that as you work on your Damage Control skills, you'll begin to see two to five strokes per round disappear from your scores.

Good luck, and lower scores to you,

Acknowledgments

THE AUTHORS WOULD LIKE to express special appreciation to the many people and facilities that have helped us so much in learning about Damage Control.

In particular we thank Porcupine Creek (Palm Springs, California), Escondido Country Club (Horse Shoe Bay, Texas), the Hills of Lakeway (Austin, Texas), and the Arrowhead GC (Myrtle Beach, South Carolina) for giving us access to superb facilities. The photographs in this book do not do justice to the incredible beauty we encountered while illustrating the fundamentals of Damage Control at your courses.

We also want to thank Leonard Kamsler, the world's best golf photographer, and our good friends at *GOLF Magazine* and the Golf Channel for their help in photographing and recording the players, conditions and circumstances of Damage Control. Special thanks go to the staff of PGA TOUR ShotLink for helping us take the world's most accurate measurements of how both pros and amateurs play the game.

Thanks also go to our friends at Myrtle Beach Golf Holiday, DuPont, the PGA TOUR Superstore, and the amateur contestants in the World Handicap Amateur Championships in Myrtle Beach South Carolina, whose games and "disaster scores" form the basis of this book.

We sincerely appreciate Sven Nilson's graphical presentations, and the many and varied roundtable discussions of the entire Pelz Golf Institute staff. We also thank Tom Sieckmann for his demonstrations and insights on Damage Control from the point of view of a PGA TOUR champion.

We thank the PGA TOUR players who demonstrated their skills and communicated their thoughts honestly and straightforwardly to us along the way. Without being able to watch you (Phil, Vijay, Payne, Lee, Elk, and Mike) up close, and study how you escape from trouble, the five skills of Damage Control may never have been recognized and this book certainly would never have been written.

And finally, we thank those particular players in the World Amateur Championship who talked to us in interviews after making disaster scores on disaster holes. Your thoughts, consternation, and honesty helped us to recognize the on-course problems you have from trouble lies, and gave us four years of pure enjoyment in figuring out the answers of Damage Control.

Grateful acknowledgement is made to the following photographers and organizations for permission to reproduce their work:

Leonard Kamsler

Joel Mendelman/Pelz Golf Institute

Eddie Pelz/Pelz Golf Institute

The Golf Channel